Sarah Harrison

Sarah Harrison always wanted to write and was the original 'scribbling child'. She read English at London University and then joined IPC Magazines where she worked on *Woman's Own*. During this time she began to write short stories, and after four years she left in order to concentrate on her first love, fiction. The author of ten novels, she has written several children's books, short stories, articles and scripts and is also a regular broadcaster on Radio 4.

Sarah Harrison lives with her family in Hertfordshire. Her latest novel, LIFE AFTER LUNCH, is also available from Sceptre.

SCEPTRE

Flowers
Won't
Fax

SARAH HARRISON

SCEPTRE

First published in 1997 by Hodder and Stoughton
First published in paperback in 1998 by Hodder and Stoughton
A division of Hodder Headline PLC
A Sceptre Paperback

10 9 8 7 6 5 4 3

A CIP catalogue record for this book is
available from the British Library

ISBN 0 340 65389 2

Typeset by Palimpsest Book Production Limited,
Polmont, Stirlingshire
Printed and bound in Great Britain by
Clays Ltd, St Ives plc

Hodder and Stoughton
A division of Hodder Headline PLC
338 Euston Road
London NW1 3BH

For friends

'Bastards!'

'I'm sorry?' asked Isla politely.

'Bastards!' repeated the cab driver, his neck reddening.

This time Isla confined herself to a small, sympathetic sigh. She sensed that the driver's outburst was due as much to a well-mulched misanthropy as to any immediate exterior stimulus, and didn't want to attract or aggravate it in any way. All through the 'Where There's a Will' lunch at the Café Royal, during which a doughty Labour baroness had given out awards to disabled high achievers, she had smiled and reacted and listened with focused thoughtfulness to a series of moist-eyed carers, neighbours and family members. It had been a cause of almost hysterical relief when one of the award-winners, a wheelchair athlete with hair extensions, had placed a hand on her knee and pronounced his joystick in full working order. Even heroes could be randy sods.

The cabbie beat out the rhythm of the 1812 on the steering wheel with both sets of fingers. 'This is just triffic,' he announced, and switched off the engine.

The northbound traffic in Regent Street was stationary. The midsummer heat, rancid with engine fumes, vibrated thickly around the cab, which was inauspiciously positioned between a bus and a coach full of tourists.

The cabbie wound down his window to its fullest extent and leaned out. He wore a jolly tartan cap which sat ill with his sulphurous expression.

'Oi!' He bellowed at some unseen figure further down the street. 'What the fuck's up, mate?'

As a drama student in the early seventies, Isla had had a brief relationship with a Mancunian Buddhist, the legacy of which was a knowledge of relaxation techniques. Now she settled the length of her spine evenly against the back of the seat, uncrossed her legs and allowed her hands to rest loosely on her thighs. She took a deep breath and closed her eyes as she slowly exhaled.

But the Mancunian's long-ago lessons were no match for a London cabbie with a serious beef. The loud exchange through the open window continued for the best part of a minute, followed by a more muted but equally intrusive burble of complaint which Isla was too polite to ignore.

'. . . don't give a monkey's that the rest of us got homes to go to and livings to earn.'

Isla opened her eyes, and caught the choleric glance of the driver in the rearview mirror.

'It's too bad,' she agreed.

'I mean, you're going to Hampstead. I live in Stockwell. That lot –' he indicated the coach to their right – 'to *Phantom, Saigon* and all points west, and what are our chances?' He made a gesture to indicate she shouldn't dream of answering. 'Don't get me started.'

Isla crossed her legs again and laced her fingers together. It was stifling in the cab, but to wind her window down would have been to admit a blast of noise and toxicity that was even worse. She gazed out through the glass, but became conscious of the cabbie peering at her in the mirror, clearly cueing the response he'd vetoed earlier.

'What do you think's causing it?' she asked.

'Lady, if I knew that I wouldn't be doing this job, I'd be in MI5,' he declared triumphantly, having led yet another sucker on to the punch.

Isla smiled a weary, empathetic smile, and transferred her attention to the neighbouring bus. Some passengers were cutting their losses and getting off to walk. One or two of those remaining sat with their heads leaning on the window in an attitude of despair, or perhaps in the faint hope that this might help them to see further up the road to the cause of the trouble. One woman on the long seat near the door did appear more optimistic – or at least less desperate. She sat slewed round, her chin resting on her crossed arms, eyes narrowed, cat-like, in the glare of the sun. She had a square jaw, a wide mouth, and the sort of thick, coarse, blonde hair that positively flourishes on inexpert chopping. Lucky thing . . . Isla adjusted her gaze to her reflection and touched her own sleek black bob, every delicately snipped and chemically enhanced inch of which set her back several pounds.

'Here we go,' said the driver, with grim relish. 'Here come the excuses.'

Two policemen in short-sleeved shirts and fluorescent waist-coats, and carrying walkie-talkies were advancing between the rows of traffic, stooping to talk to drivers as they went. One of them, a young man in his twenties, wearing sunglasses, had the most beautiful arms, Isla noticed. She couldn't help gazing as he pointed towards Oxford Circus, the rope of muscle along his forearm flexing beneath its dusting of golden hair . . .

The approach of hard information seemed to cheer the cabbie. He wound the window down again and welcomed the young policeman with a broad smile.

'Go on, surprise me. Lights at the Circus up the spout?'

'I'm afraid not,' said the policeman with scrupulous, bland politeness, glancing through the open panel at Isla to include her in his reply. 'I'm afraid we have a security alert.'

'Bomb?'

'It's a possibility. We've cordoned off the area.'

The cabbie took off his tartan cap and mopped his face and neck with it. 'So what's the choice between getting blown to bits and dying of heatstroke, officer?'

'We're organising a diversion right now mate, we'll get you moving again any minute.'

'Yes, and Gazza's taken holy orders. Is that a minute as in a couple of hours, or as in this time tomorrow?'

The policeman smiled at Isla, she saw the split-second of recognition. 'As in pretty soon.'

'Oh dear,' she said. 'Do you think we're in for a whole summer of this?'

'Let's hope not. Doesn't do anything for the tourist industry.' He tapped the roof of the cab and moved on.

'Bugger the tourists,' growled the cabbie. 'What about the

workers?' For the first time he twisted round and looked at Isla face to face. She saw that he was older than she'd thought, his face gouged with downward lines, and perspiring freely. 'Might be quicker to get out and walk to the tube.'

'No thanks,' she said. 'In these shoes, I'll stick it out.'

'Cheers, love. I switched the meter off.' As the traffic inched forward with an optimistic revving of engines, he turned back, adding for good measure a final explosive: 'Bastards!'

When Jen saw the police approaching, she disembarked from the bus. It could only mean one thing. She wasn't about to join the rush back to Piccadilly Circus for the tube, but neither did she want to be stuck in a traffic jam. With no particularly clear plan she set off, thanking God for her trusty Nikes and the bumbag which she favoured – much to her daughter's displeasure – over a handbag, for days out.

'That is such a tacky thing, I don't know how you can wear it.'

'I don't wear it, I use it. It's useful. It carries stuff and leaves my hands free.'

'For what? How many Amazonian rainforests per week do you hack your way through in Crouch End?'

Jen was used to such criticisms and accepted them in the spirit in which they were offered. They were part of the commerce of their relationship, and if she'd suddenly abandoned her bumbag, her roman sandals, her thumb ring and her Velvet Underground tapes an essential currency would have gone missing. A girl needed a fix on her mother, and in Claudia's case the fix was that Jen was an old hippy who scrubbed up well if pushed.

Now she trudged through the Burlington Arcade into Piccadilly, and then up past the Royal Academy to Green Park. A dense wedge of hot, agitated, would-be travellers packed the entrance to the tube, so she went into the park and sat down in the shade beneath a tree. She got out her bottle of Evian water – now slightly warm – undid the cap and took a long swig. She was going to be late back, but that might be no bad thing.

Jen had spent the day recharging her batteries at the pictures – first the Tate and then the Odeon Leicester Square. That was the one true perk about being self-employed – one had no need of terminally ill aunts or pressing root canal work to provide a pretext for bunking off. In fact a person in the artistic line of business positively owed it to herself to play hookie from time to time.

She screwed the top back on the Evian, and hiked down to lie flat on her back on the grass. The afternoon sun glittered between the leaves, and the irritable drone and blast of jammed traffic increased her sense of having escaped, for a second time in one day.

With which happy thought, Jen slept.

Richard Wakefield arrived in Selwyn Street only five minutes after his usual time of five o'clock, the Jag having made light work of the back roads between chambers and Crouch End. He was therefore not in the least surprised to find the house empty. Even when he was late, which was often (and with ample justification), Jen could be relied upon to be later, or to have forgotten that he was coming at all.

He had his key of course, but decided to stay in the air-conditioned comfort of the XRJ for a few more minutes before braving Number 65. There was a clarinet concerto on Radio 3, and the notes tumbled forth cool, liquid and civilised as chilled Pimms . . .

Richard gazed across the street at the house. He'd known at once that she wasn't there – the curtains in the bedroom bay window were still drawn and the downstairs living-room windows were open, but the cats, Cain and Abel, were loitering outside, a sure sign that their mistress was not at home. He had told her a thousand times about leaving the house hanging open, a welcome mat to undesirables, burglars and worse, but whichever minute tendril of DNA was responsible for caution, Jen was without it. 'If I'm around, what does it matter?' was her usual response to his admonitions, and it was no good pointing out to her that she used the term loosely. In her book, 'in' might mean anything from up the garden with Bob Dylan on the headphones, to just-popped-out to Hanif's for bread. Her insurance was minimal, and out of date, also in spite of his advice. That her house remained intact and unrobbed and her person unviolated was a source of wonder to Richard. He concluded that the local criminal fraternity must assume, from her lack of precautions, that the modest terraced house was occupied by a jujitsu coach, and protected by a sociopathic (but silent) pitbull.

Such was far from the case. As he sat there with the engine running, the cats moved to the gate (still without a latch) and stood there with their snake-like tails aloft, staring at him. Actually, Richard would have preferred a pitbull: he was more at home with dogs. Cats unsettled him, and these two treated him with a casual contempt which familiarity had done nothing to improve. Not, he observed, that this prevented them from materialising at his arrival in the expectation of access to the house, and the sarcastic hope that the Jag's boot might be stuffed with Premium Cuts.

Cain sat and began washing beneath his armpit. Abel sprawled, slitty-eyed in the small shade of Jen's dusty privet. Both were pretending to have bowled up there quite by accident, and not to give a damn what he did: Richard knew different, and took evil pleasure in keeping them waiting. In this his professional experience was of great assistance. He had met many Cains and Abels in his time, both in and out of the courtroom, and fancied he could out-cool any of them, particularly when he held all the cards – and the key. Street-cred was overrated in his view, when compared with the experience of the average lawyer.

He loosened his tie just enough, and undid his collar button: it was hot, and this was Jen-country after all. He surveyed the long rows of terraced houses with a sort of guilty fondness. More happy hours than he could remember had been spent in Selwyn Street but he was awfully glad he didn't have to live here. As with first-class air travel, it was space that made the difference. Especially undedicated, seldom used space. In his own house overlooking the heath in Hampstead it was the acreage of lawn, shaded by mature trees . . . the great, high-ceilinged hall with its leisurely curving staircase . . . the galleried landing with its many tributaries . . . the cool, leafy orangery . . . the library . . . all those tranquil, largely undisturbed expanses which enabled each occupant, even when the boys were there, to be unaware of the presence of others.

The fast movement of the clarinet concerto rippled, swirled, and crescendoed to its conclusion. A little reluctantly, Richard switched the radio off. Time to go in. The movement of his arm caught the attention of the cats, whose eyes widened slightly and fixed upon him. He supposed he was going to have to put the blighters out of their misery.

He was already out on the pavement, car locked and tie straightened, when Keith Burgess rounded the corner on his pushbike. For a split second Richard considered slapping his pockets, feigning the loss of some vital item, and making a fast getaway. But unfortunately Keith had already spotted him.

'Who-a!' cried Keith, putting a foot down on the kerb outside Number 65. 'If it isn't Rumple of the Bailey!'

'Good evening to you.' Richard crossed the road with long, unhurried strides and an air of urbane geniality. Jen's lodger was something up with which one had to put. 'It looks awfully as if she's out.'

'She expecting you?'

'Probably not, but that doesn't mean anything.'

'Ah, our Jen . . .' Keith shook his head. 'A stranger to the diary.'

He nudged open the gate and pushed his bike up to the front door, propping it against the chipped windowsill and fished his key out of his breastpocket while the cats pressed passionately against the damp course. Richard watched him with scientific interest. Keith was a primary school teacher. There were drawings in his room of women with triangular skirts and houses with loopily smoking chimneys, labelled 'TO MR BURGESS' or simply 'TO SIR'. Keith wore a nylon short-sleeved shirt, knitted tie and cycle helmet (a kagoul, Richard knew, would be neatly rolled in his saddlebag), and kept tropical fish in a tank on his chest of drawers. He was hopelessly naff and incorrigibly nice. The 'Rumple of the Bailey' shaft – all his own work – was an ill-judged attempt to show that he, too, could be one of the lads. Richard had no option but to forgive him because the alternative was too complex and painful to contemplate. Keith just Didn't Get It, as Giles would have said. Whether he 'got it' in any other sense was also debatable. Keith could only have been in his early thirties, and yet he appeared to Richard to be sexless. Perhaps he simply divided and multiplied like an amoeba, causing other Keiths, also in knitted ties and helmets, to slip out of the back bedroom window at night and go forth to populate the primary schools and prayer groups of south east England. However he managed, this lack of any overt sexuality made him an extremely safe pair of hands, which was another reason why Richard was never less than civil to him.

'There we go,' said Keith, pushing wide the door and standing back with one arm extended in an exaggerated display of deference. 'Age before beauty.'

The cats trotted ahead, tails aloft, almost tripping Richard up. Cats before chaps was the rule around here. There were two bills and a Labour circular on the mat. He picked them up and put them on the corner of the stairs as Keith followed, removing his helmet.

'Now then, who's for a cuppa?'

'No thanks.'

'You sure?'

'Quite sure, thank you.'

'I trust you'll forgive me if I do,' said Keith.

'Please . . .' Richard made a graceful, don't-mind-me gesture, and went into the living room. The cats accompanied Keith into the kitchen.

Richard drew back the over-long calico curtains on their rattling wooden rings to their full extent. The room, now bathed in full sunlight, was like its owner – indifferently maintained, tousled to just this side of slatternly, but uniquely seductive. A room to sink down into, a room in which to remove one's shoes, loosen one's tie, and to let it all, as the slang had it, hang out.

Keith appeared in the doorway, a Garfield mug in one hand.

'I hate to leave you like this, but I must away upstairs.'

'Please,' said Richard again. 'You carry on.'

'Where can she be, the dirty stop-out?'

Richard shrugged. 'She'll be back in due course.'

'I wish I had your faith!' observed Keith, going, only to pop back in again. 'By the bye, those cats were dropping heavy hints but I ignored them.'

'I'll see to it,' promised Richard.

'Okey-dokey. Duty calls. Hob-nobs in the tin.'

From an ingrained habit of caution Richard waited till he heard the door of the back bedroom close and the sound of Simply Red strike up on the other side before sinking down on the multicoloured sofa-bed, his head at one end, his crossed ankles on the other. Jen's throws, and her shawls, and her cushions, smelt faintly spicey, a mixture of joss-sticks, and hash . . . a hint of vegetable korma . . . Morning Mist Body Splash . . . essence of Jen. He closed his eyes, cradled in the room's special atmosphere. He didn't have to look to see it in all its familiar detail, from the peonies in the white jug in the hearth to the brutal female nude on the wall to his left. There was a chipped plaster statuette of a child – a charity promotion from the 1920s – and several of Jen's own sketches, hands, heads, entwined figures. The fireplace at this time of year was filled with giant pine cones from woods in southern France and flanked by the natural sculptures of silver-grey driftwood. On the chimney breast were a collection of masks, a dozen leering, slant-eyed faces in wood, ceramic, papier-mâché and metal, genial or malign according to one's mood. The wooden floor was painted cobalt blue and stencilled with creamy, lily-like flowers, but there were tufts of dusty cat hair drifting round the edges near the skirting board. The door, painted with a trompe-l'oeil second door that stood permanently ajar, was dappled with fingerprints, and the windows were smeary. The round beechwood table, the only furniture of any real value in the room, was home to a drawing board, piles of books, and a wicker basket overflowing with mail, opened and unopened. Brushes, sticks of pencil and charcoal stood in a cylindrical bamboo vase. Wind chimes hung in the window. Giant floor cushions covered in Jen's distinctive primitive (and X-rated) batiks lay in an inviting mass beneath the windowsill. A plain calico screen was covered with photographs – mostly of Jen's daughter, Claudia, some of Cain and Abel, and a small group of Other People's Pets, the raw material of Jen's livelihood. An easel bearing an oil painting of a golden retriever stood near the window.

Seeing the pictures of Claudia, even in his mind's eye, unsettled him almost as much as encountering her in real life. As a child she had been alert, detached, suspicious. As a young woman she was as censorious as it was possible to be at a distance, for they assiduously avoided one another. He could perfectly understand why – he suffered from the double disadvantage of a step-parent's apparent permanence with none of the credentials or the responsibilities. Whereas Jen had never caused a moment's twinge of guilt, Claudia was, as his sons might have said, Guilt City.

He lay on the sofa for about ten minutes until these unsettling reflections had drifted off, and then went in search of the bottle of Bells with which he made a point of supplying this plonk-swilling household. In the kitchen the cats were sitting on the gas boiler, facing each other but gazing his way, like ornaments on a dresser. Between them, three improbably red apples lay in a shallow pottery bowl that listed slightly to one side. Richard shooed a fly off the apples with a vigour that sent the cats lolloping huffily to the floor as well. He took the Bells from its place between the chickpeas and the Italian rice, poured himself a generous shot and added a finger of cold water from the tap, splashing his jacket in the process. Tutting, he removed the jacket and hung it carefully over the back of Jen's prized Shaker chair, the only one in an otherwise undistinguished and unmatched junk shop sextet.

Upstairs, Mick Hucknall (whom Richard only recognised courtesy of the boys, who dismissed Simply Red as the apotheosis of uncool) declared that he 'loved the thought of coming home to you . . .' Richard sat patiently, legs crossed, gazing out of the back door at the tangle of dog roses and rampant pelargoniums that overhung the turf in Jen's back garden. Generally speaking Richard disliked being kept waiting, and hated the arrogance implicit in unpunctuality. But with Jen it was different. Here, in the familiar snug seclusion of 65 Selwyn Street, he was perfectly content to wait.

The hall floor was made up of big black and white tiles, like a chessboard. Isla removed her shoes the moment she'd closed the door behind her and felt the coolness strike up through her tired feet and ankles. Was there, she wondered, any bliss to compare with that of taking off one's high heels at the end of a long, hot day . . . ?

Still barefoot she went into the library and pressed the button on the answering machine. The first voice was that of Marjory Dix in Bradenham.

'Hallo . . . hallo? Am I there? Sometimes your little tune plays and sometimes it doesn't, but I hope you can hear me now. I do hope your journey down won't be too atrocious, what with these beastly people up to their old tricks in London, but perhaps things will have cleared by then. Anyway, all the stuff you asked for is there, except for aubergines which were simply not to be found. The entire county must be making ratatouille. I took the liberty of getting extra courgettes instead. I prevailed on Norman to cut the grass and to get his own back he brought about a hundredweight of stick beans from his own garden which I've bagged up in batches and slung in the freezer because there is absolutely no *way* you could have eaten them all over the weekend. The sweet peas are *simply* rioting. I've put a posy in the drawing room but left you to pick more if you want to. The Fylers told me to tell you—'

At this point Marjory was cut off, and called back. 'Sorry, my fault, butterfingers! The Fylers have confirmed for Saturday night, presumably you know what for. Not much else to report. See you tomorrow. Cheers to both.'

The second message was from her husband. 'Darling, this is me on the mobile, in the Tottenham Court Road. We seem to be caught up in the backwash from this infernal bomb scare. It occurs to me you probably had the same problem, and that's why you're not back. I hope it went well, by the way. If it turns out I'm too late we'd better cut our losses and make an early start tomorrow. OK? See you soon.'

Isla stood quietly in the library, digesting this message as the tape whirred back on itself. The noble, rather sad eyes of her grandfather, the general, gazed down from his frame opposite the door. She tried to assemble the calm dignity befitting the general's granddaughter and the colonel's daughter . . . But Tottenham Court Road? The machine reset itself with a beep, and she didn't bother to turn it off. She stared back at the portrait. Henry William Munro was depicted on horseback. The horse was a snorting bay poised for the charge, nostrils flaring, mane fluttering like bunting along the perfect parabola of its neck, tail flaring like a banner, one gleaming hoof raised in anticipation, a scintilla of white showing in the lustrous eyes. Isla went closer and stood, arms folded, before the picture. She had seen family photographs of her grandfather's horse during his time in India, and it bore little resemblance to the fiery beast in the frame. The real thing, Bertie, standing with ears askew on the end of a rope held by a grinning syce, had been a stolid gelding with a hogged mane, a docked tail, and an attitude problem. Nought out of ten, in fact, for artistic impression . . . But who would deprive her grandfather of making the most of his military reputation by means of this glorious charger? Isla looked deep into his eyes, a willing conspirator. She decided not to think too hard about the Tottenham Court Road.

Jen remembered the arrangement with Richard as she hopped off the bus in Crouch Hill at a quarter past seven. Remorsefully, she quickened her pace over the Broadway towards Selwyn Street. Her chronic unpunctuality, which she was the first to acknowledge, had the unfortunate side effect of invalidating genuine reasons for lateness. She didn't suppose for a moment that even a well-attested bomb scare would remove the taint of unreliability from her record.

She saw the Jag at once, parked in its usual place opposite her gate, though at this time of day it was surrounded by the more modest vehicles of Selwyn Street's other residents, home from work. It was funny the way people's cars began to look like them. Her own white Renault Diane was by now so much an extension of herself that she fancied it cocked an eyebrow at her approach. The sleek muzzle of the Jag she equated with Richard's heavy, Roman profile, and the distinctive configuration of the rear windscreen corresponded to the slight droop at the outer corner of his eyelids which gave him his air of reflective braininess. Parked patiently at the kerb opposite Number 65, hemmed in by lesser vehicles, it seemed, like its owner, a model of handsome, intelligently confined power and understated wealth.

Jen's step lightened, enabling her to find another gear. She was practically running by the time she reached the gate, and cannoned into Richard coming the other way.

'Whoops!' He caught her shoulders, bracing them both.

'Sorry!'

'No need to be.'

'There was a bomb scare in the West End, you never saw anything like it.' He shrugged, began to put his hands in his pockets but then held them out in response to her groan of frustration. 'You don't believe me.'

'I do as it happens.'

'It'll be on the news.'

'I know.'

'Is Keith in?'

'He is.' Neither of them looked at the house, but their eyes met, trapping a laugh for later. 'He spoke disparagingly of your timekeeping.'

'For crying out loud – what's it to him?'

'Just what I asked myself.'

Jen pushed open the gate. 'Have you had a drink?'

'I fear so. Look—' She stopped, looking over her shoulder. 'I really must go.'

'OK.'

'It's not, I know it's not, but as things have turned out . . .' He tapped his watch, pulled a face. 'I really am most awfully sorry.'

'Don't be, it's my fault. As usual.'

'Even you can't be blamed for the activities of the IRA.'

'No, well, that's true.'

'I'll be in touch one day next week.'

'OK.'

He pulled the gate to and kissed his hand to her briefly. '*Au revoir* then.'

'See you.'

'Take care.'

'You too.'

He walked away from her across the road, pointing his key briefly at the Jag to unlock it. She turned in the doorway to watch him drive away. He didn't look at her, but lifted his forefinger from the wheel as the Jag purred down Selwyn Street and away.

'Sorry!' called Keith leaning back from his desk to call through the open bedroom door. 'None of my wiles worked. A man's gotta do what a man's gotta do, and do it on schedule!'

'Tell me about it,' said Jen.

The ground floor of the house was full of the blues. The gravelly moan of Billie Holliday slithered from concealed speakers to pervade the lofty space of the hall, the shadowed stairs, the wide, empty floor puddled with late evening sunshine.

'*Southern trees bear strange fruit . . . Blood on the leaves, blood at the root . . .*'

Richard stood very still. It was only when he began to move again that he found he had been holding his breath, and exhaled, a long sigh. He put down his briefcase and walked across the hall towards the back of the house. At the foot of the curving staircase which cried out, as Isla said, for Fred and Ginger, he paused and looked upwards, hand on the banisters, his head slightly tilted to catch the fine current that would tell him his wife was there. Getting nothing, he walked on.

She was in the orangery, sitting in one Lloyd-loom chair with her stockinged feet up on another. Her feet were elegant and narrow but big – a size nine. The length and beauty of her legs still brought his heart into his mouth. Her elbows were on the arms of the chair, her fingers laced loosely round a misty glass of white wine, head tipped back so that her sleek dark bob fell back from her face in a shell shape. She turned towards him as he entered, her eyes dreamy with the music.

'Hello, you.'

'Hello. Sorry I'm late.'

'It doesn't matter. We'll go in the morning.' She took his hand and held it to her cheek. 'You did warn me.'

Richard went to the kitchen and came back with ice cubes in a tumbler, and a bottle of ginger beer. Isla watched him as he glugged half the ginger beer into the glass and took the first few luxurious gulps, leaving a moustache of creamy bubbles on his upper lip. He was carrying a few extra pounds round the middle these days, but it quite suited him. The weight gave added physical presence to his great height. Here was a man of substance, in every respect. His bespoke suit – a dark grey with the faintest stripe – was rather creased, and he appeared to have tightened his tie carelessly, causing a slight tuck in one corner of his collar.

'You must be whacked,' she said.

'I wouldn't say that. What about you? Were you snarled up for hours in the West End?'

'It wasn't too good. I had a cabbie with high blood pressure so one of us had to stay calm.'

'And you're good at that.'

'Past master.'

'Mmm . . .' He bent to kiss her, his lips cool and damp from the ginger beer, and then sat down heavily on the cane sofa, carelessly crunching the disarrayed cushions, leaning back with knees apart, bottle resting on one knee, glass on the other. He caught her watching him and gave her his hot, secretive grin. He represented all that Isla liked in Englishmen – the lack of vanity that was itself slightly vain, the solid confidence, the overgrown-schoolboyishness which could be insufferable but which, when combined with intellect and charm, was irresistible.

'So tell me,' he said, 'how were the saintly sufferers?'

She laughed. 'Not all that saintly, you'll be disappointed to learn. One of them massaged my knee during the main course.'

'And was he massaging himself at the same time?'

'Don't be disgusting!'

'I only wondered.'

'Anyway, it was nice. Very uplifting.'

'For him, certainly.'

'Did I say it was a man?' For a split second she caught his shock. 'Your face is a study.'

'It was, though, wasn't it?'

'Of course.'

'Phew . . .' He took a swig. 'Only one never knows these days.'

'No,' said Isla. 'One doesn't.'

It was a sultry night with a rattle of thunder. Richard and Isla lay side by side beneath a single sheet, like a knight and his lady in marble. Generally she lay on her back, and he on his front, with one arm slung across her, until such time as he fell asleep (long before her) when she extricated herself and curled on her side. But tonight a slick of sweat had formed wherever their bodies touched, driving them apart.

'Too darn hot,' he grumbled.

'Far too,' she agreed.

'Hope it pisses down tonight,' he mumbled, sinking, 'and then resumes normal service tomorrow . . .'

He was asleep too quickly to see this hope fulfilled. By the time the heavens opened, soon after midnight, he'd been breathing deeply and distantly for nearly an hour.

Isla slipped from under the sheet and pulled on her black satin pyjamas which lay where she'd discarded them like a puddle of oil on the floor. In the bathroom she ran herself a glass of water from the tap, and then went out of the bedroom and round the gallery to the window that overlooked the heath. She sat on the windowsill with her arms clasped round her knees and watched the storm flicker and thrash over the wooded slope opposite, and the hissing curtains of rain making the wet surface of the road jump and burst as though hit by a spray of bullets.

She shared her husband's hope for the weekend. She wanted it to be nice for their visit to the boys. But she also wanted this tumultuous night not to end.

Jen woke up when one of the cats, wild and wet from the storm, leapt on to her bed and began washing with a vigour that sent a shower of cold drops flying in all directions. As she spluttered and swore into consciousness the other cat thundered and skittered up and down the stairs in an attempt to outdo the natural forces outside.

'For crying out loud . . .' Jen turned on the light and shooed Cain, for it was he, off the bed. The old-fashioned bell alarm clock said half past midnight – so it was probably about quarter to one, the clock lost a good half an hour in every twenty-four. She fell back on the pillows, her arms linked round her head. She heard Keith emerge from his quarters, speak chattily to Abel and then creak the three paces over the landing to her door.

'Art tha sleeping thar below, missis?'

'Fat chance.'

'Fancy a cuppa?'

'No thanks.'

'Well, if you change your mind I'll be manning the kettle.'

She listened to him creak away again and pad down the stairs.

Keith had his uses – mainly the forty pounds a week he paid for the back bedroom and associated facilities – and presented absolutely no threat to a single female such as herself. She was glad of him in many ways. But it was difficult, in view of all the turbulence and drama that currently crashed and howled about the streets of Crouch End, to accept that Keith was all there was.

2

Isla and Richard had bought the cottage in Bradenham six years earlier when Giles had first started at Hawtreys, the exclusive and eccentric public school favoured by Richard over his own alma mater, Winchester. It had seemed a good idea to have a country bolthole within easy reach of the school, and also of Richard's father's retirement home, where family obligations could be discharged, R & R taken, and a pleasant, undemanding, secondary social life pursued.

They referred to Brook End as a cottage, and it certainly had many of a cottage's traditional attributes – beams, inglenook, an uneven floor, and a garden foaming with honeysuckle and old-fashioned roses – but it was actually two cottages knocked through by some enterprising and far-sighted former owner, to create a spacious house. Its long, low, amiable frontage was at right angles to the eponymous brook, and overlooked a lane with only a minimum of through traffic, on the far side of which were the stately acres of The Bury (mature trees, tennis court, trout pool, and Conservation area), the property of Bill and Barbara Fyler. At the back of Brook End the garden was bordered on one side by the stream and on the other by a lovingly husbanded bank and hedge, full of wild flowers, birds' nests and small holes some of which, they had soon discovered, belonged to adders, who came out to bask in the summer sun. Giles and Marcus used to catch them with forked sticks, and hang the flaky skins up to dry.

Beyond the end of the garden, as if to remind arriviste townies of the realities of rural life, could be glimpsed the steel turrets and angular overhead walkways of Norman Brake's grain silos.

Norman was a noted misanthrope who, in common with thousands of others, had a soft spot for Isla, and had consequently allowed the boys and their friends to play 'Colditz' on and around the silos – a game in which 'prisoners' attempted to get from one side to the other without being picked out by the torches of the 'guards' patrolling the walkways. The lane circled Brook End, snuggling affectionately against the hedge, before widening fastidiously past Norman's dilapidated farm buildings and climbing the gentle hill into Silver Street, Bradenham's main drag.

This was where Marjory Dix lived, at Number 41, Heron's Holt. Richard had remarked early on, and many times since, that herons did not have holts, and that if they did they were unlikely to choose Silver Street as a site. Marjory always replied that this had been the name of the house when she bought it, that people could call a house what they liked, and it was bad luck to change it. She was someone who could truly be called 'a good woman'. She was in her early sixties, unmarried, house- and garden-proud, an upholder of family values with no family of her own, but surprisingly tolerant of the crimes and misdemeanours of 'the young', as she called them, as though they were the offspring of wildebeest or big cats. Wherever community endeavour was, there was Marjory to be found, toiling cheerfully in her dirndl and Hush Puppies, seeking neither praise nor reward. Bradenham in Bloom, suitcase sales, the clearing of the drainage ditch in the conservation area, Evergreen tea-dances and Toddler Club picnics, all would have been the poorer without Marjory's lemon curd tarts and boundless good humour. She believed in neighbourliness in its broadest sense. When the Wakefields spent their first weekend at Brook End it was Marjory who arrived with sticky bread and the village newsletter. She had befriended them at once, and continued to play the part of ex officio caretaker and housekeeper to the extent that Isla had given her a key to the cottage and their London number. She wouldn't hear of payment, but they did their best to reward her in kind with theatre tickets, and bottles of wine, and free access to cuttings from the garden. A few of the locals, the Fylers and Richard among them, laughed, not unkindly, at Marjory behind her back, but Isla refused to join in.

'She's a thoroughly nice person and I don't know what we'd do without her.'

'Employ someone we could dish out orders to without feeling guilty about it?' Richard would suggest, putting his arm round her shoulders to show he didn't mean to be cruel.

'Speak for yourself,' said Isla. 'I don't have any problem asking her to do things, and I honestly believe she considers it a pleasure.'

'And I, my darling,' said Richard, 'honestly believe that you underestimate the effect you have on people.'

This Isla conceded was probably true. She at all times resisted the idea of her own starriness, those qualities attributed to her by the press and public which ensured her a place in the hearts of both. She wasn't falsely modest, but there was a streak of canny Scots realism in her which told her that that way madness lay.

When she asked herself what she had done to deserve her modest fame, she allowed that the qualifications didn't amount to much. She'd been a quite successful model, but not in the Shrimp or Twiggy class. She'd then moved into acting, and ·played toffish young women in assorted made-for-TV films and commercials – her most notable triumph was as a lady of the manor who, jumping ship with her leather-jacketed young lover, could bear to leave everything but her Swiss oven. The final shot showed Isla, barefoot and blissful, meandering across a moorland path at dawn, with her perspiring swain trudging in her wake, the cooker on his back. The voice-over, also Isla, breathed confidingly: *She's gone with the raggle-taggle gypsies-o . . . And SCHWARTZ, of course.*

Her big break, if you could call it that, was as Sophie St George, the gobsmackingly well-bred heroine of the long-running action series *Lady In Charge*. The part could not have been called demanding. Its chief prerequisites were A1 legs, unspoiled top-drawer looks, and perfect, rounded boarding-school vowels, all of which Isla had from nature. What she brought to the part in addition to these was a humorous warmth which caused the entire viewing public, male and female, to fall a little in love with her. There was a friendly twinkle in her eye as she felled miscreants with a karate chop to the throat, a smile in her voice as she advised them to mend their ways, and a sympathetic intelligence in her eye as she warded off the half-serious advances of her partner, the lecherous rough diamond Jake Sparrow, played by Ned Braden. Ned, the housewives' fancy, was a ruggedly handsome bachelor, whose sexual ambivalence was a well-kept secret. Isla on the other hand had no secrets. She was an open book. Where other actresses complained that viewers were unable to distinguish between them and the parts they played, Isla happily admitted that, martial arts aside, she and Sophie St George were one and the same thing. Her adoring fans discovered this to be true as she opened fun days and fetes, and supported a variety of good causes, all without losing her easy, diffident charm. She was that rare and priceless thing (her agent at Prize Performers pointed out), a class act with the common touch.

Isla's modesty was genuine, for she felt she had much to be modest about. Her long line of regular army forebears and their doughty, adaptable wives, peered forever over her shoulder, reminding her that while she might nominally have a job, it could scarcely be called work. She was too much of a professional not to know by now what her assets were, but she also knew she had them by luck rather than skill or application. What she had learned to do was 'be herself' in the way that her mother had always advised. And if the self that was available on a particular occasion was not up to scratch she could effortlessly switch on the more appropriate one and put it through its paces.

It was this talent – or charm, in its magical sense – which had helped her forge an harmonious relationship with both her husband's former wives, and with the sons of the second, who even at six and eight had seemed to look down their noses at her and regarded her small store of celebrity as suspect. The fact that she had some sympathy with the latter view made it no easier to bear, but she persevered. This perseverance took the form of rigorous restraint. She was never less than kind, but also withdrawn. She did not invite or cajole, she simply allowed access, and waited. As she went about her life with

Richard she watched his mutinous offspring from the corner
of her eye. Her instinct told her that small boys were like wild
animals, shy and unpredictable, their aggression sparked by fear
rather than hostility. So it made sense to move smoothly, avoid
direct eye contact and raised voices: to do nothing, in fact, to
activate the fight or flight mechanism.

It worked. Slowly, they came round. And hard cash was the
early currency of the relationship. The day Giles asked if he
could borrow two quid to go to the cinema she knew they
were on their way. She said, did he mean borrow, or have?
He conceded grudgingly that he supposed he meant have. On
this sound business footing the lines of communication were
opened. She gave him the two pounds and was rewarded with
a certain dour appreciation. They weren't as yet friends, but
they had the glimmerings of an understanding. The next time
he used the word borrow she elicited an IOU, called in the debt,
and was duly, if tardily, paid.

Now Giles and Marcus were both at Hawtrey's, completing
their A and GCSE years respectively. Giles was smooth and lazy
and ambitious. Marcus was clever and off the wall and didn't
give a shit. In the holidays, part of which was always spent
with their father and stepmother, Giles gravitated towards 'older
women' – girls of nineteen or twenty – whose fathers owned
yachts and ski-chalets, and Marcus burrowed scowlingly into the
social equivalent of the gutter. The previous summer Giles had
wangled a holiday job at a language school – foreign chick city, as
he pointed out. Marcus got one toting stock in the warehouse at
Toys R Us, his angry energy just about compensating for his lack
of interpersonal skills. He had a half-hour lunch break which he
took outside, consuming as many Marlboros as was possible in
the time and probably (Isla thought) frightening the family
clientele with his dark and dissolute appearance.

Neither of the boys was expected to do particularly well
in their exams, but this was not a source of great concern,
either at home or at school. Richard had chosen Hawtrey's for
the 'progressive' reputation gained by the founder, Quentin
Hawtrey in the late 1920s. Richard himself had been ruthlessly
directed through Winchester and Cambridge to the Bar by
his own father, with outstanding success and commensurate

material rewards, but Richard was typically ungrateful and determined, via his own sons, to make some perverse point about personal fulfilment. Isla wasn't sure where it would all lead, but kept her misgivings to herself. As a childless third wife plucked from the domestically unstable ranks of showbusiness, it behoved her to keep her counsel.

For a woman whose public persona radiated a warmly vocal and outgoing charm, Isla Munro was good at keeping quiet, and pondering things in her heart.

Dinner at The Bury was considered locally to be something of an honour, but Isla and Richard, who had been on the Fylers' A list since they arrived, were not aware of this. Bill and Barbara's style of hospitality did nothing to confer a sense of privilege. Drink was strong and free-flowing, food plain, plentiful and filling, and chairs capacious and comfy. But in winter the temperature inside The Bury lacked only precipitation to make it identical to the one outside, and even that could be arranged when the ancient pipes played up. The kitchen was vast and weather-beaten, with a stone sink, a wooden draining board and visible mousetraps. There was a larder with a marble slab and a meat safe. And Barbara as often as not placed a milk bottle on the coffee tray with a small beaded net over the top to keep out winged invaders. The Fylers had several dogs. Bill kept springer spaniels as gun dogs, who were housed in kennels and a pen adjoining the barn. In a separate kennel, nearer the house was a vicious and unpredictable Rhodesian Ridgeback, Janus, an animal just waiting for some unsuspecting villain to trespass and make his day. But in fact neither the springers not Janus were the problem, which lay with the two indoor dogs. Portia was an ancient Rottweiler – Janus's predecessor – with sagging upholstery and halitosis that could have halted a cruise missile. To be befriended by Portia over the pre-dinner drinks was to be exposed to slow torture by proximity. Pepe, Barbara's Jack Russell, was fighting fit, and made his typical entrance through the air at lap height, teeth bared, skimming from chair to knee to Georgian whatnot at lightning speed, scattering Waterford crystal and Smiths crisps, and coming to rest on whoever had the most expensive clothes. There were cats, too, at The Bury, but they were yowling, feral creatures who fled in the headlights, gruesome remains dangling from their skinny jaws.

'Forget the council,' Bill was wont to say. 'If you've got rats you want hungry cats and a terrier.'

'We haven't got rats,' Richard would reply, prompting Bill's cavernous phlegmy chuckle.

'There speaks a Hampstead countryman! Of course you've got bloody rats, Dick, that place of yours is sandwiched in between two working farms, and old Norman's patch is completely overrun, you can betcha.'

They let this go by. They hadn't yet seen a rat and to keep cats and a dog in a weekend cottage wasn't practical, as Bill knew perfectly well. He had the genial hard-heartedness common to the landed upper class and liked to bully them a bit.

'Thought you were coming down last night!' he growled, pressing navy-strength gin on Isla and a large Bells on Richard. 'But we gather you let a spot of rain put you off.'

'No, it wasn't that,' said Isla. 'There was a bomb scare in town and it made us both late, so we decided to cut our losses.'

'Where was this bomb?'

'Suspected, only. In Oxford Street.'

Barbara entered from the kitchen. She wore a long Indian cotton dress in shades of brown, teamed with a cashmere cardigan and a plastic apron decorated with a nude female figure. Pepe circled her legs intently as she shook peanuts inaccurately into a Limoges sugar basin.

'It wasn't the weather held these two up,' announced Bill. 'It was some bloody silly bomb scare.'

'What so-and-sos they are,' agreed Barbara. 'Pepe, no, no! NO! Nut anyone?'

Pepe's beady, shark-like eyes remained fixed on the nuts as they dispersed. To avoid head-on contact with the canine piranha, Isla declined. Richard took a handful but remained standing. Bill, scotch in hand, hove alongside his guest for the usual bullish inquisition on the legal profession. Barbara sat down on the sofa by Isla.

'Poor old Portia's got the gutsache.'

'Oh, I am sorry,' said Isla. 'What do you think might have caused it?'

'Could be any of a dozen things – old age, eating rubbish, something disgusting in the fields . . .' Barbara's grimace indicated that the list was endless.

'Poor love, what have you done with her?' asked Isla, looking deeply concerned to disguise her relief.

'She's in the washhouse, looking very sorry for herself, but best place for her. If she chucks up in there it's nothing a wodge of newpaper and a damp cloth can't handle.'

'I don't envy either of you.'

'That's dogs for you.' Barbara proffered the nuts again, restraining the quivering Pepe with her free arm.

'I won't thanks. I'm saving myself for dinner.'

'I've done a massive stew, prime beef and two pints of stout.' Barbara's catering paid no never mind to seasonal changes or public opinion. 'I take it you two aren't frightened to death at the prospect of eating cow?'

'Not in the least. Now tell me,' went on Isla, touching Barbara's wrist lightly with her forefinger. 'How is Nell?'

Petronella was the Fylers' twenty-six-year-old daughter, a tall, rawboned young woman who when put in a frock looked, as Richard succinctly put it, like an Aunt Sally, but on horseback became a valkyrie.

'Nell's going great guns, I'm happy to say. She's got a flat in Lexham Gardens with Robert Scott-Chatham, did you ever meet James and Angela?'

'I don't think so . . .' mused Isla. 'They're not the ones with the water mill . . . ?'

'Good God no!' Barbara's expression was a colourful snapshot of the English class system at work, conveying in a split second that, nice though the water mill was, it was a touch too picturesque for respectability, and had been exhaustively (the unkind might say excessively) renovated with bucketfuls of spanking new money. This placed it if not beyond, at least within striking distance of, the pale, while the Scott-Chathams were comfortably within it. The greater the social divide, the greater the Fylers' dismissal of it. It was the would-be-theres who attracted their disfavour. So Norman Brake, a spitter, a cusser and a Labour voter who held his knife like a pen, might be cordially disliked but was not looked down upon. The unfortunate owners of the water mill might as well have borne the mark of Cain on their foreheads.

'. . . nothing in it, she assures me,' Barbara went on doubtfully, 'this mixed sharing goes on all the time. Not that it's any business of mine any more what she gets up to. What about your two, Richard's two?'

'We're going over to the school tomorrow, and taking them out.'

'Do use the court if you want to – it's only standing idle.'

'Thanks, that's very kind, we may well.'

'Unless of course they're at the age when they'd rather walk barefoot over hot coals than consort with the older generation?' Barbara raised an unplucked eyebrow. Isla returned a suitably rueful grin.

'A bit like that, I grant you. But I imagine they could come over on their own, if they wanted to?'

'Hell's bells, my dear, I didn't mean *you*, I meant *us*. I mean if I happen to show my face about the place will it completely ruin their weekend?'

Isla laughed. 'No. Of course not. It's a good offer, Barbara, thanks.'

'I'm going to slip away and check my greens,' said Barbara. To wish for an *al dente* vegetable at The Bury was to court certain disappointment. 'Don't let Pepe take any liberties.'

Bill replenished drinks all round. 'She told you about Nell?'

'What about her?'

'About sharing with the Scott-Chatham pillock?'

'Oh yes, she did. It sounds like a good arrangement.'

'That's just where you're wrong!' Bill jabbed an unlit cigarette in her direction. 'He's a prize toerag. I don't want him sniffing around my daughter with his eye on the main chance.'

Richard covered his eyes in despair. 'Steady on, Bill – this is the nineteen-nineties, mixed sharing isn't even new. And anyway, Nell's free, white and twenty-one, what's your problem for God's sake?'

Bill rounded on Isla. 'You know what I'm getting at don't you, gorgeous?'

She shook her head. 'I hate to let you down, but I think you're overreacting, I really do. It's absolutely the norm, and Barbara seems to be taking it perfectly in her stride.'

'Christ! Traitor!' Bill made a wild gesture which slopped scotch on the priceless but already heavily-stained Persian rug. 'You come here in that get-up, with those legs, in a cloud of some aphrodisiac stench, and have the brass neck to take their side against me? Me, your ever-genial and eternally lustful host?' Thoroughly wound-up by this tirade, Pepe sprang from the sofa and began to execute vertical take-offs, barking noisily.

'Shut up, William.' Barbara appeared in the doorway. 'You're upsetting the dog.'

'Christ . . .' grumbled Bill again, then swallowed the remaining Scotch and bore down on Isla. 'Come on, I vote we revive the old tradition of escorting the ladies to the table.' He proffered an arm the size of a well-upholstered sofa-back. 'Will you take this withered limb, my dear?'

Conversation over dinner, fuelled by a full-blooded supermarket claret, was typically noisy and contentious. Barbara's watercress soup and excellent stew saw the twilight of the old-style Tories, the tyranny of Brussels and a reprise (occasioned by mournful howling in the yard) of Portia's stomach upset; apple amber and ice cream was the occasion for a bracing work-out with career wives (the Fylers were not at the cutting edge of social change), leading as night follows day, with the Stilton and Bath Olivers, to more of the Nell question.

'I don't just think, I *know* that frightful lothario is after her,' declared Bill, stabbing savagely at the heart of the cheese.

'So what if he is?' asked Barbara. 'Cupid's dart and all that.'

'Stuff Cupid. The thought of that brainless, gutless oaf as a son-in-law fills me with complete and utter gloom.'

'You're leaping ahead a bit here, surely,' said Richard. 'A bit of nooky in Swiss Cottage's one thing, wedding bells quite another. And increasingly rare, I might add.'

'There's no telling him.' Barbara sprinkled salt liberally along a stick of celery. 'He's a dinosaur. We both are, but he's a helluva lot more of a one than I am.' She took a noisy, incisive mouthful and munched, cheeks bulging.

Once again Bill turned to Isla. 'Now's your chance. Are you going to redeem yourself after your earlier lapse, or what?'

Isla beamed, head tilted in apology. 'What, I'm afraid.'

He glared now at Richard. 'How do you stand it? So cold, so unfeeling. So bloody heartless.'

'It's a tough job,' agreed Richard, 'but some poor bugger's got to do it.'

'And as for that dinosaur dig – my own wife!'

'How do you think they died out?' asked Isla. 'Not enough mixed flats.'

'Ah. Ah. Ah. Now we have jokes!'

'I was never more serious in my life.'

'OK, all right, have it your own way –' Bill dusted his huge palms together, releasing a shower of crumbs to be hoovered up by Pepe. 'But I still don't want that Nth-rater getting his clammy paws on the Fyler fortune.'

Barbara let out a pig-like snort, and Pepe immediately leapt on to her lap and thrust his face into hers.

'I beg your pardon, my heart?' asked Bill.

'Fortune, my eye!'

'Not at all. Compared to the SCs we constitute bloated plutocrats, and as such Nell's a bloody good catch.'

'Forgive my saying so, but you're talking about your daughter as if she were a brood mare,' commented Richard, poising his knife over the Stilton. 'May I?'

'Help yourself,' said Barbara. 'If you ask me, Nell could do with a bit of a sex life, and she's not so daft that she's going to marry some chap just because he stonks her.'

Bill didn't bat an eyelid, but Isla caught Richard's eye and felt a laugh swell between them like an invisible balloon.

'Because he does what?' asked Richard in his most cool and lawyerly manner.

'Stonks her. Stonks – have I got that right?'

'You mean bonks,' said Isla.

'Do I?'

'Unless you know something that we don't.'

'But I swear I've heard people – the young – say 'stonking' in the same sort of way they say, um, fucking.'

'Language, dearest!' barked Bill absentmindedly, but it was

just as well he said something because Richard and Isla were helpless.

As they paid a good-night call on the ailing Portia before leaving, Bill placed a hand on Isla's shoulder.

'Do this poor old man a favour, gorgeous.'

'What, here?' Richard gazed wildly about. 'Now?'

Bill ignored this. 'Go and pay Nell a visit when you're back in the smog. Have a womanly word. Report any developments.'

'Don't be such a fathead,' said Barbara, making kissy faces at the dog. 'What possible excuse could poor Isla find for dragging across town to see Nell? And why the hell should she anyway?'

'Absolutely,' said Richard. 'Why should you?'

Isla cuffed him. 'Of course I will. It'd be a pleasure.'

'Good God 'n' stuff,' cried Bill. 'That was easier than I thought it would be.'

'You thought I was joking, didn't you?' said Richard in bed.

'About what?'

'About Nell.' He stroked her hair. 'But I wasn't – why should you?'

'No reason, except that it would amuse me.' Isla knew that enlightened self-interest was the reasoning most likely to appeal to her husband.

'Oh well in that case. Though I must say there's no accounting for taste . . .'

A silence spread. Or at least a pocket of silence in the creaking, whispering, squawking rural darkness. You were never alone in the country. Whereas at night in Hampstead the huge house could feel empty as a vault, and the sleeping giant of London, grumbling distantly, no company at all.

Isla felt Richard's hand cupping and pressing on her cheek, and rolled her head to face him.

'You're too good,' he said.

'Oh Lord,' she said, appalled. 'Please. I do hope not.'

'You are . . .' He was amorous.

'Too good for what . . . ?' She turned on her side, into his arms.

'For all of us. Definitely too good for me.'

'That's true.' She smiled, kissed, settled. 'But then, who isn't?'

Richard had gone after Isla with a singleminded passion which had surprised even his colleagues and his closest friends. Already separated from the boys' mother, Caroline, after eight years, and with a youthful mismatch to a fellow lawyer, Donatella, haunting his past, they'd all thought he would concentrate on being single, and sought-after. After all, he was a catch, eligibility made flesh – the grey wolf of the libel bar.

But once he'd met Isla, at a show-business party to which he'd been invited by a grateful client, that was it. He had to have her. He called, he wrote, he sent flowers. Onlookers remained sceptical. They took the view that once – if – the conquest were made he'd lose interest. Not that she played hard to get. But she was busy, a star. Part of her charm, people considered privately, was her unavailability. But when the breakthrough came, in the form of dinner at Claridges, Richard was if anything even more smitten.

'She's quite, quite the best thing on two legs,' he told Archie Stainforth, a slightly younger colleague and friend of many summers' standing. 'I simply adore her.'

'But you're not exactly alone in that are you?' Archie pointed out. 'I mean half the male population of England's infatuated with her, so she must be awfully used to it.'

'She's not in the least actressy, if that's what you mean,' said Richard. 'She's one of the nicest, warmest, funniest women I've met, and as for the packaging . . .'

Archie looked understanding. 'Yes, yes. Quite. But then – well – that is her job, isn't it? I mean, being funny, warm and beautiful is how she makes her living. A pretty handsome one, I should imagine.'

'That's an extremely unworthy observation.' Richard looked aggrieved, and Archie, a famously softhearted soul, even more so.

'I'm sorry, no offence intended. Maybe I'm just jealous.'

'You've no need to be. I'm probably making a fool of myself in the most public way possible.'

'No, no, no,' said Archie, who actually could not have borne to see his friend humiliated. 'No, no, not at all.'

Richard knew that he meant it. When Isla agreed to marry him, Archie was quite moist-eyed with delight. His was a giving and humble nature to whom the concept of *Schadenfreude* was utterly foreign. His happiness consisted of the happiness of those he cared for. When Richard visited Archie and Alison in their large, shambolic house in Clarendon Road, Camden, he always came away feeling two things – first, that they were a profoundly happy couple and, second, that whatever the vagaries of his own emotional life he was awfully glad he wasn't Archie. At some point around his late thirties, Richard had at last acquired enough self-knowledge to realise that he was not cut out for the long domestic haul. He noted the cluttered kitchen noticeboard, the forest of toothbrushes, the sluggish and hirsute au pair, the tiny cubes of Lego on the kitchen floor, the constant summons of the phone and the banging of doors as the Stainforths' various offspring, ranging in age from toddlers to teenagers, came and went, the animal hairs clinging to the furniture . . . The weird, far-off music and strange smells . . . Not that Richard wasn't distantly acquainted with some of these from the dark days of his union with Caroline when the boys were little, but seeing the selfless tolerance and cheerfulness of Archie and Alison made him realise how wretchedly inept he himself had been in similar circumstances.

His marriage to Isla was as near as possible the perfect relationship of which he'd always dreamed. So many of his male acquaintances told him he was the luckiest man alive, and he could well believe it. He could not find it in himself to harbour any regrets about their lack of children, though he suspected it might in the past have been a source of sadness to Isla. If she had raised the subject of adoption, or – God forbid – fertility treatment or in vitro fertilisation, he would of course have seriously considered the options. But she never had.

She seemed, now, to be asleep. He gazed into the dark, close, secrecy of her face. A woman with a public persona was owned, in some strange way, by everyone who knew her name. But Richard knew that much as he himself might like to do so, Isla could never be owned.

*   *   *

They arrived at Hawtrey's the following morning at eleven. The order of the day was that there were various exhibitions of the students' work, and teachers were available for consultation, though only in the presence of the student concerned. Neither exhibitions nor consultations were compulsory and Marcus, in Edward Scissorhands mode, was hanging about at the school gate hoping for a swift getaway.

'You don't want to waste time in there,' he complained through the open car window. 'It'll be the same old bollocks.'

'Why not let us be the judge of that,' said Richard. 'Hop in.'

From Marcus's look it was clear that this suggestion was on a par with tea with the Queen Mother. He withdrew from the side of the car as if electrocuted. Richard smiled coolly.

'We'll see you back here then . . .' The Jag slid forward. 'Good grief, what does he look like?'

'Memorable?'

'OK, OK, let's leave it at that.'

Isla smiled at his ashen look. 'You wanted them to find their own path, and he's finding it.'

'I'd have thought pathfinding of any sort would be out of the question with that hairdo.'

'Listen to yourself.'

'Am I being a stuffy old bore?'

'You're in danger of sounding like one. And if you don't watch out, how will people who don't know you be able to tell the difference?'

As they approached the mêlée of vehicles attempting to park outside the school's main entrance, Richard placed a hand on his wife's knee.

'True, as always.'

Giles, suave in a black polo shirt and jeans was in the front hall, sitting sideways on the edge of a table covered in leaflets. Like a TV director, thought Isla, and experienced a faint chill of precognition.

'Hi there,' he said. 'You're looking at the man in charge.'

Isla kissed him, and he claimed a second cheek as well. She wondered what he said to his friends about her.

'In charge of what?' asked Richard, taking in the milling

throng of big shirts, rugged boots, nose-studs and rumpled jackets which could contain students, staff or parents, it was so hard to tell . . .

'Today's events. Have a leaflet.'

Richard stared at it and passed it to Isla. 'We saw Marcus at the gate.'

'Poor little sod, I'm holding him up.'

'Not at all,' said Isla, 'we want to take a look round.'

'How come you're doing this, anyway?' asked Richard, unable to keep the note of suspicion out of his voice.

Giles shrugged. 'Just got lucky I guess. Plus, I'm the oldest inhabitant.'

There was no prefect system at Hawtrey's, responsibility being handed out as a cure for delinquency or a concomitant of long service. Richard suspected that if his older son qualified on the latter grounds, his younger would soon make it on the former.

Over coffee in the refectory – administered from behind a counter by two whey-faced girls with an abrasive approach to service – Richard and Isla were approached by the headmaster, Bruce Aldred. He was a burly, open-faced man in his early forties, who had once been a monk. His style of leadership was shirt-sleeved and democratic, with a muscular plain-spokenness which had helped set the tone of Hawtrey's in the 1990s.

'Good morning, good morning.' He proffered a hand like a shovel to each of them in turn, and pulled a third, spindly, green refectory chair well out from the table in order to sit down, which he did with arms folded on chest and thighs well apart. 'So how do you find them?'

'Pretty true to type,' said Richard. 'Marcus saturnine and hankering to be away, Giles in the thick of it.'

'That's your boys.' Bruce clicked his teeth, and then added: 'Playing against the role as usual.'

Richard grew wary. 'How do you mean?'

'Your wife knows what I mean.' Bruce looked at Isla with eyebrows raised and chin slighty lowered, prompting her to speak, but before she could do so Richard cut in.

'No, no, I understand the expression perfectly, but not its application to my sons.'

'Marcus is a thorn in the side of everyone over twenty in this establishment, but he's actually doing rather well in spite of himself. An attitude problem and a bit of dope do not, unfortunately for Marcus, add up to full-blown delinquency, much as he might like them to. Not around here, anyway. Giles of course is affability itself, but puts the pleasure principle before all else.'

'Oh dear,' said Isla, 'what has he been up to?'

'Pursuing a vibrant social life. Nothing wrong with that, but there's a limit to what can be tolerated in a school, even one as broad-minded as this.'

'We're talking sex, here, are we?' enquired Richard in a robust tone which Isla recognised as covering a certain amount of embarrassment. 'Good old-fashioned sex?'

'That's right. Whether it was old-fashioned or not I'm not in a position to say, but it must have been good because it woke the under matron up at one in the morning.'

'Was it another pupil?'

Bruce nodded once, lips pursed. 'That's the problem we have with it. A non-close-encounter policy is key to this operation. Once that's allowed to take hold it could create complete havoc as I'm sure you appreciate.'

'So you're keeping him busy,' said Isla.

'Well, yes, and putting him on the spot a bit. Being singled out puts him in a more exposed position, makes it a bit harder to get up to all sorts.'

'What about the girl?'

'A very together young lady in Marcus's year, her people are out in Bahrein—

'Hang on a second,' said Richard, 'what did you say?'

'Bahrein. He's an engineer.'

'No. Did you say she was in Marcus's year?'

'That's correct.'

Richard looked stricken. 'She must be under age!'

'Strictly speaking yes, she is. Was. She's had a birthday since.'

'What other way is there of speaking?'

'Richard, my dear chap – you haven't seen her.'

'If a judge said that he'd be quite properly pilloried in the right-wing press. It's illegal.'

'Yes it is, but if anyone chose to enforce that particular law half the teenagers in the country would be clapped in irons.'

Richard shook his head, massaging his temples vigorously. 'God . . .'

'Do her parents know?' asked Isla.

'Not at the moment. Or not by our agency at any rate. It may have been technically illegal, Richard, but we're not about to criminalise it. These are two healthy young adults we're talking about, and the evidence is that they were taking precautions –' Richard groaned – 'so as far as we're concerned the matter ends there.'

'But the implications are horrendous, I mean this girl's in your care, it doesn't bear thinking about in today's climate.'

Bruce made a facial shrug. 'We take our responsibilities extremely seriously, but we try to live in the real world.'

'I'll talk to him, naturally, I'll talk to him today . . .'

Isla knew that finding an opening for this sensitive exchange between leaving Hawtrey's at twelve and returning at ten p.m. would not be easy. It was clearly not a matter to be discussed in Marcus's presence, or (she was sensitive to her position) in hers, either. This was man-to-man stuff, but how it was to be achieved, when Giles's day was generally dedicated to the most accessible starred entries in his little black book, was beyond her.

On the drive back to Bradenham Giles was in high good humour, while Marcus put on headphones and closed his eyes.

'You know,' remarked Giles, leaning on the back of Isla's seat, 'this may come as a surprise to you but I can't wait to be shot of that place.'

'Is that so?' said Richard. 'You do surprise me.'

'No, honestly, Bruce and co think they're the dog's bollocks with their liberal regime, but when it comes down to it they're no different to anyone else.'

'Glad to hear it,' said Richard grimly.

Isla turned round to look her stepson in the eye. 'When it comes down to what?'

'You name it. Scratch a teacher, find a fascist.' He chuckled.

'I think they're saints,' said Isla. 'I'd need danger money to be in charge of you lot.'

'You'd be great. Want to join up? You could take drama workshops instead of Tanktop Man.'

'No thanks. Wild horses wouldn't drag me.'

Richard peered frostily in the rearview mirror. 'Had any thoughts about what you're going to do when you leave?'

'Certainly have. Chris Beales and me are going to start up as party organisers. There's serious money in it.'

'If it was as easy as that, everyone would be doing it.'

'Chris has got contacts,' said Giles, and fell back in his seat with a smile as though that closed the matter.

Much to Isla's surprise, when Richard suggested a singles after lunch, Giles acquiesced.

'Sure, if you want to get thrashed. Best of three short ones, right?'

Isla, left alone with Marcus in the garden, broke the silence.

'So,' she said. 'How were the exams?'

'All right.'

'And what about everything else?'

'Bit of a global question. What would you like to know?'

'I don't know . . . Tell me something.'

'No,' said Marcus. 'Not in the mood.' He had been lying on the grass with his ankles crossed, a can of Grolsch resting on his stomach. But now he stretched his arms in the air, can in hand, rolled forward and stood up. His shrunken T-shirt revealed a frighteningly thin torso.

'Think I'll take a walk.'

Isla forebore to offer company. She was relieved rather than offended. She and Marcus understood one another. The scrupulously maintained distance between them was a substitute for niceties and insured complete discretion.

She sat in the sun with the last of her wine. It was very still and she could hear the irregular plop of the tennis ball, Giles's voice raised from time to time in glee or despair.

'Hello there! Am I disturbing?'

'Marjory, how nice – please do – sit down.'

'Phew!' Marjory collapsed in the deck chair vacated by Richard. 'That'll larn me. I set out to cycle and it's turned wondrous warm.'

'Isn't it lovely,' agreed Isla.

'Is that your lot playing at The Bury?'

'Richard and Giles.'

'Ah yes, I saw t'other one toiling up the footpath.'

'I'm sorry, Marjory, how rude of me, would you like a glass of wine?'

'Not a drop thanks, contrary to appearances I'm not stopping, I might have a slurp of tap water on the way out. Was everything all right, by the way?'

'Absolutely. Thank you so much. As usual.'

'Fiddle-de-dee,' said Marjory. 'And did you have a nice evening with the Fylers?'

'We did, very good fun. They're worried about their daughter, though, and I've been deputed to run the rule over her.'

'*You* have?'

Isla laughed. 'Don't sound so surprised.'

'No offence, my dear, but Nell has nothing to fear does she? If she has any secrets, which I doubt, they will be perfectly safe with you.'

Richard returned looking damp and dishevelled and with a dangerously high colour.

'Who won?'

'Don't ask. I have all the technique, but he has youth on his side.'

Isla lowered her voice slightly. 'Where is he now?'

'Conjuring a date on the phone.'

'Did you manage to . . . ?'

'I did.'

'And how did it go down?'

'It sank in. I think. It's a bit hard to tell, he's so bloody affable, it's rather like leaning on an open door.'

Isla held out her hand to him. 'Well done, anyway. What line did you take?'

After a split-second's hesitation he took the hand. 'Trust,' he said. 'I played the trust card. Our relationship with him depends on trust, Hawtrey's is run on a basis of trust. And that has to be a two-way thing. Would you agree?'

'Yes,' said Isla, 'I would.'

3

Claudia Delaney descended from the passenger cab of a Dutch container lorry in the car park of a Happy Eater on the Oxford ring road. The driver leaned across to bid her farewell.

'You have my address and number. Don't forget to visit if you're in Holland. I live just outside Amsterdam.'

'I will, thanks.'

'Will you be all right now?'

'I'll be fine.'

'Good to have met you.'

'Yes,' agreed Claudia. She picked up her khaki canvas fishing bag, swung it over her shoulder, took a couple of backward steps, hand raised, to signify token regret, and began walking determinedly away. She knew the driver was gazing after her because it was a full thirty seconds before the lorry's engine started up. As it roared past her to rejoin the ring road, she didn't look up.

Claudia was a seasoned hitcher of lifts, and on a sex-pest scale of one to ten the Dutch driver had scarcely made the cut. Far too nice: earnest, interested, persistent. She was awfully glad to see the back of him, even though it had meant being dropped at an inconvenient distance from her destination – too far to walk comfortably, too close to pick up a decent lift, and not well-placed for buses even if she'd had the first idea which one to get on. A taxi was out of the question, she told herself. She had the cash on her, but there was a parsimonious streak in Claudia.

When the lorry was safely away she paused, dumped the fishing bag on the ground again and studied the road map. Kersney Court, she estimated, was about two miles from here as the crow flew, more like four as a loaded pedestrian made her way on foot. She glanced at her watch. Time, at least, was on her side. She'd left Paris at eight a.m. and it was now three. Taking into consideration the hour's leeway she always allowed herself, and the hour's lateness which was a given factor with her mother, she'd stroll it with time to spare.

A Toyota sports car pulled up by her, and a male voice said: 'Everything OK love?'

'Yes thanks.'

'Want a lift anywhere?'

'No.'

'I'll be stopping for tea.'

Claudia folded the road map and stuffed it back in her bag. The man at the wheel of the Toyota was fleshy and sleekly groomed, with a moustache and a wedding ring.

'No – really?'

Encouraged, he treated her to a roguish smirk. 'Sure. I generally go for some nice little spot.'

'Want my advice?' asked Claudia. Something in her tone caused the smirk to fade and she moved swiftly to finish it off. 'Forget it. You need to cut down.'

'Rude bitch.' He gunned the engine so hard it whooped, and the Toyota shot forward towards the road, missing Claudia's feet by inches but not causing her to flinch.

'My pleasure,' she murmured coolly, and started walking.

Claudia was twenty-one, six foot, and barely ten stone, with dark red hair and bronze eyes interestingly flecked with black. Because of her exceptional height and striking looks men – both casual predators like the Toyota driver, and hopelessly enslaved romantics – had been coming on to her since she was in her early teens. Either way they were generally rebuffed. She was not so much picky as uninterested. She had seen enough of the mess consequent upon romantic entanglements to last her a lifetime. Her own mother was a case in point – an object lesson, in Claudia's view, on the unwisdom of being too susceptible to the male of the species.

She dressed specifically to counteract what she saw as her own natural disadvantages. Her personal style was best described as trailer-trash, with a nod to wartime drudge and a dash of mad vagrant. She used no make-up (if you didn't count the tattoo of a frog on the arch of her left foot) and her hair at this moment was barely an inch long all over – it had been shaved six weeks before but she had caught the sun on the top of her head and had grown it for protection. Today she wore a brown-and-pink-printed cotton dress that drooped unevenly to mid-calf, a pair of plimsolls grey with use, and a spinach-coloured cardigan tied round her waist. No jewellery, minimal underwear. As well as the fishing satchel she carried a shoulder bag, both of them slung diagonally across her torso like cartridge belts.

Unfortunately for her, Claudia's looks were more than up to the challenge, and her determined efforts to repel only had the effect of throwing her eccentric beauty into sharp relief. Walking with head high and a long, leonine stride along the grass verge of the Oxford ring road she was the unwitting cause of innumerable changes in pulse rate and at least one acrimonious near-miss.

Claudia took her responsibilities seriously, especially those towards her mother. She loved Jen with a stern, protective passion, and despaired of her almost as passionately. How could one apparently intelligent and balanced woman get into so many disastrous emotional entanglements? How could someone who Claudia allowed was a wonderful parent, be such a lousy judge of character? And why on earth couldn't she get a grip? Because what got Claudia's goat most of all was her mother's apparent lack of concern about the mire of muddle and make-do that was her life.

Jen had always been frank – about the facts of life, about unorthodox proclivities in others, and about her past. Claudia knew that her own birth had been at least in part a response to the two abortions which had preceded it. The first of these had been the result of a liaison with a married man (not the last, as Claudia grimly reminded herself), the second had been Claudia's putative older brother or sister. That upset Claudia if she thought about it too much. She herself loathed the very idea of abortion and could not imagine any circumstances in which she would even consider such a thing. Her father, Mo, was now married to a timpanist with the Bournemouth Symphony Orchestra and had a brood of legitimate children of his own. She and Jen enjoyed a friendly relationship with all of them, but Claudia would have liked a little more order. After all, it hadn't ended there. For ages now, since she was a child, there had been Richard, who appeared to be what passed for a fixture with Jen. A fixture, but not a fitting. A very unfitting fixture . . . In the early days she'd been at primary school, it had been impossible to avoid coming into contact with him from time to time and, to do him justice, she hadn't disliked him. He'd always maintained a polite, benign distance with her which was unthreatening. But that was years ago, and it had just gone on and on. What, she wondered, could possibly be in it for her mother? How could she be satisfied with something so patently unsatisfactory? These days Claudia made damn sure she didn't run into the fat cat, with his cigars and his big swanky motor . . .

She found that her teeth were gritted as she walked along. They made a small squeaking noise and she relaxed her jaw and eased it from side to side. She knew, because both Jen and her dentist had told her, that she ground her teeth at night. And could you wonder? She had a lot to grind about.

She paused to consult the map again. She had long since turned off the ring road, and now she must take the next left into something that was no more than a squiggly thread on the page, and from there into another, straighter thread which was the private road, considerably longer than a mere drive, which led to Kersney Court.

She turned up the lane without altering her stride, homing in steadily on her destination. Claudia had been spending the weekend with her friend Ben who was studying (when the mood took him) at the Sorbonne. Ben and his Danish girlfriend Elke had occupied the futon in the bedroom and Claudia had spent two uncomfortable but mercifully short nights on a sofa nearly as bony as she was. But it had been fun nevertheless. Elke played tenor sax with an all-girl group in a bar in Bastille, and they'd gone there in the evening and hung out with wonderful-looking gay women in the sort of relaxed, intelligent atmosphere that she found completely *sympathique*.

Surprisingly it had been at this bar, the Club Copain, that a man had come up to her and told her she should be a model.

It had been such an unlikely setting for this approach, and such a hackneyed line, that she'd actually laughed in his face. But he'd been completely unperturbed and handed her a card with the addresses (Paris and London) at which she would be able to contact him or his colleagues. At the time she hadn't even bothered to look at it. But over peppermint tea at three-thirty a.m. in the flat, Ben and Elke had made her do so and they'd all three shrieked with pleasurable disbelief to see the name of a designer of whom even Claudia had heard.

She still had the card in her bag, but she doubted she'd do anything with it. It was almost certainly a fake and the man in the suit a procurer. Claudia wasn't born yesterday, and she had a combined studies degree at London to complete next year.

The hedge to her left had given way to a high wall, and now she came to two immense gryphon-topped stone pillars flanking a gravel entrance. Halfway down the right-hand pillar the words 'Kersney Court' were discreetly engraved, the indentations softened by time and silvery lichen. Claudia put the map away and turned in.

Twenty or so metres past the entrance the drive narrowed and became a recently macadamed cart track, with cattle grids at regular intervals. Fat white Charolais cows dotted the park on either side like becalmed yachts. Their presence deterred Claudia from striking out across the grass towards the house whose tall chimneys she could see sticking up beyond trees to her left.

She had agreed to come here, rather than hitch a lift straight back into town, to give her mother an excuse to escape, and map-reading support. She should of course have said no – a woman of Jen's age ought to have been able to depart and find her way home without assistance – but had, as usual, weakened and come miles out of her way to provide the necessary.

She heard a vehicle turn in off the road and come bumping down behind her, buzzing over the grids noisily, going too fast for a low gear. Claudia moved aside on to the grass without breaking stride or altering her speed.

To her annoyance a filthy Land-Rover with two labradors lolling in the back pulled up alongside. The driver, middle-aged and wearing a checked Vyella shirt, hung an arm over the side and raised his voice to counter the amiable barking of the dogs.

'Going to the house?'

'Yes.'

'Like a lift?'

'No thanks.'

'Are you sure? It's a helluva hike if you don't like cows.'

Claudia gave him a cool stare. 'I don't mind cows, and I like walking.'

'Tremendous.' She couldn't tell if he was being sarcastic or not. 'I'll leave you to it then.'

The man bumped and buzzed away, the labradors still wagging and barking in the back.

It was a further fifteen minutes before she reached the house and she slightly regretted not having accepted the lift. Plimsolls were not designed for serious walking, and hers were not in the first flush of youth. The sole of one of them was almost worn through and she had a blister. She yanked irritably on the iron bell-pull and stood back to survey the house.

Claudia knew nothing about architecture, but Kersney Court would have been perfect for the role of Great House in a TV adaptation of Jane Austen. Long windows, tall chimneys, a slate roof with parapets, an impressive pillared entrance and loads of ivy. Nice. The only jarring note was her mother's disreputable Renault Diane parked, wheels askew, bang in the middle of the forecourt.

Distant barking accompanied the opening of the door.

'You made it then,' said the man from the Land-Rover. 'Come in.'

'Thanks.' Smarting with embarrassment Claudia stepped over the threshold and into a big hall full of the evocative smell of stately oldness. The man was in his stockinged feet.

'I live here, you see,' he said, catching her glance. She nodded. 'So please – what can we do for you?'

'I'm meeting my mother here – Jen Delaney.'

'Ah.' He clicked his fingers. 'Is she the pooch-lady?'

'She's an artist,' replied Claudia crisply.

'Sorry, didn't mean to sound flippant.' She gave him a look which acknowledged the lapse but did not absolve him from it. 'She's with my mother I believe.'

She followed him across the hall and into a large room

overlooking the drive. Her plimsolls slapped on shining oak floorboards, his feet moved soundlessly in rumpled oiled-wool socks. She remembered something she'd read about the best way to polish a dance floor being to slide around it in stockinged feet.

'Sorry to interrupt the sitting,' said the man cheerily, 'but I've got a visitor for the artist.'

The room was a library rather larger than the whole downstairs of 65 Selwyn Street, and a great deal grander. A state-of-the-art Bang Olufsen television stood on one side of the fireplace. A very old, very thin woman whose neck and head stuck out at right angles to her body like a human gallows sat in a wing-back chair on the other. At her feet lay a comatose basset-hound which lifted its head glumly as they entered. Claudia's mother was kneeling on the floor a few feet from the dog, instamatic in hand. As the dog's head arose she cried: 'Oh, thank you God! Good boy! Stay—!'

Everyone waited obediently as she took a Polaroid. And then again, with rapt anticipation – feigned in Claudia's case – as the photo came into focus.

'Magic!' Jen pronounced, displaying the developed article. The old lady smiled a devastatingly sweet smile, patted the dog with a gnarled hand alight with diamonds, and turned her tortoise-like head to look at Claudia as Jen came over to embrace her.

'Red, great, so you found it all right.'

'Yes, no problem.'

'Now then,' said the man musingly, 'I should probably effect a few introductions but I'm at a bit of a disadvantage here. You two obviously know each other . . .'

'That,' said the old lady to the man, 'is my nice Mrs Delaney.'

'And this,' said Jen to everyone, 'is my daughter Claudia.'

'And over there,' said the man to Claudia, 'is my mother Lady Olivia Saxby. Which only leaves me and I'm Anthony Saxby. How do you do.'

He held out his hand, first to Jen, then to Claudia. The basset hauled itself on to its feet and waddled over. Claudia thought of a heavy roll of carpet being carried by two very short men.

'Hang on,' she said, crouching to pet it. 'Who's this?'

Three voices answered at once: 'That's Horace.'

'He's the business.'

'Which is why he's having his portrait made,' explained Jen.

Claudia made a fuss of Horace who stood staring wretchedly into her face as though this were his very last fuss before facing a firing squad.

'What about some tea?' asked Lady Olivia with a vague, unfocused imperiousness.

'I'm gone,' replied her son. The door closed behind him.

Claudia rose and lifted an eyebrow at her mother.

'Well, actually we should be going,' said Jen.

'In a minute, in a minute.' Lady Olivia peered at the cherub-encrusted clock on the mantelpiece and jerked bent fingers at the sofa. 'It's ages 'til my nice chef comes on the box. Sit down.'

They sat. Horace, after a moment's tragic indecision, waddled back to his mistress. Lady Olivia stared at Claudia with the unabashed appraisal of a two-year-old and then asked: 'Now where do you get your looks from?'

Jen laughed. 'Not from me!'

'I can see that. Your father?'

'My father's very tall,' replied Claudia. 'But my colouring's like Mum's.'

'Really?' Lady Olivia peered. 'I assumed you dyed it. What there is of it.'

'No, I dye mine,' said Jen. She reached up a hand and rubbed ruefully at Claudia's stubble. 'But honestly – this is a darn sight more than there was a month ago.'

Lady Olivia scratched and scratched at Horace's loose neck, sending him into a trance. 'Are you an artist too?'

'No, I'm at university.'

'Anywhere I might know?'

'London.'

'Ah yes, I dimly remember. And what are you studying? It's all a mystery to me, I had no education myself.'

'Nor me,' said Jen. 'I got into Hornsea on the strength of a few pictures and I've lived on my wits ever since.'

Lady Olivia pursed her lips and lowered heavily-veined eye-lids. 'On your talent, my dear. I had only the Saxby millions on which to get by.'

Sensing the beginnings of a mutual admiration society, Claudia stepped in firmly. 'In answer to your question, I'm taking Combined Studies.'

They both looked at her, Jen fondly, Lady Olivia with a frown. 'What is that – a bit of everything?'

'Pretty well.'

'Sounds just the ticket.'

'I'm hoping so.'

The door swung open, pushed by Anthony Saxby's foot, and he came in carrying a high-sided butler's tray with tea things. As he put it down on a paper-strewn table in the window, Lady Olivia asked: 'Couldn't you be a *rock star*?'

Jen snorted with laughter. Anthony said: 'I hope you're not addressing me.'

'I'm talking to Cleo—'

'Claudia.'

'– don't you think that's what she should do?'

'Yes,' said Anthony, handing an unmatched porcelain cup and saucer to Jen. 'Good idea. Sugar?'

'I've been telling her for years,' said Jen, 'but she won't listen.'

Claudia smiled thinly and declined tea. Her life seemed to be flashing before her eyes. What was she doing here? She tried to conjure up an image of Ben and Elke and the Club Copain but they seemed like memories of another life, in another dimension. Except, of course, for the designer's card.

'Perhaps,' she said, 'I'll be a supermodel instead.'

They all laughed, glad she'd taken the joke on board.

'Would anyone care for one of these?' asked Lady Olivia, fumbling with the lid of a silver cigarette box. 'Because for me tea is not complete without one.'

'Yes please,' said Claudia.

'They're not low-anything, I can't be doing with it. They're – what are they, Ant?'

'Marlboros.'

'There you are then. Named after a fine old public school. Cleo, help yourself.'

'So, Mrs Delaney,' said Anthony. 'Tell me, I'm interested – is doing dog portraits profitable?'

'I don't only do dogs. And that's a bit of a leading question under the circumstances . . .' Jen smiled at Lady Olivia, who was applying a Crown Derby table lighter to her cigarette with a quaking hand.

'Ah . . . !' Lady Olivia exhaled luxuriously. 'I don't see why. I'm paying her two hundred pounds plus expenses. Cheap at the price.'

'I'd have thought so,' agreed Anthony Saxby. 'I imagine you need danger money with some sitters.'

Claudia, embarrassed by money-talk, looked down at her knees, holding her cigarette between herself and her mother, who predictably gave her rich, meat-and-potatoes chuckle.

'*That*'s true. And by the way, I hate to be picky but I'm not Mrs.'

Oh please, thought Claudia. Oh no. Gimme a break.

'Who is these days?' commented Anthony Saxby with what even Claudia conceded was a deft touch, giving Jen the opportunity to leave it there . . . Which of course she didn't.

'Not many it's true, but I never was. I was before my time.'

Claudia smarted. If she could actually have covered her ears she would have done so, but the Saxbys laughed. Lady Olivia's laugh became a cough. Through her wheezings, Anthony said smoothly:

'By middle-class standards perhaps, but you'd have to be up early to beat us. The Saxby escutcheon is so besmirched it's barely legible.'

'Cleo—!' rasped the old lady.

'Claudia . . .'

'Don't let it embarrass you—'

'She's not that easily embarrassed,' put in Jen, 'are you Red?'

'Well—'

'Our family tree,' Lady Olivia continued, 'is absolutely littered with bastards.' She jabbed her cigarette at Anthony. 'Him over there, he's one.'

Claudia couldn't look up, let alone catch his eye. Her teeth were gritted. She heard him say smoothly: 'So you tell me, Ma, so you tell me.' He leaned towards Claudia. 'But we don't talk about it.'

*   *   *

Jen was apologising before the Renault had rattled over the first cattle-grid.

'Oh, Red . . . what can I say?'

'Nothing.'

'On a scale of one to ten how cringe-making was it?'

'About nine point nine.'

'Oh God . . .' Jen put an arm round her daughter's shoulders, causing the car to make a detour through the cowpats. 'Oops! I'm so terribly sorry. I can be so crass . . . I don't know what comes over me.'

'It's OK. Forget it.'

'I would, except that I know you won't. Another black mark against the old dear in the great book of life . . .'

'No it's not.'

'I just hate it when people make assumptions.'

'I know.'

'Can you forgive me?' An anxious, pleading glance, another bone-shaking swerve.

'Watch out! Yes!'

Between the final cattle grid and the right-hand turn into the road, Claudia realised that her mother's assessment was exactly right: Jen had put the matter behind her, but she herself couldn't, quite. She was an honest young woman, and had to admit that the reason for this was Anthony Saxby, her fellow-bastard.

By the time they were hacking across log-jammed north London, Jen had negotiated the treacherous waters of her daughter's disfavour and had succeeded in breaking the huff and making her laugh.

'That Horace,' she said, 'is the sitter from hell. The only time he got above brain-dead was when you came in. And I'm expected to create an affecting study of doggy character and devotion from one measly polaroid and a couple of sketches of him with his eyes closed! What's a serious artist to do?'

'Make it up?' suggested Claudia. 'Everyone likes flattery.'

'Damn right, Red – I'll make that fleabag look handsome and heroic if it's the last thing I do. Never let it be said that I couldn't prostitute myself when the occasion demanded.'

Almost at once she regretted her choice of words. Claudia's

answering laugh lacked warmth, and she turned away to look out of the window.

That evening they ate Jen's special macaroni cheese, piggily and deliciously mixed up with bits of crispy bacon and fried onion, in the living room. Keith was out. Not, as Jen conceded, that he ever intruded, but his excruciating self-effacement – creeping down the stairs, running taps at half-strength, closing kitchen cupboards so slowly that they clicked twice – created a kind of uneasy backdrop to evenings in.

'Where is Norbert?' asked Claudia.

'What day is it?' Jen glanced abstractedly at her empty wrist. 'Tuesday? It's karate.'

Claudia stayed her fork, lowered it to the plate. 'You're telling me he teaches martial arts? That we have Karate Keith?'

'No, I think he's got some kind of more peripheral connection with it – opens up the school hall, makes the orange squash, that kind of thing.'

'Orange squash sounds a bit flash – how about lemon barley water.'

'Right. And potted meat sandwiches.'

'Anyway, it's nice he's not around. I don't know how you put up with it, it'd drive me crackers. It does drive me crackers.'

'Now come on, Red. He's no trouble and his money is as good as the next man's and always on time. A dream lodger in fact.'

Claudia put her plate on the floor. 'A nice single white female would be better.'

'Yes, well, one didn't apply. To be honest I don't see Keith as either male or female – is that awful?'

'Realistic.'

'No, it *is* awful . . .' Jen used her knife to pick up what remained of her cheese sauce and licked the blade with long, catlike strokes. 'Now then. Who cares about him? What about you? You were being terse with me in the car. What else happened in Paris?'

Jen was a good listener, because she was genuinely curious. Claudia knew that what might have seemed an affectionate token question in anyone else was a matter of real, consuming interest to her mother. Now that she felt more relaxed it was a pleasure to talk about her weekend to someone who was, when they were alone together, so absolutely on her wavelength.

She talked for three quarters of an hour and Jen sat curled up on the end of the sofa, a model of attentiveness. Claudia knew she'd remember every word, not just from maternal instinct but because she was a clever woman with a selectively retentive memory – much too bright to be turning out idealised pictures of over-indulged animals.

'I like Ben,' she said at one point. 'He's *sympatico*. A nice man.'

'Yes he is,' agreed Claudia, adding just in case: 'And he seems to be very happy with Elke.'

'Oh, I wasn't suggesting anything.'

'Perish the thought.'

They exchanged sidelong smiles of understanding. 'Mind if I smoke?'

'I suppose not . . .' Jen sighed. She was a serial giver-up of the weed. 'Shall I have one too . . . ?'

'Don't shift the responsibility. It's all yours.' Claudia struck a match, aware of her mother's envious gaze.

'I think I will. In fact I will. Thanks. Aah . . .' Jen inhaled with sensuous relish. Claudia sometimes thought that her periods of abstinence were simply a way of intensifying the pleasure of resumption. Jen would never succeed in giving up permanently because she was not only a hopeless addict, but a congenital optimist, incapable of seriously entertaining the idea of her own mortality. She sat with knees bunched up in the corner of the sofa, her shock of dry fair hair pushed back behind her many-tiered Indian earrings, her nose, the tip of which seemed to have been pushed upwards expressly to savour the scent of tobacco, her broad mouth wreathed in smiles and smoke – patently delighted to have failed once more.

'Guess what age that old dear was this afternoon – Lady Saxby.'

'I don't know. Old. Eighty-odd?'

'Ninety-four.'

'You're joking! I hope I'm half as feisty as that at her age.'

'And puffing on Marlboros like there was no tomorrow,' remarked Jen with evident satisfaction. 'Not that I suppose there are that many tomorrows to get het up about at that stage in the proceedings. Just the same,' she tapped her ash into the extended lid of Claudia's packet. 'It does make you feel, what the hell.'

The last three words should have been on the Delaney coat of arms, thought Claudia. She felt indulgent towards her mother. 'There is one funny thing I haven't told you yet,' she said.

'Oh God, Red – you didn't get married, did you?'

'Don't be ridiculous. No, it was – hang on, let me show you.' Claudia bent down to get the designer's card from her bag. As she did so, the phone rang.

'Hang on, don't go away, I'll be back in two ticks.'

Claudia laid the card on the sofa. In the hall, her mother lifted the receiver.

'Hello?' She never said the number, it was always just hello. 'Oh, *hello*.' She never said the name of the caller, either, one had to guess who it was from her tone of voice and the general tenor of the conversation. But she wasn't secretive, she didn't do it to dissemble. Claudia had a pretty fair idea who this might be.

'So how was the weekend? How were they? Good . . . Claudia's here with me at the moment as a matter of fact, we were having a natter about Paris. Yes, that's right. Well tonight definitely, which will be lovely, and then back to the flat I suppose, I don't know . . . I haven't asked her. Yes. Yes, that sounds like the best idea, why don't you do that. OK. OK. Me too. Bye.'

When Jen came back into the room there was a subtle but unmistakable change in her manner that confirmed Claudia's suspicions.

'Richard?'

'How did you guess.' Jen sounded unabashed, but didn't catch her daughter's eye. 'So come on then – what were you going to show me?'

'It doesn't matter,' said Claudia, palming the card. 'It was nothing exciting.'

After he'd put the phone down, Richard went to the window and looked out. Isla was doing one of her evening ambles in the garden, walking round very slowly, with her arms folded, pausing now and then to gaze, or listen. She wore a long off-white dress, and flat sandals with a criss-cross strap at the ankle. In the garden setting she looked faintly Grecian – classical, somehow, the shallow folds of the cotton dress appeared heavy and solid, her interrupted movements were so slow and graceful she appeared like an animated statue. Not a woman turned to stone, but stone brought to life. Her warm, friendly, open beauty seemed in the blurry, late evening light cool and wise – a little unsettling. At the end of the lawn she turned to walk back towards the house and paused for a moment, facing straight ahead. In the dusk, he couldn't tell if she was looking at him or not. He hadn't turned the light on in the drawing room, and for some reason he remained very still, and held his breath, not wanting to be seen.

She walked on, and he exhaled slowly, his breath trembling slightly as it sighed out into the darkening air.

4

Isla didn't in the least mind yomping across town, as Richard put it, to visit Nell Fyler. She enjoyed such projects, and was flattered to be asked to undertake them. Especially at the moment, when a vague unease was closing in on her, like a long-term stalker becoming ever more threatening.

She'd engineered the meeting by ringing Nell and saying she was going to be down in her area for a dinner one evening the following week, and could she drop in beforehand? Nell had reacted in her rather offhand way.

'I don't see why not. I think I'll be around.'

'Well obviously,' said Isla gently, 'I shouldn't bother if you weren't going to be there.'

'No, I suppose not. But Scotch is always about and he's as capable of filling a glass as the next man.'

'I'm sure he is.'

'Anyway, I should be.'

'Oh, good.'

Isla drove down to Swiss Cottage. She did in fact have a dinner to attend, but it was a private one with the Stainforths, at whose house she was meeting Richard at eight-fifteen. In consequence of this she was not dressed up, but wearing loose khaki peg-top trousers and a cream silk shirt. This casual ensemble was not missed by Nell.

'Come on in. Not a black tie affair, then.'

'No, not this one . . .' Isla bumped cheeks. 'Just friends, at their house.'

'Yes, but I know your friends, they're all high court judges and scions of noble houses and what have you.'

'Come come, not *all*,' said Isla teasingly, following her into the living room. 'We know you.'

'Yes, true. Grab a pew,' said Nell. Isla lowered herself on to a sagging hammock of a sofa. Alan Clarke's famous taunt about having bought all one's own furniture could never have been levelled at Nell, whose house was packed with Bury overspill. It was odd sitting in this room off the Finchley Road, with the growl of metropolitan traffic and the whiff of kebabs coming through the open sash window, and yet to feel that one was in the drawing room of some backwoods rectory in Dorset, surrounded by frayed Persian rugs, chintz covers, threadbare tapestry cushions, hunting prints and thin-lipped family portraits.

'I just got in,' said Nell. 'What can I get you?'

'No really, I'm fine.'

'I usually have a g and t.'

'Go ahead.'

'Suit yourself,' said Nell bluntly and went into the kitchen. Isla watched through the open door as she sploshed a liberal measure of Gordons into a tumbler and topped it up with flat tonic water from the fridge. She was a big, rawboned young woman with broad shoulders, a slim waist and muscular slightly bandy legs. Her carroty shoulder-length hair was cut straight and sensible, and no mascara enhanced her sandy-lashed pale blue eyes. For work at her unadventurous but expensive gallery in Belgravia she wore a navy suit (one of those safe, expensive mid-range labels, Isla surmised), scuffed navy court shoes, the outer edge of each heel badly worn down, and a black velvet hairband. No rings, but a string of mumsy pearls, and pearl studs, all undoubtedly real. Isla liked Nell, but it was difficult to see her as the defenceless object of some young man's ungovernable lust, or as the innocent victim of a predatory gold-digger. She did not come over as a young woman one would choose to cross.

'Are you sure you won't change your mind? Tonic on its own? Orange juice?'

'No thanks.'

'Salt and vinegar crisps?'

'Now you're talking.'

Nell came back into the room holding two packets of the crisps, one of which she tossed unceremoniously to Isla. 'Scuse fingers, simplest way.'

'Where's your flatmate?' Isla asked, tweaking at the packet. 'Still at work?'

'Still at the office. I'm not sure he goes in for anything as taxing as work.'

'Really? What sort of office is it?'

'Public relations.' Nell sucked her teeth. 'I ask you. Look, it is nice to see you. Sorry if I was a bit brusque when you arrived.'

'Were you?'

'Have you seen the aged Ps recently?'

'Yes, as a matter of fact we were in Bradenham for the boys' open day last weekend, and we went round there for dinner. That was what made me think of you when I realised I was coming down this way.'

'How did they seem?'

'Very bullish, except that Portia's not well and your mama's obviously worried about her.'

Nell sighed. 'Mummy will have to get over it. The old bitch is on her last legs.' For a split second Isla misunderstood this observation, and it must have showed. 'Portia I mean. She's fourteen – that's a colossal age for a Rottweiler. I remember the day we got her. She was supposed to strike terror into the hearts of gyppos and Jehovah's Witnesses, but she was a complete busted flush.'

'I don't know much about it.'

Nell warmed to her theme. 'The trouble is, Mummy likes to think of herself as a hard nut, but she's completely ridiculous about Portia and Pepe.'

'It's understandable. I can remember when we left Malaya when I was a child and my father sold our boxer to the neighbours. I don't think I've ever been so heartbroken.'

'It's no use breaking one's heart over animals,' said Nell. 'They have a shorter lifespan than us and that's all there is to it. One simply has to move on. But I've got a super idea for Mummy's birthday present this year.'

'Now look,' said Isla, realising that time was limited and the more straightforward she was the less suspicion she would arouse. 'I didn't come here to talk dogs. How are *you*?'

'Fine. In rude health as always.'

'Still fancy-free?'

'Yes.' Nell shot her a piercing look, very like her father's, from beneath ginger eyebrows. 'Who wants to know?'

'I do. You know me, I'm a trivial sort of person. I like gossip and romance and affairs . . .'

'Then you came to the wrong place. No, I have one or two jolly girlfriends who give nice dinner parties and in the autumn Scotch and I plan to push the boat out if we're spared and do a lunchtime drinks.'

'Scotch being Robert?'

'That's right.'

'And is he good at PR?' asked Isla, not meaning it seriously, trying to elicit a more personal opinion. But Nell was rock-solid.

'At the moment. I don't think it's a career, or anything like that.' There was the sound of the front door opening. 'Anyway, you can see for yourself.' She raised her voice. 'In here, you! I want to introduce you to an old friend of my mother's!'

As she shook hands, Isla realised that whatever she had been expecting this was not it. Later she realised that she had built up a picture of a fair-haired smoothie not unlike her own elder stepson. Either that or a prototypical, ferret-faced, hollow-chested rat fink. But Robert Scott-Chatham was neither of these things. He was tall and toned with a sculpted bad-boy face, almost-black eyes and fetchingly scrubby hair: blue suit, open-necked white shirt, highly-coloured tie protruding from jacket pocket; must-have Gucci belt, or cunning imitation of same and any-old-how black lace-ups. Isla, accustomed by experience to assessing the success or otherwise of image-promotion, recognised an adept and witty practitioner when she saw one.

Still beaming delightedly, he flopped down in a chair and professed himself gobsmacked.

'No disrespect to Nell's esteemed parent, but when she said an old friend of her mother's I didn't picture anything like –' he swept a hand up and down, 'you.'

'And I bet,' called Nell from the kitchen, replenishing glasses, 'she didn't expect anything like you, either.'

'No,' confessed Isla, 'I didn't.'

Unusually for a man (and Isla considered herself something

of an expert), Scotch did not take this opportunity to talk about himself. Instead he propped his head on his hand and continued to gaze at her through narrowed eyes.

'Am I allowed to say that you're even more stunning in real life than in your pictures?'

'You're definitely allowed to say it. In fact as the decades roll by you're positively required to say it! Thank you.'

'Are you working on anything special at the moment – are you going to be on the box?'

'Not unless my agent does some very fancy footwork. I mainly do rent-a-face these days.'

'She's far too modest,' said Nell, returning with the drinks. 'You do all this charity stuff now, don't you? She's working on her OBE.'

'Oh yes, I'm Our Lady of the Good Causes,' agreed Isla, laughing. 'I eat a lot of mediocre food, have my photo taken with the bravest and the best and make a few undemanding speeches, that's all. I'm not required to dirty my hands with any real work.'

Scotch frowned. 'Why do you run yourself down?'

'I wouldn't want to overstate my usefulness.'

'You couldn't, I'm sure. You must be one of the best-loved actresses of your generation.'

'Even if you're right, which I doubt, serious actresses want to be best-respected, not best-loved.'

'Maybe you never were a serious actress—'

'Scotch!' barked Nell. 'Give over.'

'No, I meant no offence.'

'None taken,' said Isla.

'What I meant was that perhaps this – what you do now – is your real vocation. And just because you're not emptying bedpans or swabbing pus doesn't mean it's not useful.'

'That's a jolly good way of looking at it,' conceded Isla. 'I shall remind myself of that next time I'm on rubber-chicken duty.'

'Tell me something,' asked Scotch. 'Who does your PR?'

When she left fifteen minutes later Isla looked forward to describing the encounter to Richard, and to telling the Fylers at the first possible opportunity that their daughter would have to be mad or made of stone not to succumb to her flatmate's charms, and that such a consummation was devoutly to be wished and would make her the envy of every woman she encountered.

Supper with the Stainforths was taken in the kitchen because their eight-year-old had been given a Scalectric for his birthday and it had been set up on the dining-table. But since supper had been taken in the kitchen for as long as anyone could recall anyway, this excuse rang a bit hollow. Archie was upstairs officiating at a bedtime which sounded like a student uprising while his wife prepared supper.

The house in Clarendon Road, though not as large as the Wakefields' in Hampstead, was a substantial residence that would, at some unimaginable point in the future when Archie and Alison were on their own, realise a good profit. But before it did so, reflected Richard, an army of experts was going to have to move in and make good the ravages that decades of Stainforth family life had wrought. It was a source of wonder to him that, just as Jen got by un-burgled, so Archie managed to appear in chambers each day looking halfway decent and able to represent his clients perfectly creditably. How, out of all this chaos and clamour, was it done?

Having arrived first, by taxi, Richard sat on the wheelback chair with the wonky leg, drinking a gut-wrenching Bulgarian red (his own bottles of pleasing claret would be accompanying supper) and submitting to Alison's interrogation as she chopped economy-sized carrots to accompany her 'special' chicken *chasseur*. He hoped the 'special' didn't mean half the chicken being replaced by chickpeas or some other disgusting pulse . . .

'So how are your brood?' asked Alison. To her, children were always a brood, or a tribe, a primitive species to be subjected to benign dictatorship. 'All well?'

'Yes, we saw them the other day—'

'My goodness, Richard, you don't know you're born! Think of us, seeing all of ours, every blessed day!'

'Believe me,' said Richard humbly, 'I do.' Archie was several years younger than him, and Alison younger than that, but she had the knack of making him feel like a schoolboy.

'But they were in good fettle?'

'Marcus always looks terrible, but appearances are deceptive. Giles—' Richard paused fractionally before deciding not to spill the beans, 'Giles plans a career as a party organiser.'

'Really?' said Alison brightly, scraping the carrot chunks off the chopping board into a saucepan with a splash, and bending to retrieve one from the floor. 'Like Lady Elizabeth thingy?'

'Not like Lady Elizabeth Anson, no.' Richard watched the piece from the floor join its fellows in the saucepan. 'And the money raised won't go to charity unless you count the Giles Wakefield Benevolent Fund.'

Alison began on potatoes. 'Still, all jolly fun,' she said vaguely, adding: 'We wouldn't be without them, would we?' There was a tremendous thud from above, followed by roars and shrieks and a thunder of footsteps. 'I wonder if Archie needs a hand, will you excuse me for a mo?'

'Please, of course.'

Alison beetled into the hall and up the stairs, calling as she went: 'Archie, Archee . . . ! What's going on up there, I'm coming to sort you out!'

Richard sipped his fiery red with pursed lips. At least there were no animals about, thank God . . . The Stainforths had plenty, but they were all of the small, caged and penned variety – rodents, fish and reptiles – who shared bedrooms with their various owners. Only once, that he could recall, had there been an unsettling incident with a pied rat, and that was many years ago . . .

The front door bell made its distinctive sound, like a football rattle being swung slowly. From the hurly-burly of the upper reaches Alison's voice came faintly: 'Richard –! Be a dear and get that . . . !'

Richard rose and went to the door.

'Ri-chard!'

'I'm there, I'm there!'

Isla stepped in and kissed him. 'Where is everyone?'

'Upstairs, mostly, doing bedtime.'

'Oh good, in that case I've got to time to tell you about—'

'Hello Isla, down in a tick!' came from upstairs.

'Hello – lovely!' Isla raised her voice, then lowered it once more: 'I've got time to tell you about Nell and her flatmate.'

They went into the kitchen. Richard lifted his glass. 'Rocket fuel?'

'I'll wait. Listen.' Isla sat down opposite him at the table. 'He's an absolute sweetie.'

Richard raised his eyebrows. 'Isla . . .'

'No, he is. Trust me –' she laid her hand on his. 'I know about these things.'

'Go on.'

'He's handsome and charming and altogether delightful.'

'Do you realise, my darling, that you have just described Bill Fyler's worst nightmare?'

'No, no no,' she shook her head impatiently. 'You don't understand. How can I describe it . . . ? He's actually very, very *nice.*'

'Holy cow.'

'Be serious. You know me, I'm not particularly gullible, I'm a pretty shrewd judge of character and –' she stroked his hand again – 'I'm a connoisseur of male beauty.'

They laughed quietly at one another, their faces drawing closer together, and kissed. Archie pounded across the hall.

'Sorry – oh! We needn't have worried about leaving you two alone for five minutes!'

Isla got up and hugged him. Archie blushed furiously. 'That's nice – can I have another of those?'

'Later. What have you done with Alison?'

'I handed her the baton. Twins' bedtime,' added Archie, pulling a comical face. 'You haven't got a drink.'

'It's all right, I'll wait till dinner.'

Archie poured himself a glass of wine. 'So tell me where you've been. I could do with a bit of vicarious glamour. At some glittering show-business do? A champagne reception for the great and the good?'

'Not at all. I've been in a flat off the Finchley Road visiting the horsey daughter of very old friends.'

'And vetting the bloke she shares with,' added Richard, 'whom her father suspects of having less than honourable intentions.'

'Well,' said Archie, joining them at the table, 'call me newfangled, but I didn't think that was much of a cause for concern these days.'

'It's not,' agreed Isla, 'but the father in this case is a bit feudal, and he thinks this chap is after the family silver.'

Archie shook his head. 'It's another world.'

'Don't trouble your pretty little head about it, Archie,' suggested Richard. 'And behold the lady wife, hot from the battle.'

'Archie!' protested Alison between kisses. 'You never turned the veg on!'

It was a jolly enough evening: the chicken *chasseur* was reasonably unadulterated and the *charlotte russe* exemplary, having been bought (Alison was not proud) from the frozen-food specialists who called door to door. Accompanied by Richard's stylish claret it was a nice dinner, and Archie and Alison were always droll company. From time to time during the meal one or other of the younger children would appear, trailing shawls or featureless stuffed animals, occasionally with damp pyjamas, and the parent whose turn it was hustled them away and got them back to sleep. At eleven-thirty Amanda Stainforth returned.

'Come in here darling,' called Alison, 'and say hello to Richard and Isla.'

Footsteps trudged across the hall and Amanda appeared in the doorway. She was a well-built girl of fifteen (going on twenty-eight in Richard's opinion), wearing jeans and a checked shirt. Her expression of contemptuous impatience cracked into a smile when she saw Isla.

'Oh, hi.'

'Where have you been?' asked Isla. 'Anywhere interesting?'

'Just hanging out with friends.'

'It's the best thing, isn't it,' agreed Isla, including Archie and Alison in the remark. 'You do look nice, by the way.'

Amanda glanced down at herself. 'I do?'

'Yes. Doesn't she?' Isla prompted Richard.

'She does. Super.'

'You can't beat 501s on a smashing young figure.'

'Can I have a drink, Dad?' asked Amanda, now completely won over.

'Um, well—'

'No,' said Alison. 'Off you go, school in the morning.'

The thunder threatened to return. 'I wish you wouldn't say that as if I was ten or something.'

'I'm not, darling, I'm saying it as if you were fifteen.'

Isla caught Amanda's eye and smiled regretfully. 'You'll be glad one day.'

'I'll take your word for it!' Only partly mollified, Amanda stumped off.

Archie leaned to watch her go. 'Night, petal!'

'Night.'

'She's not a bad kid,' he said, addressing Isla and Richard, 'but I wish I knew what "hanging out" involved.'

'Nothing half as sinister as your worst imaginings, I'm sure,' said Isla.

'Probably not,' agreed Alison. 'Still, there are times when we envy you the luxury of having your two safely banged up in boarding school.'

Something less than a look, lasting only a nanosecond, passed between Richard and Isla before Richard said carelessly, 'If they have no-good on their minds they're going to get up to it wherever they are, believe me.'

'You only have to look at her,' said Isla, 'to see she's not doing drugs or OD-ing on alcopops. The odd ciggy perhaps, but then who didn't at that age? She's an absolutely lovely girl.'

'She is, she is . . .' Archie got up to recharge the coffee cups. 'But that doesn't stop us worrying. Goes with the territory, doesn't it?'

Alison's brow furrowed. 'We think – what if she has a secret life?'

'On that score,' said Archie, 'I draw some comfort from the fact that Amanda's like the rest of her ilk, pretty lazy, and conducting a secret life would be far too much like work!'

They agreed amid laughter, and moved on to another subject.

Richard didn't consider that he had a secret, or even a double life. Nor did he consider himself duplicitous. On the contrary, he thought himself honest, open and truthful, on a need-to-know basis. That this species of honesty entailed a great deal of day-to-day concealment was a fact he chose to overlook. He was not an introspective man, but one exponentially suited to his calling as a barrister. His ability to rationalise, justify and validate the behaviour of his clients stood him in good stead when it came to the salving of his conscience. He had made out his own case to his perfect satisfaction.

His relationship with Jen predated his marriage to Isla by fully two years. He had met her during the period of his divorce from Caroline. She had been nothing short of a lifesaver. After the Mediterranean storms of Donatella and the maternal neuroses (as he saw them) of Caroline, Jen was bliss. It was some years since he had felt any sense of peace – both his marriages had been a cause of painful friction. In the case of Donatella, the friction had created a positive bonfire of passion which had burned them out; in that of Caroline it had worn them away so that in the end they barely touched. With Jen, their complementary curves and spaces of body and mind fitted snugly together. By the time they had known each other for a week, it was impossible for Richard to imagine what it had been like before. In her company he relaxed, and in doing so realised that he had not relaxed properly in years. Here, at last, was a woman who accepted him absolutely as he was – who was not overwhelmed by him, and was neither resentful of his strengths nor waiting to pounce rapaciously on his weaknesses. He had never known whether she loved him in any romantic way, but oddly that didn't seem to matter. She seemed to see herself, as he did, as a safe haven, a place from which he came and went at will, without obligation. She was always pleased to see him, and there was a calmness about her pleasure, as though he had only gone out a short while ago and she was happily surprised to see him back so soon. Her door was – literally – always open, and her life did not change because of him. Richard's peers would have been astonished to know that this made him feel safe.

Physically, Jen was not a woman to induce an awed quake of desire, like Isla, but one to melt into. In fact, he often failed with Jen, but it felt less like failure than a sort of release. What he experienced with her was an animal warmth and cuddliness, an infinitely comforting closeness. What their love-making lacked in grandeur it made up for in a snuggling intimacy that Richard had never known, even in childhood.

Perhaps, he thought, on those rare occasions when he attempted to analyse the relationship, that was what it was all about. All that bracing fortitude, the firm grip of so much parental aspiration, steering him towards his destiny. It had worked, of course. Without a trace of vanity he could say that he was one of the smartest lawyers of his generation. He could name his price. But he hadn't chosen this. It had been chosen for him. He could not remember having had childhood ambitions in another direction and he resented what he felt to be the theft of these dreams. Where were the rugby heroes, the war correspondents, the writers, the painters – the *engine drivers*, for God's sake – who should have peopled his boyhood? Strangled at birth, he sometimes reflected grimly, while acknowledging that he had the luxury of picking up these grudges when he felt like it and dropping them in the corner when he didn't.

He was an only child, the focus of much expectation but very little attention. His mother, Sylvia, who had died before she was sixty, was a widely respected and admired scientist – quiet, clever, soberly dressed, self-sufficient. Now that there was only him and his father left, he realised how little his mother had needed either of them. Unusually for her generation she lived for her work. She was not an unkind woman nor as far as he knew (though only Richard's father could confirm this) a cold one, but she was utterly preoccupied.

Alec Wakefield was an orthopaedic consultant at Tommy's, the last of the real ocean-going consultants as contemporaries often commented, who cruised the wards with a voice like a foghorn and a flotilla of nervous housemen. He was a tall, corpulent, florid, man with bright blue eyes and a mane of wavy hair. He was not preoccupied in the way that Sylvia was, his manner was extrovert and unfettered, but he was no more accessible to Richard. Noisy and genial and a poor listener, he crashed about the Wakefields' domestic life as little as he could, itching to escape back to a larger stage.

But different though his parents were, they were united in one thing – their only son should want for nothing, and get to the top. It was fortunate for all of them – especially Richard – that he was bright. A less academically able boy would have endured the long, small torture of being a disappointment. As it was,

Richard was not just clever but good-looking and socially adept – like a well-flighted arrow in the hands of a skilful marksman, he shot towards his starred first at Oxford and pupillage at the most distinguished chambers in London. Before he even left university he was being talked about as a star of the Union, with a dry, worldly wit beyond his years and a Midas touch with women. By the time he encountered Donatella they were both tearing headlong along the fast-track and the result was the sort of colourful collision that fuelled the dinner-party conversations of mutual acquaintances for years to come.

Donatella Speranza was, poetically enough, a divorce lawyer. Richard's dealings with her had finally convinced him of what he had always suspected – that when it came to blood and guts divorce law left the criminal courts for dead. To describe Donatella as hawkish in this already bellicose milieu was to be unfair to hawks. She was feared, and her name spoken in hushed tones by vengeful wives, tight-fisted husbands and serial adulterers everywhere. She was a small, short-waisted, big-breasted woman with a shock of black hair and hot, dark eyes that could melt hearts of stone or scorch the unworthy depending on her mood. She was in her early thirties when she met Richard, five years older than him, but in spite of twenty years' residency in England her grasp of the language remained erratic and her accent, gestures, and mind-set irretrievably Italian. This furious foreignness, combined with a razor-sharp mind and a deadly grasp of the law made her quite terrifying, not just to the unfortunate opposition, but to her clients, whom she perceived as equal partners in the enterprise, with a job to do and no prisoners taken. You – or more often the Legal Aid Board – paid Donatella, but you did not call the tune: she did.

Richard had been bowled over from the moment she was introduced to him at a party and said, in her husky, resonant voice, fruity with red wine and tobacco: 'I have been looking at you for some time across the room. You are a very sexy Englishman of a particular kind. You have beautiful hands. I believe we shall make love soon.'

Richard had laughed nervously, but took note of the fact that others standing around, who already knew Donatella, did not join in. There were some faint, wry smiles, but it was clearly not a joke. Her eyes rested on him like a couple of hot coals. He experienced a shockingly vivid premonition of what it would be like to have her blunt, beringed hand holding his cock in its commanding grasp. Hopelessly taken aback he had resorted to verbal fencing – a course which, had he known Donatella better, he would never have followed, and which quickly caused a small crowd of onlookers to gather.

'What makes you believe that?' he enquired caustically.

'You are nervous. If you are nervous you are susceptible.'

'You're making, if I may say so, a great many assumptions.'

'Yes.'

'Assumptions, in my experience, are the product of arrogance.'

'Certainly.'

'QED.'

'You don't wish to go to bed with me?'

The burning look, the flaring nostrils – the haughtily raised eyebrows . . . Richard hesitated. Fatally as it proved. She gave a short, grunting laugh and turned away, tossing over her shoulder as she did so: 'QED.'

From that moment Richard was ensnared. The strong drink of being propositioned by a renowned older woman and a focus of half-admiring, half-appalled general speculation would have turned older and wiser heads than his. If he had suddenly taken up with Julie Christie he could not have courted celebrity more surely. The affair with Donatella was intoxicating: the subsequent marriage an unmitigated disaster.

With hindsight and greater experience he could see that it was Donatella, not he, who had been trapped into marriage. Her Latin heart entertained a fantasy of hearth, home, ever-ripening sex and well-nourished *bambini*. But her lawyer's brain could not, in the event, cope with any of it. Well before the *bambini* stage (a fact for which Richard often thanked his Maker) hearth and home had become a howling wilderness and sex had shrivelled and died in the atomic blast of Donatella's discontent. It wasn't until post-Caroline that Richard was able in some small way to sympathise with his first wife and what she must have gone through. For Donatella, in spite of her passionate espousal of the rights of children following divorce, was not cut out for domestic intimacy and could not tolerate the company of the young. She liked children at a distance – through glass, from a car, over a fence, on a screen. But put her in a room with a three-year-old, be he ever so winsome, and she would be a twitching wreck within five minutes. In the face of this almost clinical aversion, she persisted in the idea that she and Richard would have a family, a contingency from which probably only her relatively mature years saved them. Added to this she was to homemaking what Joe Frazier was to needlepoint, and could not cook. The mess infuriated her, but she hadn't the smallest skill, nor even the trace of an instinct, as to how to put it right. She would simply stride about, roaring her displeasure, while Richard protested vainly that it wasn't that bad, before taking her to yet another restaurant where she would chain-smoke black cheroots, glug down red wine, eat enough for an army and finally become amorous. To begin with, that was. After six months or so the dinners began to be taken elsewhere and with other people, and she would come home too exhausted and the worse for wear for anything as strenuous as sex. It would fall to Richard to help her undress, bring her the mug of strong, syrupy tea she craved, and watch most of it go cold as she drifted, snoring slightly, and woozily murmuring his name among others, into oblivion.

Now, when he saw her, as he often did, cruising the room at legal gatherings, swooping on the unsuspecting objects of her predatory fancy, he felt a perverse tenderness for Donatella, whose fierceness made her vulnerable, and who had been without doubt his first grand passion.

Caroline followed as the night the day. Cool, fair, moon-faced Caroline, conventional and in control, a woman to rely upon and take for granted, a woman with high standards and a low sex-drive, a soothing tepid bath after the white-water ride of Donatella. Richard mistook relief for true love. This was how it was supposed to be: he would be free to scale the legal heights and Caroline would always be there, behaving impeccably and oiling the domestic wheels.

To be fair to Caroline, she was always there. She did not suddenly begin to behave out of character. It was simply that

Richard had never envisaged the way in which life would change when the children came along. With the birth of Giles he felt a slight, unsettling shift in the centre of gravity; within weeks of the arrival of Marcus he realised he had been marginalised. Caroline was not cruel or cold; she was exemplary in the kitchen, on the phone, at the dinner table, even, when required, in bed. In fact she was a good wife in every way, except that she did not love him half as much as she loved the children. Their house in Muswell Hill, though it continued to be impeccably run, was completely dominated by the demands of these two small pampered tyrants. The qualities in his wife which Richard had perceived as perfectly complementary began suddenly to rush the two of them in opposite directions. Caroline – and her clucky home-counties mother – were the undisputed experts in all things connected with the nurture and upbringing of children. Everything from teeth to table manners, taking in bowels, diet and reading along the way, they claimed as their sovereign territory. Their calm, unshakable assurance sapped Richard's confidence. Not caring to risk being wrong, he left them to it, and without really meaning to set about becoming the kind of distant, work-obsessed father that Alec had been. He had a few guilty flings, including a brief sentimental journey with Donatella, upon whose luxurious bosom he had all but wept with frustration.

'I think I've made the most God-awful mistake, and the trouble is she's done nothing wrong . . . I have no cause whatever for complaint.'

'Except, Ricardo,' growled Donatella, stroking his hair, 'that she does not love you.'

'No, I believe she does—'

'But not enough. Not like I did.'

Even in his distressed state Richard could see that it would be best not to comment on this assertion.

'She is a mother first and a wife second,' she went on. 'Very English. Very organised. She will organise you out of your very self. To hold on to your soul you must let her go.'

Donatella's style of spoken English had a melodramatic ring, but there was a kernel of truth in what she said. Richard absented himself still further. When the final break came it was more or less a case of formalising a situation that already existed. Money was not an issue, because there was plenty of it. They were sad, and Caroline cried, and the boys, then aged five and three, looked on with round-eyed tolerance. But they all accepted the inevitable with a gentle mutual understanding. And of course it had been for the best. Because now Richard was able to be a better father. With distance his affection, which had never been in doubt, grew stronger, and his hopes and fears for his sons clearer. He talked to Caroline for the first time about how he didn't want them processed, pushed through a particular system, and why, and to his surprise she was understanding, and agreed with him. Their boys would have a different experience.

'Why didn't we have this conversation before?' he'd asked, rhetorically really.

'Because we were married, perhaps.'

'But surely that's a reason to talk, not the other way round.'

'Yes, it should be . . . If you're happy.'

He looked at her in astonishment. 'You weren't happy?'

She shook her head, turned her wedding ring, gave a little sniff. 'I was always much too dull for you, Richard. It's awfully sad not being able to make someone else happy.'

He was devastated.

Caroline had not remarried, but they had remained friends. And he had Jen.

He had met her when his car – a Merc back then – broke down in the Archway Road on the way to Marcus's primary school nativity play. He had stood in a biting east wind gazing at the car's intransigent engine in a fury of ignorance. Jen alone among the hundreds of passers-by had come to stand next to him. Shrouded in a huge black duffle coat with a hood, like a small Darth Vadar, he hadn't even been sure whether it was a man or a woman till she spoke.

'Has it simply packed up?'

'Yes . . . blasted engine died on me at those last lights.'

'What a lousy thing to happen – and in this car, too.'

'It happens to the best of us.' He leaned forward, as if a halo of flashing lights might suddenly advertise the problem. She too leaned slightly forward, pushing back the duffle hood and releasing a shaggy chrysanthemum of fair hair.

'Is there anything I can do?'

He glanced at her. 'Why, do you know about engines?'

'No.' She sounded rather surprised. 'But I'm sure someone does.' Before he could prevent her she'd turned and addressed the hurrying throng on the pavement. 'Does anyone know about cars? We're at our wits' end – can anyone help? Please?'

'I am a member of the AA . . .' muttered Richard, mortified. But already two men, with Jen in between them, were competing vociferously under the Merc's raised bonnet. In less than five minutes a petrol-feed problem had been diagnosed – 'muck in the carburettor's favourite' – some mechanical sleight of hand performed, and advice given to top up with petrol at the first opportunity to avoid 'recycling the gunk'.

'I can't thank you enough,' said Richard, gratitude outweighing embarrassment as the men went their separate ways. 'Or you,' he added. 'I'm afraid misplaced pride would have prevented me taking the obvious course of action.'

She pulled a nicely judged aw-shucks grin.

'Look, I've got to dash, I'm going to Highgate – can I give you a lift?'

'Thanks.'

He went into the nearest filling station and topped up with four-star. When he got back in, he asked: 'Where would you like to be dropped off?'

'Where did you say you were going?'

'St Mark's in Highgate West Hill – it's my sons' school—'

'Near there'll be fine.'

During the short drive he found out her name, that she was a painter, and that she herself drove a VW beetle which was kept on the road by a friendly Senegalese mechanic named Sam Blanche. It was a small amount of information, but she delivered it in such an unself-consciously droll, circuitous way that Richard was sorry to say goodbye.

'Where are you going now?' he asked as her hand was already on the door handle.

'Back home. Crouch End.'

He frowned. 'But that's miles away.'

'Sorry. I'm afraid I only wanted a ride in your car.'

Laughing, not at him but at herself, she climbed out. He leaned across to stop her from closing the door.

'May I buy you dinner some time?'

'You certainly may,' said Jen.

And then there was Isla.

Isla whom he worshipped, and wooed, and who finally came his way. Isla with whom children simply 'hadn't happened' as the euphemism went, much to his secret relief. Isla, the luminous glow of whose popular fame somehow set her apart from the ordinary messy travails of human relationships. Isla whom he idolised, and who, against all the odds, loved him in return.

He often wondered if Isla knew about Jen, and usually concluded that she didn't. After all, there had been no sudden changes in his behaviour, no differences that she would notice, no cooling in his behaviour.

Jen had always been there.

5

'Everything's fine,' Isla told Barbara over the phone. 'Really. Trust me.'

'Oh, I do,' said Barbara. 'And Bill does too, insofar as he trusts any woman. Unfortunately he believes we're all easily led. I tell him he flatters himself but it makes not a blind bit of difference . . .'

'You're going to have to remind him that fluffy little dinner party guest though I may seem, I have made my way in the villainous world of show business and I'm a reasonably good judge of character. And it was he who asked me to go, after all.'

'That's true. But I think he thought you'd take his side.'

'Easily led . . . ?'

'Precisely.'

'Well, anyway, I'm not just going to leave it there,' said Isla. 'I thought I'd invite the two of them to dinner, to see how they perform in company.'

'The trouble with that,' Barbara protested, 'is that it presupposes they're a couple.'

'No it doesn't, it presupposes they're friends – which they obviously are. But to be honest I'd be amazed if something wasn't going on. And if there is, you should encourage it. He's an absolute charmer.'

'Yes, but Nell isn't,' said Barbara with bracing frankness. 'So if he's bedding her it's got to be for some ulterior motive, surely.'

'Bar, I despair of you – did you never hear of beauty being only skin deep?'

• Sarah Harrison

Barbara grunted. 'There, if I may say, speaks a woman who's always been able to take the top layer for granted.'

Isla called Ned after that.

'Ned, it's me.'

'How are you petal? It's so great to hear your voice. What brought this on?'

'I wonder if you'd come and have supper in a couple of weeks' time – we could make it a Sunday if you're working.'

'Do what?' Ned gave his fruity Welsh chuckle. 'I'll come any bloody night you like, my lovely.'

'Saturday fortnight then.'

'You're on. Any particular pretext? Anything I should know?'

'No, a mixed bag of people . . . nothing grand.'

'That's just as well, girl, because I don't do grand. As you know.' Another choice chuckle, ripe with cigarette smoke. Isla could picture the bared teeth, the slightly rheumy narrowed eyes, the cheeks scored by deep vertical lines . . . the face for which, not so long ago, the phrase 'handsome devil' might have been invented. There were times when she missed her *Lady In Charge* days.

'So how's himself?' he asked. 'Saved any good reputations lately?'

'That business with ex-King Stanislas.'

'Ah yes, the Ruritanian royals, I was glued to the papers. A famous victory.'

'It was. He's the man to beat at the moment, I'm very proud of him.'

'As he is of you I'll be bound, girl.'

For a treacherous second her throat closed and her eyes filled with tears, but when she spoke her moment's weakness didn't show in her voice.

'I'm really looking forward to seeing you, Ned.'

'Me too, petal. Can't wait.'

Ned put the phone down and exhaled a rippling stream of smoke, brushing an invisible speck from his jeans with long, sweeping movements. Poor lady. One of the very best . . . but not entirely happy.

*   *   *

Richard couldn't believe it.

'You're here! And no one else is?'

'Only the cats.' Jen grinned. 'Ain't you the lucky one.'

'Where's Claudia?'

'Back in hall, for the last few days of term. Make the most of it. But she's got a job in Pleasurelands for the whole of August.'

'Pleasurelands?'

'Honestly, you lead such a sheltered life, you do. The holiday people.' She made a banner gesture, pronouncing in a film-trailer voice: 'Pleasurelands. The family holiday with only one thing missing – the stress.'

'Means nothing to me. What will she be doing?'

'Looking after cabins, I suppose.'

'It's on board ship?'

She clapped a hand to her eyes. 'Just don't worry about it. Drink?'

'I think I will.' Richard rolled his eyes to the ceiling. 'So where's he?'

'School trip to Amsterdam, he was telling me all about it.'

'And that,' Richard reminded her, pulling off his tie and undoing his collar, 'was *before* he went. Imagine what it will be like when he comes back with several films of photographs and a host of colourful memories.'

Jen handed him a whisky. 'I don't believe they'll be all that colourful. Unfortunately.'

'Oh, I don't know . . . Even Keith could get led astray in Amsterdam.'

'Not with thirty-odd ten-year-olds to mind, he couldn't. Or not if he wants to keep his job. Poor Keith . . .'

They began to laugh. She flopped down next to him, slopping wine on her shirt and wiping at it with her hand. He wiped too, his hand strayed, they were laughing helplessly now, she undid her shirt and hugged him to her, head thrown back, hands in his hair, her strong, prehensile toes pushing at the waistband of his trousers. One-handed, he helped her. The rhythm of the laughter became the rhythm of sex. It was broad daylight and the living room window was open on to the street, but they neither of them thought of that.

*   *   *

While Richard and Jen lay together in Crouch End, Isla was attending a photo-call at the Hawkes Road City Farm in Bethnal Green for the animal charity Gain Without Pain. It was not one of the causes on whose letterheads she regularly appeared, but they had told her that a mere hour of her time, being photographed in jeans and a T-shirt surrounded by lambs, rabbits, and children from the local play group, would give their campaign an incredible boost. She'd been happy to oblige and was enjoying herself. Things had gone slightly wrong, which added zest to the occasion. A shetland pony had deposited a pile of steaming manure not once, but twice in the area to be photographed. The children were excitable townies, not confident with the animals. The play group leader could not conceal her irritation with the whole exercise and paced the periphery of the yard muttering venomously about media circuses. There was a problem with the light. The representatives of the press and those of the charity had subtly competing agendas. The journalists wanted the best possible shot of Isla and the children, the charity the best one of the animals. During protracted negotiations, Isla, as the only adult facing the lens, had the difficult task of remaining composed and photogenic while regulating the behaviour of several dozen under-fives, rabbits, chickens, guinea pigs, kids and lambs. The yard of the Hawkes Road farm was small and overcrowded; the day was hot. Isla, as everyone said, was an absolute brick, the consummate professional and a natural den mother. By midday three rolls of film had been taken, the children were piled back into their minibus, and the animals were herded away to be fed and watered.

'We can't thank you enough,' said the press officer from Gain Without Pain, 'you were a star in every sense.'

'Don't thank me, I had fun.'

'Well, you say that, but . . .'

'It's true. Honestly.'

'She means it,' said another voice. 'Believe it or not.'

It was Robert Scott-Chatham. 'Scotch? What are you doing here?'

'PR, don't you know.' The press officer absented herself with a discreet smile. 'And no one calls me Scotch except Nell, though I give you permission.'

'Well thanks.' She smiled up at him. 'So whose image are you burnishing, today?'

'City Farm's. It's actually a mutual image-booster for our firm – shows we're on the side of the angels, but no bucks in it, as you may imagine. Fancy a drink?'

It took Isla less than a second to decide, and when she declined it was because she wanted to go. 'I'd have loved to, but I have to dash.'

'Fans to please, fêtes to open . . .' He was teasing her.

'No, but a home to go to and a husband to feed. Look, Scotch, I have to make my goodbyes.'

About ten minutes later they met again, out in the road. 'What does he do, your husband?'

'He's a QC.'

'Ah, so an actor *manqué*.'

'Not at all. Richard's a star in his own firmament – a much more important one than mine, and a much bigger star.'

'There you go, selling yourself short again. Taxi! Want to share? I take it you're heading north, there's nowhere else to go from here.'

'Thanks, but I've got a car booked.' The limo slid alongside as she spoke. 'Can we offer you a lift?'

He held up his hands. 'Er – no. People might talk.'

The driver opened the door. 'I'll see you soon, I hope,' she said. 'I'm going to ask you and Nell to dinner.'

'Sounds a blast, we'd like that.'

Isla noted the 'we'.

The driver from the limo firm – one she used often – was experienced enough not to make conversation. Isla thought about her husband, making his way back to their house from wherever he'd been. Not in court that afternoon, that much she knew. He'd mentioned a routine day, quiet, nothing much happening. His words had made chilly water lap around her heart.

She had always known, instinctively, that there was someone else. Or a series of someones, she wasn't sure which. It had not been a case of accepting it tamely so much as realising that this other life was an integral part of Richard, something that had been there long before she was, and which was not going to go away. From time to time she despised herself for putting up with these fears and suspicions but she simply could not bring herself to confront Richard with them. Such a scene was unimaginable. It was not just that she could not summon up the right lines, but that she did not want to see Richard, whom she loved and admired, compromised; and if that meant she was a tacit collaborator in whatever was going on, so be it. Besides, she never for a moment doubted the strength and passion of Richard's love for her. From the moment he had come after her she had seen it in his eyes and felt it in his touch – she was adored. Isla was used to being desired but this had made her more, rather than less, sensitive to the real thing. She was minutely attuned to nuances of approbation, from simple liking to carefully disguised lust, and with Richard she had found pure gold.

And yet . . . there was this secret which ran through their life together like an underground stream. She tried not to think about it, to torture herself with futile questions. She was happy, she was loved, she had many friends, and she enjoyed great comfort and security. What would have been the point of digging beneath the surface in order to uncover something she would be better off not to know? There was a straightforward answer to this question, but she shied away from it.

As she had got to know Richard and his friends and colleagues, he had never been characterised as a womaniser, rather as a man who had been through the mill of two disastrous marriages and to whom she (they assured her with shining eyes) represented likely salvation. His fearsome professional reputation seemed at odds with his notably unsuccessful private life, a tension which struck a chord with her, and which she found attractive. She enjoyed the physical evidence of this tension – the explosive, grunting laugh . . . the slightly harrassed frown of concentration when listening to other people talk . . . the verbal ease combined with a manual clumsiness . . . the bespoke tailoring worn with scuffed shoes. She was a little in awe of Richard, but also amused by him. After years of actors who resorted to everything from gyms to make-up to alter their appearance she appreciated a man upon whom an embarrassment of physical gifts were left to go hang. Richard was six foot four with dark, greying hair worn, through idleness, a little over-long, and brown eyes with a sardonic droop at the outer corners. He had always been built on an heroic scale: the god-like physique displayed in old school photographs had been allowed to romp unchecked over successive decades. His attachment to good food and wine and his aversion to exercise for its own sake had resulted in a distinct bulge around the waistband of his trousers. If Isla teasingly grabbed the bulge, he would frown anxiously: 'Does it disgust you?'

'No.'

'You,' he would add, also teasingly, 'who could have any man you wanted?'

'Do I seem disgusted?'

'But you're an actress.'

The exchange usually ended in a kiss, at least. Isla's only real concern was for Richard's health. She did her best to lower fat and raise fibre, but there was nothing she could do about the wine and the weed, and references to exercise led as often as not to furious bouts of squash with young turks from chambers which were at best injudicious, at worst downright dangerous.

Isla was sure that if she had not met Richard she would never have married. It was not something she had ever considered enough to know whether she wanted it or not. It was only after she had accepted Richard's proposal – his fifth? or was it sixth? – that she realised no one else had asked her. Those men – mostly actors – with whom she had had relationships of any duration had all professed to worship her more than life itself, but none had proposed, and she would have been surprised had they done so. But Richard, against all the odds, believed in wedded bliss. She had been touched by his faith in an institution which had so signally let him down on two previous occasions. Her pride was challenged – having accepted him, she wanted very much to be the wife of his dreams.

And that, she supposed, as the limo began the climb up towards Hampstead Heath, was what she was being. The perfect wife.

The phone was ringing as Isla let herself in. Caroline's voice began to leave a message as she entered the library, and picked up the receiver.

'Caroline –? I just walked in.'

'Oh, hello . . .' As always there was that faint hint of disap-pointment, of former-wife's rank-pulling. No more than a trace, but enough to imply that Caroline had hoped to speak to Richard direct. 'Is Richard there?'

'I'm afraid not, shall I get him to ring you when he gets in?'

'If you could, Isla.' The chill began to come off Caroline's voice, she was basically a nice woman. 'I'm so worried about Giles.'

'Oh dear, what's he been up to?' Isla knew better than to imply even a glancing acquaintance with the problem.'

'Probably nothing . . .' Caroline sighed. 'Sex, it's always sex, isn't it?'

'Very often,' agreed Isla.

'And I've got nothing against it in principle. They have to sow their wild oats . . . you can't protect them from life . . .'

'No.' Isla had never looked on Giles as a young man in need of protection but that, she supposed, was a mother's perspective.

'But they absolutely should not be doing it at school!' con-cluded Caroline. 'And in my view Hawtrey's should be ensuring that they don't.'

'They certainly have a responsibility to try.'

'They do, don't they? I've had the head on the phone today, waxing confidential on the subject, as though there were any-thing I could do when the boys are seventy miles away under his care! What does Richard think, do you know?'

'I'm not sure,' said Isla carefully, writing RING CAROLINE on the phone pad. 'I believe he wanted to speak to you about it. The impression he got from Bruce was that Hawtrey's were pretty calm and collected about it all—'

'Well I'm not!' Caroline's voice became shrill. 'I think Giles should be given a proper, official roasting, and Richard should do the same to Aldred.' She never called him Bruce.

'Perhaps you're right,' said Isla. 'Actually, now I come to think of it Richard did have a serious heart to heart with Giles the other day—'

'Much good may it do either of them.'

'And I'll make sure he rings you, this evening if possible.'

'I would be grateful, thanks.'

Caroline went on to express an interest in Isla's work (the

only thing she could reasonably show an interest in, when you came to think about it) and to sign off in a tone which, though careworn, was noticeably brighter.

On the way home, Richard, having pulled up at a red light on the corner of Archway Road, stared at a flower stall and debated whether to buy flowers for Isla. He could see the white trumpet lilies and creamy stocks that she adored, and he would like to have given her some. But if one said it with flowers what, exactly, might she think he was saying? If they could have reached her at this very moment by other means – by fax, say, or delivery – he would have given in to the impulse. But to arrive with the bouquet in his arms would inevitably prompt the question, full of delight: 'What are these for?' And the message might not accord with something in his eyes . . .

The light turned green and the flower stall slipped smoothly out of sight.

Just before he reached the round pond, Richard pulled over and got out of the car. He retrieved his jacket off the back seat and shrugged it on, then locked up and strolled a little way down the broad, sandy track, an expedition he often made when travelling direct from Selwyn Street to Hampstead. There was a seat a couple of hundred yards from the road where he sat down and lit a cigar. As he lifted the lighter he inhaled briefly, to detect what of Jen remained on his sleeve. Unlike his wife, she did not regularly use the same scents. In the daytime Isla wore Calvin Klein; in the evening, Jean Patou. Jen's was more of a mixed-bag aroma, the essence of her day-to-day preoccupations. He thought he could still detect on his cuff a whiff of turps.

The sun beat down. For the past couple of weeks the weather had continued relentlessly perfect. An elderly couple in odd, unseasonal clothes – waistcoats, walking boots – trudged with bright, enthusiastic faces up the path. He liked to think that they were good, old-fashioned Hampstead Fabians, filled with an innocent idealism and intellectual fervour. A naughty world needed people like those. Sitting high on the wooded hill over-looking London, waiting for the heat and the cigar smoke to burn off the traces of Selwyn Street, and anticipating the shady, seclusion of his garden at home, Richard was happy.

Now that he'd gone Jen, too, was out in the sun. She lay flat on her back, eyes closed, Abel crouched sphynx-like on her solar plexus. Her patch of luxuriant, uncut grass grew smaller as the summer progressed and the surrounding vegetation encroached. Seen from above at this moment Jen fancied she would have resembled a leaf floating on the surface of a green and overgrown pond. She actually felt that she was floating. The drone of distant traffic, the buzz of wasps over fallen greengages and Abel's rattling purr created a kind of aural whiteout. Added to which was the deep, deep peace of Keith's absence.

She thought, tranquilly, about Richard, and the wife to whom he had returned. Even if Jen had been a devotee of newspaper and magazine gossip columns, which she was not, she was unlikely to have known the identity of Mrs Richard Wakefield. This was because Isla had made a point of keeping her marriage as private as possible. Only her closest friends had known about the wedding, and many others only came to hear of it months later. There had been no press at the ceremony and she had continued to use her own name even when attending legal functions with Richard, when she remained scrupulously in the background. From time to time the most friendly and least-investigative show-business reporters would trot out their 'Who Is the Most Envied Man in England?' headline, with much reference to 'the best-kept secret in showbiz', but the answer was never aggressively sought. The most that usually appeared was a row of eligible bachelors of a certain age with 'availability' and 'likelihood' ratings represented in stars, and an implicit understanding that none was a serious contender.

But Jen didn't see these and so had not even the opportunity to put two and two together. She was, as Claudia often remarked, shamefully ignorant of current affairs. She might just have been able to come up with the name of the prime minister if pushed, but the topics which set social gatherings alight all over the capital were only hazily comprehended by her. She was continually astonished by other people's grasp of these matters, impressed by their ready and well-informed opinions and their far-reaching frame of reference.

'How on earth do you *know* all that?' she would ask Keith as he delivered one of his statistic-laden diatribes against government policy on schools.

'I'm at the sharp end, is how,' he would reply grimly, a man of sorrows and acquainted with grief. 'When we have to put on a suitcase sale in aid of basic classroom tools, you know it's time for a change.'

'I suppose so,' replied Jen humbly. 'But it is incredible how you seem to know what they're thinking.'

'Huh!' said Keith.

It was the same with Richard. Earlier in the year he had, apparently, been defending some out-at-trouser deposed European king. She had known nothing about it except what he told her, which were the merest snatches of wry observation. 'So who's he?' she kept asking. 'What's the beef exactly?'

'You haven't read about it?'

'Well . . . no.'

He had explained with painstaking thoroughness. But as always she had been so much affected by his wisdom and fluency that her attention wandered after a few minutes. So when he got to the end she was really none the wiser.

Some weeks later he brought a bottle of Krug.

'We won.'

'Won what?'

'The case? His banished Majesty versus Sir Freddy Lancaster?' She frowned back at him in confusion, until he added gently: 'The one I told you about . . . ?'

'Oh – *that* one! Well done!' He held the champagne to one side as she embraced him. 'You are just so dead clever.'

His laugh shook both of them. 'You haven't the foggiest idea what I'm talking about, have you?'

'Yes I have. I do remember now.'

'Sure, sure. Let's drink to blissful ignorance, shall we?'

Jen was not proud of her ignorance of Richard's work, but she considered it a positive advantage where it concerned his present wife. She knew he had been married twice before – he was not long divorced when she first met him – and it had been more than two years before she realised he had married again. A 'we' had slipped back into his discourse and there were references to an unmistakably shared social life – friends for dinner, Sunday lunches, the Pizza on the Park . . . a holiday in St Lucia. Jen should have been shocked and outraged, but she wasn't, and couldn't pretend to feelings she didn't have. She took on board the messages, asked no questions, and carried on as before. She had never either wanted or expected marriage, and she felt herself to be secure in whatever part of Richard's affections she, uniquely, held sway.

But lying in the sun this late afternoon her thoughts did drift in that direction. The last thing she had ever wanted was to hurt another woman, but the situation that prevailed had not presented her with any of the orthodox choices. How often did it happen, she wondered, outside of the ruthless world of mediaeval history, that the mistress preceded the wife? What was a woman supposed to do when she found she was the other woman by default?

She also knew that Richard loved his wife, and she was glad of it. Jen's grasp of current affairs might be tenuous, but her instincts were unerringly sound, and she realised how much worse it would be to be having sex with a man who had entered into some kind of marriage of convenience, but who still needed her to spill his seed into a couple of times a week. As it was, she gleaned a certain self-respect in knowing that she was the mistress of a happy man. But that didn't stop her from indulging, from time to time, in idle curiosity.

A shadow came between her and the sun and she opened her eyes and squinted up from under cupped hands.

'Sorry, can't see a thing, who goes there?'

'It's me.'

'Red, sweetheart—' Jen sat up and patted the ground next to her. 'Come and sit down.'

'No, Mum, you've got a visitor,' said Claudia.

'Oh God. Where?'

'In the hall.'

'Who?'

'How on earth should I know? We just met by the gate.'

'Oh God,' said Jen again, scrabbling to her feet and dusting herself off distractedly.

'It's not Richard, in case you were wondering.'

'No, I know, he only left an hour ago.'

Claudia followed her mother, at a distance, back into the house. She remained in the kitchen, chugging apple juice from a carton, while Jen went to meet the visitor.

'I'm awfully sorry to descend on you like this without so much as a phone call. Only I've been carrying around your leaflet for weeks, and when I found myself in the environs I thought I might as well drop in.'

'That's OK.' Jen shook the proffered hand. 'Come on in.' She led her visitor into the living room. 'Excuse the mess.'

'Home from home. How do you do? Petronella Fyler.'

Claudia went up to her room. She had come home this afternoon to rummage through the clothes which she'd left here, in the hope of finding something suitable to wear.

The bedroom had always been spartan – the only room in the house that was – even when she'd been living in it. She didn't care for clutter. The wooden bed, made by her father, was covered with a durrie striped in shades of red and yellow. A threadbare woven rug with a picture of a mad March hare lay on the floor, which was otherwise bare boards. There was a long mirror propped against one wall and two Indian prints bluetacked on another. The small black iron grate was still usable, but was now full of apple cores and fag ends. Claudia wished she had some music to play.

The wardrobe was an old-fashioned, freestanding one with a speckled mirror on the front and slightly uneven legs. The door was stiff, and as it jerked open the wardrobe teetered threateningly and emitted a faint jangle of wire hangers. As a child Claudia had always considered that this was the cupboard in which the proverbial skeleton was most likely to lurk.

Some of the clothes were still on their hangers but most, having been haphazardly arranged in the first place, had fallen to the floor to join a collection of dusty boots, flattened espadrilles, odd trainers and chewed-looking belts. Having riffled through and discounted what was hanging up, she scooped up a large armful of the rest and dumped it on the bed.

She began raking through it with her fingers. Her eye was occasionally caught by something and she tweaked out an end with her finger and thumb and drew out whatever it was to set aside for a closer inspection: a purple Indian scarf with a silver thread running through it . . . a man's threadbare green velvet waistcoat . . . a big, old (it was Edwardian), white collarless shirt in coarse cotton, with a couple of singe marks on the sleeve . . . The rest she swept on to the floor, and took out another armful, dripping shoes.

She spent very little on clothes, and most of what she did buy was second-hand. She liked odd, broken-in things that did not speak of sex – a look that was interesting, occasionally picturesque, often challenging, rather than alluring.

In this pile she saw a flash of something green and glimmering, shot with blue. Her pecking hand fell on it and dragged it forth, like a blackbird disinterring a worm. It was a dress, something vaguely ethnic, a market buy from a couple of years ago, now creased and crumpled beyond recognition. She gave it a few vigorous shakes and held it out at arm's length. It was a good colour, and seemed to have some beading round the neck, not just embroidery, but pendant beads that quivered and caught the light. She kicked off her boots, removed her overalls and tugged the dress over her head.

The speckled mirror revealed a tall streak of brilliant green like a reed. The dress wasn't lined and it clung to Claudia's legs almost to the ankle. She tugged at the creases, some of which were stuck together with damp, revealing weals of discolouration when separated, but she quite liked those. It took a good deal of imagination, but it might conceivably fit the bill. Given a wash, of course . . . handwash probably . . . and hanging up to dry . . . A few of the beads dangled at different levels on long threads, like musical notes . . .

Still wearing the dress, she pulled her boots back on. The pleasing incongruity was what decided her. This would do for going to see the designer. Standing sideways on to the mirror she put one fist on her hip, the other to her forehead, and with one foot forward and knee bent, arched her back. She held the pose for a split second before yanking off the dress in hot rush of utter embarrassment.

'She's a lovely old thing,' said Jen, looking at the photograph that had been handed to her. 'I can see why you'd want her portrait done.'

'Well, as I say, it's for the parents. Well, my mother really. She's a very practical, hard-hearted country woman in most ways, but she's terribly soppy about her dogs.'

'She's got more than one?'

'Oh there are scads about the place, but just the two indoor dogs – Portia and Pepe.'

'What's Pepe?' asked Jen.

Nell pulled a long face. 'Don't tempt me. But he's registered as a Jack Russell.'

'Do you think your mother would like him in there as well?'

'I don't know, but anyway, she's not getting him, he's got years ahead of him, more's the pity. It's poor old Portia who's on the last lap.'

Jen handed the photo back. 'I'll need some more of those. Quite a lot if you want it to be a surprise. Normally I work from photographs that I've taken myself, so I have seen the sitter in the flesh at least once.'

'I've got a whole film in the car – of course they may not be good enough – hang on—'

In a moment she was back, clutching a paper folder. 'There you are.'

Jen took them out and leafed through them. 'These should be fine. What's a typical pose . . . ?'

'Comatose,' said Nell, 'bordering on moribund. But we want to be kind, so perhaps it would be best to go for sitting up, head lifted, silent upon a peak in doggyland, you know the sort of thing.'

'Mm . . . like this.' Jen held one up.

'Yup, perfect. She could probably hear a tin being opened but no one's going to know that. Look, I hate to be pushy, but how quickly could you do it?'

Jen replaced the photos. 'How quickly do you want it?'

'Well, my mother's birthday's actually the end of next week . . .' Nell grimaced, half grin, half scowl. 'Sorry!'

'I'm not busy,' said Jen disingenuously, 'I can do it by the end of this, if you can sort out framing – my chap's snowed under.'

Nell clasped her hand. 'Thank you so much. You are a sport. I'm so glad I decided to drop in.'

Claudia waited till she heard the front door close, and the car pull away from the kerb before coming down, the green dress scrunched up in one hand.

'Fancy a glass of wine?' called Jen from the kitchen. 'Sun's over the whatsit.'

'No thanks, I'm off.'

Jen appeared, glass in one hand, bottle in the other. 'So soon? I thought you'd be staying for supper.'

'No, I want to get back, I've got an essay to write . . .'

'Oh you found that dress.' Jen put down the bottle and came over to her. 'I always loved you in that.'

'Yes, well . . . it needs a wash, but it'll do . . .'

'Got a date?' Jen touched her daughter's cheek, disarming her haughtiness.

'Sorry to disappoint you.'

'No! Hold it right there!' Jen took a gulp of her wine and ran back into the kitchen, returning with a scrap of paper which she waggled at her daughter. 'Red, you may very well go to the ball.'

Claudia took the paper. 'What's this?'

'He called to speak to you, but I was very discreet and said I'd pass a message so you weren't caught on the hop – he's a bit old for you, but I'm not bitter.'

'Who, for heaven's sake?'

Jen flipped the edge of the paper, 'Red – Anthony Saxby.'

'Who?' asked Claudia again, loudly, to disguise the thunder of her heart.

'You know,' protested Jen. 'Your fellow bastard.'

6

Richard enjoyed artistic spats, professionally speaking. Though not always as profitable, a good dirty fight between creative types was infinitely more satisfying than the self-righteous whingeing of pompous politicians or the injured dignity of redundant Ruritanian monarchs. Certainly more edifying than pop stars spitting tacks. As he parked the Jag in the select area behind chambers he felt his usual enthusiasm for his work edged with a keen, bright happiness at the thought of the award-winning author whose damaged reputation it was in his power to restore.

Of course, reputation, that nebulous thing, was the currency of this particular job, but only in the various artistic arenas was it so tender and hypersensitive. Sifting out the tiny particles of justifiable truth from the heterogeneous mass of cross-referenced imaginings and half-submerged connections was exquisitely pleasurable. The importance to those concerned was out of all proportion – compared to other types of case – with the material or emotional damage to be sustained by losing. He could never quite understand why some of his clients in this area had gone to law in the first place. How, he asked himself, could it possibly be worth it? But they, thank heavens, continued to do so.

He paused as Archie's red Nissan Frontera lurched round the corner and stopped with a slight bounce next to the Jag. Richard was conscious of an unworthy twinge of anxiety as the door was carelessly pushed open. It bumped slightly, but not fatally, against his immaculate paintwork and a wince tweaked the corner of his eye. Perhaps because of this he was especially genial as Archie advanced towards him, an overstuffed briefcase clutched in his arms like a baby.

'Morning, old man.'

'Richard . . . Christ –' Archie lost his grip on the briefcase and grabbed it as it slid down his chest. 'You know – I sometimes think about you as I'm getting ready to leave home.'

'Do you?' asked Richard. 'Why's that?'

'I dunno . . . I think of you sitting with Isla at the breakfast table, sipping freshly ground coffee and perhaps the odd forkful of smoked salmon and scrambled egg – a violin concerto playing in the background – Isla in something pale and satiny . . .'

Richard pushed open the door and allowed Archie through. 'I hate to tarnish your fantasy, but the most I'm ever allowed for breakfast is cereal, and Isla left for Sainsbury's – in jeans – while I was still shaving.'

'Violin concerto?' asked Archie hopefully. 'No?'

Richard shook his head. 'Travel news on the tranny. Sorry.'

'Don't mention it.' The two men began the ascent of the narrow stairs, made narrower and extremely dusty by plywood partitions masking the refurbishments which were currently in progress. 'All I know is I bet it's paradise compared with Casa Stainforth of an early morning.'

Richard didn't counter this speculation. 'We're seeing you tonight, though?'

'Yes!' exclaimed Archie, his face lighting up as he recalled this to mind. 'Oh, excellent! I can't tell you what a difference knowing that has made to my day already.'

Archie's enthusiasm caused him finally to drop the briefcase in the reception area. Richard left him to pick up the drift of loose paper with the assistance of Mrs Colley from behind the desk, and went into the clerks' room. All were present, and at their desks with cups of coffee, except the senior clerk, Terry Goldman, who was watering the plants on the windowsill. Goldman, a slick, bright thirty-year-old from Basildon, made Richard think of some palmier era when gentlemen had gentlemen. Theirs was an entirely harmonious relationship based on an underlying agreement to differ on absolutely everything that did not pertain to these chambers and the running of Richard's professional affairs.

'Good morning,' said Richard. 'Those are nice.'

'Morning,' replied Goldman, who cultivated a dryly democratic air with his superiors – they the gifted, scatty children, he
the level-headed adult. 'Yes, that's the general idea.'

Richard put down his case and riffled through his pigeonhole
with a slight frown. He relished the prospect of his day, but didn't
wish to betray that relish to Goldman. 'What time's our first?'

'Ten a.m.' Goldman stood back from the plants and, without
looking at Richard, added: 'Literary lions – perlease.'

By lunchtime, Richard was tempted to agree with this assessment, but that hadn't tarnished his enjoyment of the morning's
conference with the senior of two Booker-winning brothers. It
was clear to him that this was a straightforward case of sibling
rivalry – this older and more academically brilliant brother being
rapidly overtaken by the younger and more popular one, coming
up on the inside. The younger was the plaintiff. Richard's client
took the deepest exception to remarks quoted in a Sunday
paper to the effect that his work was 'stuffy, self-serving and
derivative'. There had been other, more personal insults, but it
was these about his work which had caused blood to heat and
tempers to flare.

Generally speaking, with a dinner party in the evening, he'd
have contented himself with sending the junior clerk over the
road to fetch a brie-filled baguette from the likable Sloanes at
Goodies to Go. But feeling gregarious after his session with the
growling lion he strolled down Clock Street in the sun as far as
the Waterford wine bar.

He was looking foward to the congenial company of colleagues, a smattering of professional gossip and a decent bottle
of the Waterford's special, a Wollamboola dry white. What he
hadn't bargained for was Donatella in full prandial cry.

'Ricardo! Mm!' She stood on tiptoe, her heels rising out of
her black stilettos, to take his face between her hands and kiss
him smackingly on the lips. Richard was engulfed in her usual
scent, 'Bud', a man's *eau de toilette* from America. The feel of
her hands on his cheeks, and the nudge of her fiercely-suited
but still astonishing bosom against his shirt-front stirred him
momentarily in spite of himself.

'What a nice surprise,' he said, leaving his free hand on her waist for a second to show how unperturbed he was. Her coarse dark hair was greying slightly but her large eyes were still lustrous and her eyebrows jet black against her sallow, unmade-up skin. 'How are you? You're looking wonderful.'

'I am awfully well.' She flicked his stomach with the back of her fingers. 'But there is rather more of you.'

'Pointless to deny it . . . Look, can I buy you a drink?'

'No, no, no, no, no.' She wiped out the very idea with a two-handed gesture like drawing curtains back. 'You came in here to talk with the men, and I have a thousand things to do. A million.' She was a curious and compelling mixture of ball-breaker and traditional Italian mamma. Now she fixed him with a dark importunate stare. 'But I want to know if you are happy?'

'More than any chap has a right,' he said. 'All that heaven will allow.'

She nodded sagely, the stare in place. 'I see.'

'We must have lunch some time,' he called after her as she swung away, and she raised a hand without looking back. There were two young lawyers whom Richard vaguely recognised standing near the door, deep in conversation. She halted and waited, motionless, until they moved aside, held the door, blushed and shuffled in apology. Richard sighed admiringly. She hadn't lost her touch.

'Who else will be there?' asked Alison, licking her finger and scrubbing at a mark on her lapel. 'Do we know?'

'No. Richard didn't say, and I didn't think to ask.'

'But it's not just us, or they'd have said.'

'Presumably.'

Alison held her arms away from her sides. 'Do I look all right?'

Archie detected the tremor of genuine anxiety in his wife's voice and hastened to reassure her. 'You look absolutely wonderful.'

She gave a rueful smile. 'With all due respect, love, I never look absolutely wonderful.'

'To me you do.'

'But I have to be at the very least presentable in that company.' She brushed briskly at her skirt, a snip from the mid-season sale in her favourite catalogue.

'You'll be far more than that,' said Archie stoutly, sensing that the moment's vulnerability was at an end. 'I'll go down and turn the car round.'

Unusually for her, Isla couldn't decide what note to strike. She firmly believed that the job of a hostess was to provide a background – albeit an attractive one – against which others could shine, particularly on an occasion when a young couple were among the guests. She wanted to be able to sit back and observe, knowing that everyone round her table was happy and confident. On the other hand, if she was completely honest with herself, she hoped to deserve another compliment from Robert Scott-Chatham.

Changing her mind, she removed the blue shantung shirt-waister, threw it on the bed, and put on a short, sleek grey silk shift from Ghost. It was a dress of perfect minimalist beauty. She added minute pearl drop earrings and silver sandals.

'I say,' exclaimed Richard, dropping the *Standard* over the side of his chair. 'Have some pity, woman.'

'Too much?'

'Quite the reverse.'

'That's what I thought.'

'Don't change!' called Richard, as she crossed the hall in the direction of the stairs. 'Why change?'

'What's he like?' asked Scotch as he and Petronella sat in traffic in Belsize Park. 'A boring old fart?'

'Far from it, he's extremely eminent.'

'Eminence doesn't preclude a chap from boring farthood, surely. Generally speaking it's one of the prerequisites.'

'Not in this case,' said Nell firmly. 'So hard Cheddar.'

'Hard Cheddar!' Scotch glanced fondly at her. 'I love you, Petronella.'

Ned Braden took the bus to South End Green, for both social and economic reasons. He wanted to be able to have a drink, and he couldn't afford a cab. His professional status at the moment was ill-defined – he had a name, certainly, though increasingly it rang bells only with an older audience, but it was a name based on past successes, notably *Lady In Charge* and his will-they-won't-they on-screen relationship with Isla. Since then Isla had forged a new career based as far as he could see on being an all-round good egg, doing PAs, and advertising upmarket groceries on TV. He loved her to death, but she was wasting her talents. He'd stuck with acting, and to begin with the outlook had been quite promising. After *Lady In Charge*, they'd given him his own comedy drama series, entitled *Sparrow in the Treetops*, following the future fortunes of the character he'd made his own. When it failed to take, they came up with something else, *Lockwood* – who was just Jake Sparrow by another name, and in another job, the CID. But by now roguish charm was giving way to gritty reality, and coppers were more or less indistinguishable from villains, so it was inevitable that after one series *Lockwood* left the screens never to reappear. Roguish charm was making a comeback now, but Ned himself was viewed as a mite too old to play that card. Since then he'd done guest spots in other people's series and appeared from time to time on celebrity panel shows which his agent assured him were excellent exposure but which he and everyone else knew were no more than a gulag for has-beens and trying-to-get-backs.

But he wasn't downhearted. He loved the business, he still had his looks, more or less, and a trickle of work, and every so often some woman would come up to him in Waitrose and ask, with shining eyes, for his autograph.

He wondered who else Isla would have over tonight. The uphill walk from the bus stop had left him slightly out of breath. As he paused at the entrance to the Wakefields' drive a car came up behind him. He stood aside for it to pass, but it stopped next to him and the passenger window hummed down at eye-level – it was one of those family four-wheel drives. A homely sort beamed out at him.

'Sorry, was that a bit close for comfort?'

'Not at all, you weren't to know.'

'Going in for dinner?'

'I do hope so, or it's the homeless men's shelter for me.'

She gave a cheerful, honking laugh. 'See you in there.' The driver – her husband presumably – was a large, dim background presence. As husbands so often were.

The car moved on. He sometimes wondered on which alien planet Isla met these people.

Of course they all fetched up on the doorstep together and the woman saw to the introductions. The husband, Archie, was one of those distrait owl-of-the-remove types with a hot handshake and a high shine. But when Richard opened the door in his no-contest toff's kit of cream jacket and flannels, neither of them in the first flush, it was Archie who got the shoulder slap.

'Hello, hello! Archie old man . . . Ali, mm . . . And Ned, it's been far too long. Come in and have a Pimms without further ado.'

They went through to the wonderful faded, tangled orangery, where the doors stood open and Isla – with impeccable grace and timing – was walking towards them across the grass with a tangled wreath of uprooted pink and white convolvulus trailing from one hand. Had she, Ned wondered, actually stage-managed that – nipped down to the end of the garden when she heard the doorbell in order to present this picture of exquisite, artless informality? She wore a brilliant blue dress with a crisp shirt neck, some green beads, flat green pumps. What a pro . . .

'Look who I found,' said Richard. 'I take it everyone will have one of these . . . ?'

This time Alison got the first greeting, Archie the second, himself last, but he was confident her kisses had been meted out in ascending order of importance.

'You look absolutely stunning,' he said.

'Doesn't she always?' asked Alison, and Ned thought he detected a moment's embarrassment in the husband.

'I tell her that,' said Richard, distributing tall glasses rustling with ice, mint, cucumber and borage. 'But she won't listen. She went and changed five minutes before you all got here.'

'I did,' agreed Isla, 'I wasn't happy.'

'Some of us never are!' declared Alison. More embarrassment from Archie. Why, thought Ned, did some plain women have to make things worse for themselves by parading their plainness like bleeding stigmata? And Alison was no dog – just pleasantly ordinary. He couldn't resist stirring the tiniest bit.

'Tell us what we missed,' he suggested.

'Let's think . . .' She thought about it. 'I was very grey. Very muted.'

'She looked like Ondine,' said Richard. 'But clearly considered it was too good for us.' He brushed his wife's cheek with the back of one large hand.

'Your garden is amazing,' said Archie, walking past them and out on to the mossy terrace. 'How do you do it?'

'Don't look at me,' said Richard. He hung back slightly as Archie, Alison and Isla ranged themselves overlooking the garden. 'How are you Ned? Plenty of work?'

Ned always suspected that Richard took a fairly dim view of what he probably called 'theatricals' – his wife excepted, of course – so it took a considerable effort not to feel patronised.

'Plenty, no. Enough – just about.'

'It's a cruel profession you're in.'

'And you.'

'Not really – ah, I see what you mean.'

'Nothing personal,' explained Ned. 'But wielding so much power . . . it would frighten the living daylights out of me.'

Richard smiled and said something self-deprecating, but he was irritated by Ned. He didn't consider himself homophobic, but there was an unmistakable streak of bitchiness which wasn't helped by Ned's past association with Isla. Underpinning any exchange was the playing of the shared-history card, as if the acting profession were a mystical brotherhood the roots of whose allegiances went deeper than mere marital ties.

He was listening with exaggerated politeness to Ned's florid – and scarcely original – analogies between show business and advocacy, when to his great relief the doorbell rang.

'Will you excuse me?'

'Ned,' called Isla. 'Alison's suddenly realised why you look familiar, come and meet another of your fans.'

Richard's reaction on opening the door, bearing in mind his wife's assessment of the situation, was that if these two were a couple they were an exceptionally odd one. Nell Fyler, though handsome in a rawboned way, had if anything even less idea about self-presentation than Alison, and was done up as a sort of Railway Child writ large in sprigged Laura Ashley, which clashed with her crunching handshake. Robert Scott-Chatham was self-possessed and stylish in the unshaven manner of the times. Richard tried to remember what he did for a living. Media, he supposed, in that suit.

'Come on through,' he said, 'and meet the others. We're a small, select group this evening – only the best people invited.'

'For God's sake don't tell him that,' boomed Nell, 'his head's quite big enough already!'

When the second round of introductions had been completed, Isla withdrew to the kitchen. She was happy because things seemed to be going well. The best present your guests could give you, she reflected, was to be seen to enjoy themselves. The only tiny worry she had was that Ned might drink too much. She had invited him out of genuine affection and because she had faith in his judgement of other people, but she was the first to admit he was a loose cannon.

Ned looked across at Robert Scott-Chatham as Richard circulated once more with the Pimms. This, by God, was a horse of an altogether different colour. Things were looking up.

Jen had got out a video. It was a white-flannel production starring all the usual suspects: a cultural warm bath of floppy hair, clear skins, blushing and stammering. She intended watching it on her own, accompanied only by the lees of her latest winebox and some seafood sticks.

But in the event she felt rather mean about Keith, who had returned from Amsterdam with a raging toothache and had been enduring root-canal work for most of the afternoon. Like someone about to bungee-jump – with every nerve and fibre telling her not to do it – she climbed the stairs and tapped on his door.

'Keith . . . ?'

'I'm here . . . just about . . . Come in.'

She put her head round the door. He was lying flat on his

back on the bed with a sweater rolled up and cushioned against his left cheek.

'Are you all right?'

'Let's put it this way . . .' his voice was slurred, 'I'm sure I shall be.'

'Poor you. I was going to watch a film, do you want to come down?'

'Oh, I don't know . . .' for a moment, hope sprang up in her, but he rallied. 'But why not? It might help to take my mind off it.'

'Good,' said Jen. 'I'll see you down there.'

On the way back down the stairs she tried to persuade herself that she was storing up treasures in heaven, but since heaven wasn't a concept she acknowledged, it didn't work. She would have to get by on the notion that she was adding in some small way to the gaiety of nations.

She fast-forwarded through the trailers and the censorship chat and pressed pause. Keith entered with the sweater still bundled at his cheek and sat down gingerly in the armchair.

'Oy,' he mumbled. 'Watch your plate.'

Cain was tucking into the seafood sticks, his head turned to one side, eyes slitted, jaws snapping greedily. Jen took a swipe at him and chased him from the room, fishy pink shreds scattering in his wake.

'Bad luck,' mumbled Keith. 'Just as well I'm not eating.'

Jen pressed play.

'Hey,' said Keith, 'what have you done with the trailers?'

'I by-passed them. They're nearly all dog films anyway.'

'Thass why I like them,' he said. 'It's like being at the cinema.'

Teeth gritted and with only herself to blame, Jen pressed rewind.

Isla was not a natural cook. That is, she didn't much care for cooking, though she did like to entertain. She got round this by a means only available to the affluent, which was to use the very best ingredients. She aspired to a simple, unadorned lavishness, perfectly presented.

Tonight the dining room was lit by tall ivory church candles which gave off a faint scent of honey. Flowers were white and cream, blooming amongst wayward greenery. There were rose velvet curtains, polished oak, softly gleaming silver and white china edged in red and gold: a decor mellow and traditional, but also sleek and spare. Isla and Danielle – a sophisticated Belgian help of the kind only to be found in Hampstead – set out heaped black pearls of caviar in a silver bowl, melba toast, lemon wedges on green Wedgwood. In the kitchen there awaited saddle of lamb, tiny new potatoes shining with butter, starred with parsley and mint, *al dente* sugar peas and baby carrots; blackcurrant fool in tall, fluted glasses with Jersey cream; a gold-crusted half-moon of brie, oozing ripeness; spears of pale celery; misty black and green grapes . . . The sensuous beauty of food that was only itself delighted Isla. Confronted with the true cook's challenge of a bag of bones and some market sweepings she confessed herself utterly, miserably defeated.

'I hope you have the very nicest guests,' said Danielle, 'who are going to appreciate all this.'

'Don't worry,' replied Isla. 'They are. They will.'

Another reason for inviting Ned was that a spare man introduced a note of informality, a tacit assumption that this was not a couples-only event. There might well be some languorous young luminary of RADA or the Central School in Ned's life at present, but his role tonight was that of single white male. The table was a long oval, and Isla had arranged the places elliptically, with no head of the table. She didn't have a seating plan either, preferring to see how people arranged themselves.

In the event Scotch and Nell separated, which she took to be a promising sign, an indication that they were close enough to be comfortable apart. It had become surprisingly important to her that these two *should* be an item. She found herself between Ned and Alison, which demanded a high level of sympathetic diplomacy. Alison hadn't a mean bone in her body, but she was as tactless as Ned was touchy.

'Why didn't they go on with that police thing?' asked Alison. 'We loved it.'

'A lot of people did. But not, unfortunately, the powers that be.'

'Still, presumably you don't need to worry.'

'Sorry?'

'You made your pile with Isla here, surely, in 'Lady St George'. I mean, everyone watched – you were stars.'

'Lady In Charge. And there was no pile involved, I do assure you.'

'Really? How's she done it then?' Alison jerked her head in Isla's direction.

Ned's complexion darkened ominously. 'Clever management?'

'I married money,' said Isla. 'It's the only way.'

As Alison laughed, Ned thanked God for true friends.

Scotch addressed Richard. 'This is the most beautiful house. Would you consider leaving it to a total stranger?'

'There's a waiting list,' replied Richard dryly.

'I can believe it. It's wonderful.' He leaned across the table. 'Don't you reckon, Nell?'

'Yes indeed.' Nell gazed around. 'Very grown-up, I always think.'

Archie laid a confiding hand on the table next to her. 'You make a good point there. We have a perfectly good house, but it's stuffed to capacity with kids and their effects.'

'My parents' place is like that,' said Nell. 'My mother will allow her dogs to do more or less what they like, as Richard well knows.'

'Your parents are among our dearest friends,' responded Richard with ambiguous gallantry.

'I want to meet them,' declared Scotch. 'But she won't invite me out there. What is it you're afraid of, that I'll use the wrong fork or something?'

'Absolutely.' Nell speared a new potato from the dish. 'That and the fact that you'd hate each other on sight.'

'I bet you're wrong about that,' put in Archie. 'Opposites agree and all that.'

'Listen to the man,' said Scotch. 'I want to be shown around the gun room. I've even got the waxed jacket.'

Nell rolled her eyes in horror. 'It's brand new, from Simpsons – can you imagine?'

'I'll take the darn thing to Wimbledon Common and distress it comprehensively before I come.'

Ned leaned across. 'I beg your pardon. Am I missing something interesting here?'

'He's referring to his Barbour,' explained Archie, 'and the fact that it's too pristine to pass muster in an authentically rural environment.'

Isla got up to clear, and Nell pushed her chair back. 'I'll help.'

'No need. Danielle's out there.'

'But I'd like to.'

As Danielle loaded the dishwasher and she took the fool from the fridge, Isla scrutinised Nell from the corner of her eye. Her face had gone rather red under the influence of Richard's wine club selection, but beneath the ill-chosen sprigs she had a nice figure, and her eyes were bright with enjoyment.

'I'm so pleased you could both come,' she said, decanting the cream. 'We have so many dinners with legal eagles with a tendency to talk shop. Fascinating shop, but it's nice to have an evening in really relaxing company.'

'Ditto,' replied Nell. 'You have no idea.'

'Scotch is a dear.' She chose her words to convey an older woman's indulgent approval.

'Isn't he?' Nell picked at the leftover sugar peas with her finger and thumb. 'He was an absolute find. He and I are thick as thieves.'

'Anyone can see that.'

'There's nothing whatever in it, Isla. We're just pals, really.'

'Well that's even better,' said Isla imperturbably, holding the door for Danielle with the tray. 'Loving don't last – liking do.'

She was rewarded by an incandescent grin which only confirmed her in her view that there was Something Going On, and that whatever it was could be the making of Nell Fyler. Lucky girl, finding it all out for the first time, she thought, following after with the cream.

They went out into the garden for coffee. Generally Isla preferred to keep everyone round the table, so as not to break the delicate spiderweb of connections which had formed during dinner, but this time the moonlit summer night was too good to miss.

She'd put two iron lanterns on the stone wall at the edge of the terrace, and left a lamp lit in the orangery. She watched the way people lifted their faces slightly as they walked out, as if they were subject to the benign tidal pull of the moon and its far-flung net of stars. Richard glanced at her and she knew he smiled, before sitting down. Alison sat near him on the wall. Nell, Scotch and Ned wandered down the shallow mossy steps and across the lawn. Archie came to stand by her.

'We're like Shakespeare *al fresco*,' he murmured.

'Isn't it lovely?'

'You did that,' he added solemnly. 'Aren't you clever?'

'I can't imagine what he thought he was doing, drinking.' The voice of Keith's dentist, an abrasive New Zealander, came over the line like sandpaper. 'He shouldn't have been near alcohol after an IV and on what he was taking.'

'He only had a few sips,' protested Jen.

'That's like saying he only used one match.'

'I'm sorry,' she said humbly.

'Yes, well. It was bloody stupid, pardon my frog. There's nothing I can do. Make him warm and comfortable, try and get him to drink some water, if you're really worried take him to your nearest A and E.'

'OK – oh! What about the other pills?'

'What about them? For Christ's sake, don't stuff anything else down him for the time being. I dare say even Mr Burgess would rather be in pain than dead.'

Jen went back into the living room. Poor Keith was hunched over in the armchair like a rag doll, his arms dangling by his legs, his face resting sideways on the arm of the chair. A trickle of runny vomit came from the corner of his mouth to form a smelly damp patch on Jen's treasured Afghan throw. His breathing was stertorous – but at least he was breathing. In the background the actors who had promised such a tranquil evening of enchantment – she with a white parasol, he with a striped blazer tossed over his shoulder – ran waist-deep through meadow flowers. Jen zapped them.

As she began to minister to Keith with kitchen towel and cold water, she spotted Cain, sitting in the log basket, wiping the last morsels of seafood from his whiskers with a languid paw. She hurled a cushion at him.

The sudden movement must have startled Keith, who now threw up in earnest all over her feet.

'In the library,' murmured Danielle discreetly over the coffeepot. 'Will you go?'

'Yes.'

Danielle glided away. The others were still out in the garden, playing their parts to perfection. Isla walked slowly to the door of the orangery, and more quickly once through it. She almost ran across the hall, pushed open the library door and whisked it to, soundlessly, behind her.

Marcus stood with his back to her, apparently looking up at the general's portrait. In the adaptable way of portraits the old man's expression now seemed to be one of studied detachment, as though he was only too aware of the unpleasantness beneath his large, fine nose.

'Marcus . . . ?'

'Yeah?'

'What are you doing here?'

He turned round and she was shocked by the whiteness of his thin face, burning with a kind of angry exhaustion. 'Nothing. I'll go if you like.'

'No! No, please don't.' Boldly she went over and took him by the shoulders, kissing him on the cheek. He didn't respond, but neither did he resist. 'Are you all right?'

He shrugged. 'Sure.'

'Does the school know where you are?'

'I left a note. I told them I'd get back in touch.'

'Will they – I mean, will that satisfy them?' Isla was aware that this was not her territory.

'It'll have to, won't it?'

'What about your mother?'

'She doesn't know.'

'Well, she should, don't you think? She'll be worried sick if the school rings.'

'Maybe . . .'

'Of course! We'll contact her – Richard will.'

He mumbled something. It sounded like 'suit yourself'.

'And Giles?' she asked.

'What's it got to do with him?'

'Well . . .' She floundered. 'It could put him in a difficult position.'

Marcus's eyes glittered with disdain at this suggestion, but his expression became wary again as Richard appeared.

'Look who's here,' said Isla.

'I can see. What's up?'

'I was pissed off, I didn't want to be there. I had to get out of that place!'

'He's left them a note,' explained Isla. 'But we should call Caroline.'

'Yes, we will in a minute.' Richard went over to his son and stood before him, looking enormous. Only the fact that he kept his hands in his pockets prevented him looking threatening. 'How are you, old boy?'

'Pissed off, like I said.'

'Fancy something to eat?' he asked. Marcus shook his head. 'Want to come through and join us?'

'I don't mind.'

'Come on then.'

Richard placed a light hand on the boy's shoulder and accompanied him from the room.

'Darling,' he said to Isla en route, 'could you give Caro a brief call? Tell her everything's under control and I'll speak to her properly in the morning.'

'And Hawtrey's . . . ?' she mouthed.

'I told you,' said Marcus irritably, 'I left them a note.'

'Let's leave it till morning unless they contact us.'

A few minutes later, having phoned Caroline ('Oh God! What is the matter with them all?') Isla returned to the garden. Everyone was on the terrace, sitting together, some on the wall, others on chairs of different heights. Nell and Ned were smoking. Richard, cigar in hand, was circulating with a bottle. Marcus had been absorbed into the group. He wasn't speaking, nor was anyone talking to him directly, but the soft glow of the lantern showed his face to have quietened as he listened to the others.

The scent of her husband's cigar reminded Isla of how much she loved him.

At about eleven Keith came round and was sufficiently *compos mentis* for Jen to think of getting him upstairs.

'Keith – Keith! How are you feeling?'

'Terrible . . .'

'I think you'd be better off tucked up in bed, don't you?'

He groaned, and his head flopped back. 'Can't be arsed . . .'

'None of that, I'm going to help you. Come on. Get up.' She hauled on his arm, which had all the responsiveness of a sack of coal. 'Come on Keith, co-operate!'

'Leave me alone for crying out loud . . . !'

'No!' Losing all patience, she braved his sour breath and shouted in his face. 'You've already ruined my evening! You ought to be in bed, and so ought I! Make an effort, Goddammit!'

With much grunting and groaning on both their parts, she got him to his feet. Cain and Abel, gathered to see the fun, watched from the doorway and scampered off, tails waving as she staggered towards the stairs with Keith weaving and lurching beside her.

They ascended in short, painful stages. At one point he began to retch again and she dumped him unceremoniously against the wall, with her knee pressed to his chest.

'If you dare be sick I'll let you fall – is that clear? Keith? Got that? Barf and you're dead meat!'

He belched ominously, but kept his mouth shut. After a few seconds' respite she lugged him upright again and manhandled him to his room. The cats had preceded her there, too, and slithered beneath the bed like naughty schoolboys, taking little dabs at Keith's ankles as she manoeuvred him into position. When she dropped him on the mattress they shot out and thundered down the stairs. Jen wished she could get rid of the idea that they were laughing at her.

She removed Keith's shoes, jacknifed his legs and pulled the duvet over him. She absolutely drew the line at any further ministrations. But as she stood catching her breath, he opened one jaundiced eye and mumbled lecherously: 'Aren't you going to undress me . . . ?'

Jen was shocked. It was the first time in an association of some four years that there had been so much as a ripple in the dull, cosy propriety of their relationship.

'I'll pretend I didn't hear that,' she said with only a slight tremor in her voice, and snapped the door shut, firmly.

Downstairs, the living room smelt like a public convenience – unpleasant odours overlaid with cleaning fluids. Cain was back in the log basket, Abel was curled asleep in Keith's recently-vacated warm patch. Jen wished that dear Red, even with her slightly reproving air, was here. She needed an understanding ear. Just for a moment she wished she were somebody's wife.

7

The following morning, Jen was making headway with the Rottweiler portrait when, at about eleven, she heard Keith moving about, and braced herself. He shuffled to the loo, returned to his room – leaving the door open – and then came creaking with zombie-like slowness down the stairs. To her considerable relief, he did not come into the living room right away but went to the kitchen and put the kettle on. No radio for once, she noticed, with vengeful satisfaction. A few minutes later he tapped on the open door and she said, 'Come,' without taking her eyes off the canvas.

'Mind if I sit down?' His mouth sounded full of cotton wool.

'I should think you'd better.'

He crept round the sofa, one hand on the back to steady himself, and sat down. Jen sneaked a look at him as he took a tentative sip of tea.

'Sorry . . . would you have liked one?'

'No thanks.'

Another sip. He lowered the mug to his lap. He had a cardigan on over his pyjamas, and tweedy, checked slippers with beige rubber soles. His face was still swollen, poor sod.

'Look . . . I'm really sorry.'

At once she felt some stirrings of remorse. 'What about?'

'You know, last night.'

'I don't remember last night.'

He groaned, took another sip, more of a gulp this time, winced. 'I wish I didn't.'

'It doesn't matter.'

'Do you want me out?'

'Of course not. Honestly. Forget it, Keith.'

He sighed heavily, she continued to paint. Had she been too forgiving? Was he – dreadful thought – about to enlarge on something?

'The thing is,' he said, 'I should never have had a drink.'

She was conscious of a small sweat of relief. 'No,' she agreed, 'your dentist said that. It was pretty stupid of both of us.'

'Not you,' said Keith, shaking his head mournfully, 'not you . . . You're the most sensible person I know, underneath.'

Hawtrey's was characteristically understanding about Marcus. He shouldn't have gone AWOL, of course, and that much would have to be acknowledged on his return; but they appreciated it hadn't been an easy term, and the academic year was nearly at an end. They'd expect him back on Sunday night.

Richard didn't worry about it too much, either. His younger son was given to these sudden urges to escape and they all, school included, had learned to live with them. Marcus slept for most of Saturday and Caroline came over in the evening to run the rule over him, bristling with a disturbing mixture of maternal anxiety and suspicion.

'But there must be something the matter!' she insisted over supper. 'And you must tell either me or your father about it, or what can we do to help?'

Marcus was predictably tight-lipped. 'There's nothing the matter.'

'Come on darling, we weren't born yesterday—'

'Then get off my case, why don't you?'

'There's no need to bite my head off! Richard . . . ?'

Richard said: 'I'm sure he'd let us know if it was anything important.'

Marcus pushed his chair back. 'I'm going for walk.'

'What?'

'I wonder, if you're going out,' said Isla, also rising. 'Would you do me a favour and pick up a pint of milk? I've miscalculated.'

She went with him into the hall, gave him some money, closed the door after him, returned.

'Well done,' said Richard.

Isla cast an apologetic look at Caroline. 'I thought the milk might be a hostage to fortune.'

'What if he doesn't come back?' Caroline's voice wobbled. 'I feel as though I do everything wrong at the moment. Everything.'

'I think you're wonderful,' said Isla. 'He'll come back. I'm going to make coffee.' As she left the room Richard rose and went round to sit by Caroline, who had covered her face with her hands.

Out in the kitchen Isla found she was trembling.

Marcus was back inside an hour and went to bed. He even managed a 'Night, Mum' from the hall, which went some way towards mollifying Caroline. The next day Richard drove him back to Hawtrey's, in the first rain anyone had seen for weeks. Small patches of green seemed to appear before their eyes on the dessicated brown verges and fields. And in the same way, little by little but discernibly, in the humming privacy of his father's car, against a background of the mutually acceptable Crowded House, Marcus unbent.

'Will Mum be OK?'

'Of course. You saw for yourself. She's already OK.'

'I didn't mean to have a pop at her.'

'Yes, you did,' said Richard.

Marcus pushed his fist against the walnut facia of the glove compartment. 'All right, I did. I couldn't help it.'

'Yes, you could.' Richard glanced at him with a reproving half smile. 'But she couldn't help worrying, however annoying you may find that.'

'She goes on and on, she wants to get everything organised, she's not happy unless someone gives her an answer,' protested Marcus. 'It does my head in.'

'Yes. Well, it does your mother's head in not being able to help,' said Richard. 'And I must say I'm with her on that score. We're on your side, we want to be made use of.'

'I came to your house, didn't I?'

'I'm pleased you did.'

'Yours was the closest,' added Marcus, to wipe out any hint of favouritism. 'My ride had to drop me at Platts Lane.'

· Sarah Harrison

'I'm sure Mum understands about that, don't worry.'

'I'm not worrying.'

'Glad to hear it.'

The A1 hissed by in a steam of oily spray. The windscreen wipers arced back and forth, slicing smooth semicircles in the deluge. Richard let the silence expand and wash round them, covering the tracks of the last exchange, before asking: 'How's Giles?'

'How should I know?'

'I assume since you attend the same boarding school,' said Richard unable entirely to curb his impatience, 'that you might run into each other from time to time.'

'Not if I can help it. He's an idiot.'

'Is that what you think?'

Marcus cracked his knuckles explosively. 'It's what everybody thinks.'

'Do they?'

'Poncing around . . .' muttered Marcus venomously, 'reckons he's the dog's bollocks . . . screwing Fay Gadney . . . Idiot!'

Something clicked inside Richard. The tension eased. Just occasionally life wasn't complicated. Like the warring authors, it was as simple as sibling rivalry.

'Giles won't be there much longer,' he pointed out.

Marcus muttered something which ended in the words '. . . too soon for me', but though his brow was thunderous Richard recognised a moment of truth. To test the theory, he exchanged Crowded House for Mary Black, and was, astonishingly, unopposed.

It was this sense of crisis over which persuaded him, after returning Marcus, calling on Giles, and having a brief bloke-to-bloke with Bruce, to go and call on his father at The Hayes, Lettaford. En route, he first rang Caroline to assure her that the panic was over.

'Thank God,' she said. 'But why must he always be such a drama queen?'

'It gets it out of his system,' suggested Richard. 'I believe drama's quite healthy, psychologically speaking.'

'Healthy for him, maybe. I feel about a hundred and fifty and completely shot to pieces.'

'Well if it's any consolation, you don't look it.' Richard squinted at a road sign – he feared he needed specs – 'you're looking marvellous at the moment.'

'Oh get on with you,' said Caroline, mollified. 'Anyway, thanks for doing the honours, I appreciate it. I'm quite sure if it'd been me neither of us would've kept our tempers.'

Richard then called Isla. 'They feed them disgustingly early in that place,' he said, 'so I'll have something to eat with the old boy and be back about ten.'

Isla told her husband that she loved him too, and continued to gaze blankly for a moment at the pointing, mouthing and chuckling of the television antiques experts whom she had silenced when the phone rang. Some particularly revolting vases, gilt-scrolled and rose-bedecked, perched on pedestals and barnacled with overweight cherubs, were occasioning much interest. From idle curiosity she raised the volume in time to hear the verdict of the twinkly-eyed connoisseur.

'. . . to hear that you should have these insured for no less than five thousand pounds the pair.'

You couldn't blame the lady owner for being delighted. If she had any sense, thought Isla, she'd rustle the twin horrors round to the auction rooms at the first opportunity. But no, here she was, quite moist-eyed, explaining how she'd never dream of selling them because they were part of the family. Which all went to show, Isla told herself as the closing credits rolled, heralding the black hole of TV religion, that there was no accounting for taste.

The Hayes was a 'spacious Georgian house set in beautiful grounds with many mature trees, and within easy distance of the pleasant market town of Lettaford'. Richard's father, now ninety, had lived at The Hayes for the past five years without passing comment on either architecture or surroundings. This studied lack of interest was the most scathing criticism available to a man hitherto famous for having an opinion on everything. When Richard and Isla had first presided over Alec's move from the flat in St John's Wood where he'd lived since his wife's death, they had tried to draw his attention to The Hayes' many outstanding features, from its imaginitive cuisine to its classical music club, but to no effect. He had acknowledged with silent stoicism, the necessity of the move, but he didn't have to like the place, and he was buggered if he was going to. That was the message, and they'd received it loud and clear.

Richard had the chance of a quick word with Karen, the matron, whom he encountered in the hall.

'How is he?'

'Physically, doing well. He loves his food,' said Karen. 'But like all of us he has his good days and his bad days.'

'And which is this?' asked Richard.

'I can't tell a lie – not so good,' admitted Karen, but added, on seeing Richard's trepidatious expression, 'I'm sure all that will change now you're here.'

He wished he could be so sure. He followed Karen's neatly-belted waist and bobbing ponytail up the staircase. The flower arrangement on the windowsill halfway up was artificial, but was changed to fit in with the season – anemones today.

'Will you be having dinner with your father?' asked Karen on the landing outside Alec's room.

'Would that be possible?'

'Vegetable curry or haddock mornay?'

'Haddock sounds nice.'

'Haddock. Apple and peach crumble or chocolate surprise?'

'I think I should enjoy the element of surprise . . .'

'And then Alec always has his cheese and biscuits.'

'Excellent.'

'In the dining room? Or upstairs?'

It was like one of those childhood games involving a paper snapdragon that opened and closed, offering endless options. Richard wondered what his selections might be saying about him.

'What does he usually do at the moment?'

Karen sighed regretfully. 'We can't dig him out – but you might be able to.'

'I'll do my best. If we're coming down, I'll let you know.'

'If you would.' Karen tapped and opened. 'Alec! You've got a visitor.'

'Oh, God! Who . . . ?'

'And I do hope you're going to offer him a drink.'

With a look that said 'we know how to deal with them', Karen withdrew, closing the door.

'Hello Father.'

'It's you. Excuse my not getting up, I don't get up much these days.'

'Don't even think of it.'

Richard went over and patted his father awkwardly on the arm. Alec was sitting in his armchair before the bay window, a tumbler of whisky in his hand, legs planted firmly apart, feet in corduroy slippers, stomach jutting forward taut as a bass drum, a green cardigan held across it by one straining button. Because of his girth, he still conveyed an impression of bulk, but Richard knew that one of the reasons he refused to struggle to his feet was that age and arthritis had shortened his bones. He still had a fine head of hair, though – thick, wavy and iron-grey, worn a little long out of vanity, so that it curled on the collar of his checked shirt. The room was large and well-proportioned and smelt faintly – not unpleasantly – of the life that was lived in it: food, toothpaste, tobacco, clothes. Many of Alec's own things were here, they'd insisted he have them, though Richard knew he was probably being truthful when he said it was a matter of indifference to him – he wasn't sentimental about things any more than he was about people. A photograph of Richard's mother stood on the chest of drawers next to the ivory hairbrushes: Isla had found it in a drawer and had it framed. There was another of Richard, aged about six, standing on a beach in droopy woollen swimming trunks. 'It'll give the staff a laugh,' she said.

'Take a pew,' said Alec. 'Get the weight off your feet.'

'Thanks, but I've been driving. I'll stand for a bit.'

'Suit yourself. Help yourself to a drink, by the way. Scotch or scotch.'

'Think I'll have a scotch.'

'Good choice.'

Richard went over to the drinks tray. It was the salver presented to his father on his retirement, engraved with the signatures of other doctors; kept brilliantly polished, he was pleased to note. He poured himself a small whisky and topped it up with water from the basin tap.

'There are some monkey nuts in the cupboard,' said Alec, 'if you can be bothered.'

Richard got out the nuts, opened the packet with his teeth and put it on top of the *Daily Telegraph* on the table next to his father.

'They've offered me dinner,' he said casually, 'which was nice of them. Shall we go down to the dining room?'

'I wasn't planning on it.'

'No – but as I'm here. You won't have to sit with anyone else, because you'll be entertaining me.'

'Let's cross that bridge when we come to it,' suggested Alec.

They crossed the bridge and went down to the dining room at six-thirty. Richard persuaded Alec to put on his shoes for the outing.

'The staff don't give a monkey's what you wear,' Alec pointed out testily. 'This is a bloody rest home, not a *palais de dance*.'

Richard didn't argue. The dining room was high-ceilinged and elegant, with hot plates on an oak sideboard, respectable water colours, George Stubbs table mats and linen napkins.

'How nice to see you Alec,' said Karen, showing them to a table in the window. 'Are you going to have some wine?'

'Why not?' said Richard.

'I'll tell you why not,' muttered Alec as Karen bustled off. 'Because it's *Krautischewasser*.'

'I'm sure it'll hit the spot.'

Nevertheless Alec brightened up considerably over the haddock mornay, and downed the despised German white with only a token grimace.

'How's the wife?' he asked. 'Or should I say wives?'

'There's only one, and she's fine.'

'Bring her next time, she's extraordinarily decorative. And a sweetie, to boot.'

'She is both of those things, you're right.'

'And my grandsons?'

Richard had anticipated this question, and how to pitch his reply. 'Chasing women, smoking, drinking – business as usual.'

Alec gave his wheezy, bellows-like laugh. 'Glad to hear it. Any chance of getting a look at them some time?'

'Come and have Sunday lunch next time we're at the cottage. You ought to get out, and they'd like to see you.'

'I take leave to doubt that, but we'll see . . .'

Pudding arrived. The chocolate surprise was, not surprisingly, a slab of gâteau.

Alec poured custard over his crumble with a self-satisfied air.

'Bad choice. There's always one out of a packet, and you got it.'

'It'll be fine.'

'It'll be like cotton wool and shaving cream,' said Alec, a prediction which turned out to be wholly accurate.

They went back upstairs for coffee, brought by a pale, nervous teenager, the armpits of her green auxiliary's uniform damp with sweat.

'Oh dear,' said Alec loudly before the door had even closed. 'Oh dear, oh dear, where do they find them?'

'She's new, I expect. Shall I be mother?'

'Yes, and there's some chocolate. Same cupboard as the nuts.'

Richard fetched it and handed it to his father who broke off a generous chunk. 'No? You realise you can't smoke in here? It's not a wonder I'm getting so damn fat, a chap needs oral gratification and there's only one route open around here.' He gave Richard a sly look. 'How are all the others?'

'All what others?'

'Caroline. And the Latin lover.'

'Donatella.'

'How's she? See anything of her?'

'I ran into her just the other day as it happens—'

'What happened, did you bounce straight off again?' More bellows. Alec had always had a streak of lewdness, which Richard chose to ignore.

'She's doing very well.'

'Why wouldn't she?' agreed Alec, putting in more chocolate and munching. 'And what about you?' He tapped the *Telegraph* with his forefinger. 'Saw the piece about Stanislas. Congratulations.'

'Thank you. Yes, it was very pleasing.'

'And very remunerative.'

'That too, although –' Richard was about to make some point

about money, which he always felt compelled to do with his father, when the phone rang. It was on top of the cupboard containing the chocolate and monkey nuts, but Alec got up quite spryly to answer it.

'Isla, my darling, we were just talking about you! Saying what a wicked, sour-faced dragon you were . . . Ha, ha! Yes! Do you want to speak to the old man? I suppose I'd better not keep you.' He held out the receiver. 'Your wife.'

He sat down heavily as Richard took the phone. 'Hello.'

'I was thinking about the two of you, and felt the urge to ring. How is he?'

'Excellent. We had a nice dinner and we're just having some coffee upstairs before I have to push off.'

'Well . . . drive carefully, won't you.'

'I always do.'

'Give him a kiss from me.'

'I'll convey it somehow or other, never fear.'

'See you later.'

Alec was consulting the television page and didn't look up as he spoke. 'See she's checking up on you, then.'

'Isla? Hardly. Why on earth would she do that?'

Alec peered down his large nose at the listings. 'Don't know old boy. You tell me.'

On Tuesday morning Claudia skipped a lecture on the poetry of Thomas Hardy and presented herself at 32 Marsham Street, W1, the London address of *Atelier David D*. She told herself she had nothing to lose. This was her city, her stamping ground, and she was perfectly happy with her degree course and the way things were. These people were interested? they'd have to make the running.

She wore the green dress, the sprucing up of which had proved rather trickier than she'd anticipated. The hanging beads had got in a nightmare tangle, and some of them had come off and gone down the plughole. Also there were parts of the hem which were so worn that they'd given up the ghost and she'd had to cut them with sharp scissors and hope they didn't fray too badly. But the overall effect, with the boots, was pleasing, and she borrowed some earrings off a friend – twin blizzards of small brass stars that chinked confidingly when she moved her head. On the tube she was stared at – something she was already used to, but which she supposed she'd have to learn to suffer more gladly.

Atelier David D was on the first floor, part office, part warehouse, pale, spacious and radical, with high ceilings and long, uncurtained windows. In the reception area a middle-aged woman sat at a large wooden table which had nothing on it except a computer and a bonsai tree. She wore a white shirtwaister with epaulettes which made her look like a nurse. She gave Claudia a penetrating look over half-moon glasses.

'Yes?'

'I rang – I made an appointment with –' Claudia couldn't remember who with, and rummaged in her fishing bag – 'I was given this card in Paris – damn! Hang on . . .' The woman continued to stare, chin lowered, eyebrows raised. Claudia found the card. 'It was Olivier Marc who gave me the card, and my appointment's with Jane Porter.'

The woman held out her hand for the card, flicking the fingers with a suggestion of impatience, and looked snootily down her nose at it.

'Wait one moment.' She rose. 'Do sit down.'

Claudia now saw that there was a row of spindly steel and plastic chairs against the wall behind the door. Like a doctor's waiting room. Her hackles rose. 'No thanks.'

The woman glanced at her for a nanosecond before disappearing. It was fully five minutes before she returned, accompanied by another, younger woman, in black leggings and a white shirt.

'Hallo Claudia, I'm Jane Porter, come on through.'

The contrast with the receptionist could not have been more marked. Claudia strode past the receptionist's table with her head held high and followed Jane Porter into another cavernous room, half full of clothes on rails, with an office space at one end.

'You understand we're the *prêt-à-porter* end of things here.'

'Yes,' said Claudia, who hadn't the faintest idea.

'Would you like some coffee?'

'No thanks.'

'Bun?' Jane Porter offered a cardboard carton containing three jam doughnuts. They looked delicious, and Claudia had had no breakfast, but she wasn't sure whether this might be some sort of test to see whether she was really model material, or the sort of girl who stuffed her face with sugar and saturated fats between meals.

'Don't worry,' Jane gave the box a little shake. 'Models eat like pigs.'

'Well – thanks.'

She took one and bit into it. Wonderful. Jane Porter did the same, and put on horn-rimmed specs before speaking through sugar-coated lips.

'Olivier is one of our Paris PRs, and he acts as a kind of ad hoc scout. I expect you thought he was in a prostitution racket, I've told him before about sidling up to strangers and slipping them our card.'

'I did wonder,' said Claudia, 'but I have heard of David D, so I thought why not?'

'Absolutely. And I'm so glad you did. I'm sure you don't need me to tell you that you're absolutely stunning.'

Claudia could think of no appropriate response, so simply gazed unblinkingly back.

'We're always on the look out for unusual girls to model at our rail sales. They're informal fashion shows for favoured regular customers. Do you know anything about it?'

'I'm afraid not.'

'No, that's fine.' Jane rubbed her mouth with a Kleenex and pushed the box across the desk in Claudia's direction. 'Have you ever modelled before, even non-professionally?'

'No.'

'OK. Now you said you knew about David D . . . ?'

'I've heard of him.'

'Them. Jean David and Dieter Gras. You know the sort of clothes?'

Claudia searched her memory frantically. She had never thought to do any homework. 'No. I hardly ever shop and I don't see fashion magazines.'

'The look is classic – a sort of continental view of Englishness, really. Englishness with attitude. What the English country lady would wear if she didn't have a big backside and too many dogs.'

Jane reached behind her for something and slapped it down on top of the Kleenex box. 'That was our autumn/winter collection, don't bother to look at it now, take it with you. The point is that we like to cast our models against the role. Have the strongest, wildest, most individual girls to show just how wonderful the clothes can look. I mean, for instance, I can see you in our cream twill breeches and green hacking jacket – perhaps with those earrings and a really mean-looking whip . . .'

She laughed. Claudia laughed too. Jane said: 'I hate to ask you to do this, but would you mind standing up, and walking away from me as far as the door, then turning and walking back. Don't pretend to be a model, just walk as you normally would.'

Claudia got up and walked to the door. Turned on her heel. Walked back.

'Fine, that's great . . . I do like what you're wearing.'

'It's all ancient.'

'I can see that. But it suits you. And the boots are magic.'

'Yes, they're good boots.' Claudia looked down at them. 'I dug all of this out of the bottom of the wardrobe back at my mother's house. And the earrings belong to a friend.'

'So – by the way, what do you do?'

'I'm a student.'

'Doing what?'

'The last year of my degree, here in London.'

'Could you manage to do a couple of shows in the early autumn, in London? They'd both be here. We'd want you in for a rehearsal before that. Then afterwards, we'll see.'

'Yes.'

'We'll sort out your travel and expenses, and I'll get someone to send you a contract. Linda Evangelista wouldn't turn over in bed for it.' Jane gave a wry little smile. 'But you never know.'

When the Jag pulled up alongside and then kept pace with her as she headed for Oxford Circus, Claudia was too buoyed up by the interview to pay it much attention. Taken up with her own thoughts, she presented its driver with the totem-pole profile which was usually quite sufficient to see off kerb-crawlers in broad daylight in a busy street. But this one was persistent, even lowering the window and leaning across to accost her.

'Excuse me—'

She didn't look, or break stride. 'Get lost, hmm? You're holding up the traffic.'

'Claudia—'

'Are you deaf? Sod off.'

'It's me, can I give you a lift anywhere?'

It was Richard. Now, defeated, she stopped. Embarrassment and her rather satisfactory afternoon made her more apologetic than she would normally have felt inclined to be.

'Oh, I'm sorry. No thanks.'

Leaving the hazard lights on he got out and joined her on the pavement.

'How are things? Did you enjoy Paris?'

'Yes, it was good.'

He nodded, his eyes on her face, benign but aloof. What on earth did he want from her?

'Do you have time for a drink – glass of wine, cappuccino, anything?'

'I'm afraid not.'

'And that's as it should be, of course,' he said. 'I'll let you get on with it, whatever it is. Goodbye my dear.'

'Bye.'

Richard glanced at her in the rearview mirror as he pulled slowly away in the stream of traffic. She was an impressive girl, formidable even, and he would have been grateful for her understanding if not her respect. But it was never going to happen. What he had was her disapproval – the slappingly self-righteous disapproval of the young and carefree – and he would just have to wear it.

On the tube on the way back to the flat Claudia cleared the meeting with Richard right out of her head by studying the David D catalogue. She got the picture instantly. There were tweed micro-kilts, massive caped overcoats, sleek velvet breeches and tailored satin shirts with moleskin waistcoats, all modelled by ethereal teenagers with big, black, exhausted eyes and spiky hair. Interesting. Claudia's only fear was that she would be by several years the oldest model on their books. Still, hard cash just for walking up and down was not to be sniffed at, and the poems of Thomas Hardy would still be around when she received her bus pass . . .

She raced up the steps from the tube station two at a time and the side seam of the green dress finally gave up the ghost, revealing a length of pale, slender leg that nearly caused a seizure in two elderly vagrants sitting on the pavement outside.

An invitation to Barbara Fyler's birthday celebration on Sunday week arrived, written in Bill's large, shambolic handwriting that completely obscured the discreet 'At Home' and continued on to the back:

'. . . a bit late, I know, but absolutely rely on you to turn up to leaven the village mix. The old dutch will have notched up three score, so drink will flow. Some sort of pottage for a select few afterwards. B.'

'Sounds jolly,' said Richard. 'But you know their do's – we'd better stay the night.'

'Let's go out on the Saturday and the boys can join us.'

'Now why didn't I think of that?'

'Because,' said Isla, stroking his face, 'you were hoping to slip out there, get pie-eyed at the Fylers' expense, and slip back again, without facing up to your parental responsibilities.'

'I've been parental only recently,' Richard pretended to grumble, 'and even filial, entirely off my own bat. Couldn't I be let off for once?'

'That's not how it works,' said Isla, 'and you know it.'

8

For someone who had come to marriage in her thirties, and who had no children of her own, Isla had an idealistic approach to the family, and a desire, almost a need, to do right by her stepsons, their mother, and even in some curious way Donatella. She put this down to her own extremely happy childhood as a daughter of the regiment. She was a team player from a long line of team players, and her whole experience of acting – especially in a long-running TV series – had underlined for her the importance of teamwork. The whole was only as strong as its component parts.

Sometimes she rather fancifully wished she had been given the opportunity for heroism, to find out if she were capable of it. This would happen when she looked at her grandfather's portrait, or when she remembered her parents, both of whom had died some years ago, her father from peritonitis, her mother not long afterwards from a sort of starvation of the heart. They had lived in Malaya, in Singapore, in Hong Kong, Muskat and Germany. Her father was adored by the men under him – when they sang 'Onward Christian soldiers' in church she had always as a child supposed that they were singing about him. Much later when she heard clever, enlightened people pour scorn on 'militarism' and make jokes about army officers she strove to counteract them, to say that good, brave, imaginitive people – people with a sense of humour, even – could be and often were soldiers, and believed that they were fighting for what was right. She said that it was easy to decry people who were in effect doing your dirty work for you – for someone had to fight when fighting was called for. But mostly she met with a sympathetic evasiveness.

People could forgive Isla most things, even her quirky views on the army.

But Isla clung to her memories of her parents. Her mother, Zoe née Nicholls, had been a sassy, ambitious London secretary in peep-toe shoes and fitted jackets when at twenty-three she fell for thirty-year-old Lieutenant Jimmy Munro of the Argyll and Sutherland Highlanders. And who could blame her, or him, thought Isla when she looked at their photos – she with her Betty Grable hair and legs, he with his dark, poetic eyes, counteracted (in those days) by a slightly caddish black moustache. The pictures displayed her sparkling grin and her penchant for mad, witty little hats – his slightly teasing sobriety, knowing he was the envy of brother officers. They were a dazzlingly romantic couple and if their marriage had been through rocky patches (her mother had occasionally referred in passing to 'ups and downs') then Isla had been completely protected from them. She never had the slightest doubt, throughout a childhood spent in a succession of charmless married quarters and in the most trying of climates, that she was secure in their affections, and they in each other's.

She had had a younger brother, Ewan, born when she was two, and killed in a swimming accident at the Tanglin Club in Singapore. She must have been about seven when it happened. She could remember with sickening clarity her father and his friend Bob splashing around in the middle of the pool, her mother standing on the side, her hands pressed to her face below anguished eyes, another woman's arm round her still-wet shoulders . . . And then Ewan being brought out and laid on the grass, and the peculiar quietness in spite of all the people as first her father, then the army doctor, tried to bring him back to life. The grown-ups had crowded round but she'd wormed her way through the forest of legs to watch. She remembered Ewan's skin, a tawny yellow from the tropical sun, his lips and baby-thin eyelids grey, his fair hair greenish with constant exposure to the chlorinated pool – a fairy child lying limply on the grass, a boy destined never to grow up.

She had missed Ewan, but she was too young to feel the loss acutely or for long. It was the experience of her parents' devastation that cast a deep shadow over her life in the months following the accident. There was a funeral at the Anglican cathedral, but she didn't attend, spending the afternoon playing halma with her ayah, and eating chocolate bourbons out of a green ant-proof tin purchased at the Cold Storage. Afterwards a few of her parents' friends came back and she sat on her father's knee in the steamy garden while they drank, and talked in quiet voices. That night she woke up, startled and sweating and lay in the dim cocoon of her mosquito-net, listening to her mother cry, and cry, and cry . . . awful gut-wrenching, uncontrolled sobs that rose and fell in the room across the landing, while in her own room a huge fluffy moth fought and failed to escape from the muslin shroud.

Isla had gone to army schools and then, at eleven, to a boarding school in Berkshire. Zoe and Jimmy had come back to England, first to Catterick and then to Wiltshire. Friends had come to stay for the holidays, and she'd gone to them, but the best time was always to be had at the Munros. She'd had first unsuitable boyfriends (always made welcome), then a spell of suitable ones, then had gone to the Central School and found the people – men and women – she liked best. She was not alone. Zoe regarded her friends with unashamed, adoring envy – their youth, their looks, their talent. She told any of them who would listen that their freedom, both professional and personal, was to be prized and guarded fiercely, but these strictures rang hollow coming from a woman who was a walking advertisement for the institution of marriage. Jimmy professed himself baffled by the whole thing but his manner was one of ease and confidence. They regarded her success as both proper and predictable, a cause for wonder, not for surprise.

They had, however, wanted her to marry. It was perfectly natural. They wished for her happiness and in their book marriage was a prerequisite. Not that they would ever have dreamed of mentioning it, but when Isla reached thirty her sensitive antennae picked up a wistfulness in her mother's manner and a certain tender confidentiality in her father's. She felt that she should do or say something to address their feelings without the embarrassment of open acknowledgement. So she made do with plentiful references to job satisfaction, to many and wonderful friends and the surrogate family of the long-running TV series.

It was all true, and yet hearing it with their ears it struck a false note. They liked Ned, but were far too sophisticated to be fooled on that score. And her other admirers she kept separate because there was none whom she regarded as a long-term prospect.

But perversely, when fate stepped in in the large, eligible and distinguished form of Richard Wakefield, her parents were the tiniest bit wrong-footed. Somehow this urbane and twice-wed QC wasn't quite what they'd expected. They'd become used to her louche, lovable acting friends, they'd set their sights in a particular context and Richard had zoomed in from out of field. In fact, though Richard would never know it, his built-in element of surprise was a factor in her agreeing to marry him. It had been a rite of passage – the moment when she grew up and ceased to dance, however discreetly, to her parents' tune. Once she was Richard's wife, she was never quite so close to them again, and her devotion was tempered by an awareness that she was, first and foremost, her own person, capable of surprising not only others but herself. Their deaths within eighteen months of each other had hit her hard, but not as hard as they would have done before her marriage. She had cut the cord.

But the memory, as the song went, lingered on, and with it a fond, even romantic, ideal of how family life should be. Her own, she was aware, fell far short of this ideal because of its unorthodoxy, but she still aspired to the warm and humorous harmony she remembered from her own. And from time to time she reflected that even tragedy – what her stepsons would call 'the bad stuff' – was part of the warp and weft which could, in time, enrich the pattern of the whole.

She was in a mellow mood when she drove out to Bradenham to attend Barbara's birthday party. The only pity was that Richard was under the weather with a fluey and unsocial cold and so had opted not to come. In consequence, they'd abandoned the idea of going for the whole weekend and she went bearing his apologies and the Ultimate Gardening Book, a trophy from Waterstone's in Hampstead. She had spent almost as much time selecting the paper and card from the V&A collection as she had choosing the book, and the wrapping was a labour of love, complete with a silk flower and an airy rustle of fine paper ringlets – presentation was one of her strengths.

She hadn't liked leaving Richard who did, in truth, look rather rocky: on the other hand she harboured a guilty feeling of pleasure that Nell would be there, and might have brought Scotch. She had no idea what she expected from such an encounter. Nothing, really. Certainly the last thing she wanted was to place in jeopardy a relationship which she wished to see thrive. On the other hand . . . she craved the soft brush of flirtation's wing as it passed by on its way to somewhere else.

Having dozed through Isla's departure, Richard was roused by the sound of the Sunday papers arriving. On the way downstairs in his pyjamas he noted a dull, heavy day outside. He collected the paper, made himself a mug of tea and trudged back up to the bedroom. He was perspiring slightly by the time he got there, and pushed the window open, but still pulled the quilt over himself when he got into bed.

He leaned his head back on the pillows and closed his eyes. He hadn't got much of a cold, though that was his pretext. He just felt tired 'unto death' – a melodramatic expression of which he now appreciated the meaning. He reached for the paracetamol which Isla had left on the bedside table, and took a couple, cursing at having to gulp the boiling tea. He hoped he felt better tomorrow, he was due to be in court and it was a dry, difficult case that would require a clear head and a sharp mind. In his present state, he reflected unhappily, he might as well advise his client to cut out the middle man and hand over negotiated damages to his opponent right now.

He sighed and picked up the paper. In the gossip column there was a small piece about the war between the two literary brothers, which cheered him up. He snorted mirthfully to himself as he read it. All good sport, and it would probably be a last-ditch, out-of-court settlement without loss of face on either side.

He read on, scanning and discarding supplements, but there was nothing else half as interesting. War, famine and the resulting harvest of desperate refugees made him turn the page quickly, as did the disappearance of a nine-year-old girl on holiday in a seaside town, and sleaze in high places. There seemed to be a lot of bile about, even in the more frivolous sections. An ageing rock star's long-suffering wife cried 'Enough' . . . an Olympic hurdler's former lover displayed their love-child . . . a vituperative restaurant critic worked over an inoffensive provincial hotel . . . Richard told himself that it was a sign of advancing years to long for good news.

It started to rain – a muffling summer drizzle that blurred the unopened half of the window and drew a sharp, mouthwatering scent from the parched grass and trees outside. He dozed again, the papers sliding off the quilt on to the floor as he curled on his side. But his sleep churned with garbled dreams of anxiety and confusion – Isla in court on some nameless charge and he unable to defend her or even to speak, and then being late for something, something to do with the boys, and very hot sun, and rows of traffic simmering in the heat . . . He woke up – or returned to reality, it hadn't felt like sleep – sweating and aching. There was a jug of lime juice by the bed and he poured himself some, his quaking hand making the lip of the jug clink against the glass. Childishly, he wished he wasn't alone in the house. He took a long drink of the lime juice, held the glass against his forehead for a minute, then put it down and picked up the phone.

Isla had a good journey. It rained for a while as she toiled through the outermost reaches of north London, but by the time she put her foot down on the motorway the sun was coming out. She arrived in Bradenham with half an hour to spare and headed for Brook End, planning to park there, freshen up and air the cottage before walking round to The Bury. As she drew up she saw the front door was standing open and a lady's bicycle was propped against the wall.

Marjory appeared almost at once. 'I'm so sorry – caught in the act!'

'Not at all, it's lovely to see you.'

'It suddenly occurred to me you'd be coming out to Barbara's bash, so I skipped family service in favour of a whizz round.'

Isla felt humbled to have been the unwitting agent of missed worship. 'You shouldn't have done that.'

'It's my pleasure. Now I'll get out of the light.'

'No, please don't dash off – stay and have a coffee or something, there's plenty of time.'

Marjory sighed, then beamed. 'Go on then, you twisted my arm.'

They went together into the house. It was spotless, and there were roses in the hall and sweet peas on the kitchen table.

'Where's the lord and master?' asked Marjory as Isla put the kettle on.

'Off sick, poor old chap.'

'Nothing serious, I hope.'

'Not serious, no, but he was feeling lousy enough to stay in bed.'

'Ah,' said Marjory, raising a finger, 'but whatever the illness, isn't there always one strain for females and another more virulent one for the male of the species?'

Isla laughed. 'You do have a point. But he's not actually a hypochondriac, and he really wanted to come to the party.'

'Of course. That was most uncharitable of me.'

Isla put the coffee mugs on the table. 'You were dead right in the general, but not in the particular. Are you coming, by the way?'

'No, no, no, no!' Marjory scoffed modestly at the very idea. 'One of the inner circle I am not. I shall be working away in my garden to the accompaniment of Radio Four while you lot are carousing, and very happy I shall be.'

Cain and Abel lay on the sofa. They had come in from Selwyn Street through the open living room window. Keith had thoughtfully set down twin saucers of tuna chunks in the kitchen before going out, and now the brothers were replete. Their bulging stomachs vibrated with soporific purrs, their downward drift into sleep was punctuated only by the occasional swipe of tongue on fur: rest would be unthinkable while a single wisp remained uncleansed . . .

When the phone rang – for the third time that morning and at even greater length – their heads lifted, Cain's a little more than Abel's. Their eyes widened in well-bred surprise as Keith's key clattered in the front door and his slightly breathless voice answered the call.

'Hello . . . ? Oh, hello there, how are you? Yes I just got back from chapel – that's all right, I'm here now . . . No, as luck would have it she's visiting clients, somewhere countryfied . . . yes. Shall I give her a message? Are you sure? Okey dokey, then. BFN. Bye.'

Keith appeared in the doorway. The cats' eyes were already closing. He retreated to the kitchen. Their heads sank down once more, and they slept.

Before walking round to The Bury, Isla rang Richard. Rather to her surprise, the line was engaged. She rang off and pressed 'Redial' a couple of times, but it was still engaged. The third time she got her own voice explaining that no one was available to take her call. She closed the door behind her with an easier mind – if he was up and about, she concluded, he must be feeling better.

Having got only Keith, Richard turned on the answering machine, pulled on last night's clothes and went to sit in the orangery with some court papers. He wished now that he had gone with Isla, if only to remain at Brook End while she attended the party. Sundays were depressing enough on one's own without feeling as rough as this. Inside half an hour he had fallen asleep, slewed uncomfortably round in the wicker chair, his head sagging to one side, the papers drifting, one or two at a time, to the floor.

Despite Marjory's reference to the 'inner circle', Isla noted a certain number of what might be termed political invitees among the thirty or so guests gathered in the drawing room and garden of The Bury. For instance, Norman Brake (chairman of the parish council, well worth keeping sweet); the ambitious rector, Brendan Mather and his loyally smiling wife, Joyce; and – more surprisingly – the Scott-Chathams. Whether this last denoted an epiphany on Bill Fyler's part or a cunning attempt to wrong-foot the younger Scott-Chatham, whom she could see by the French windows, Isla couldn't begin to guess.

She left the gardening book and its accompanying card with other presents on a table near the door, and took a glass of champagne from a passing tray. Barbara was at her side immediately.

'Isla, how lovely of you to come all this way!'

'Happy birthday, Bar.' Isla kissed her friend's weather-beaten cheek which smelt incongruously of Joy. 'You smell gorgeous.'

'Oh God, yes!' Barbara snuffed noisily at her own wrists. 'The old man bought it for me, I just hope it's not an indication that he expects French knickers tonight, I'm far too long in the tooth for all that.' She saved Isla the embarrassment of a response by peering exaggeratedly to left and right. 'Where's your other half?'

'Not well I'm afraid. Took to his bed. But he's devastated not to be here.'

'I should think so indeed! Doesn't he know the best way to see off bacteria is to hose them down with alcohol?'

'He sent his love, and asked you to have one for him.'

'I shall – several, probably. Now who do you know, and who don't you . . . ?'

'Don't worry, I'll fend for myself.'

'Well your face is your fortune my dear, so that will probably be less trouble for you than the rest of us. You circulate and I'll go and tell Bill you're here.'

Isla regarded being a good guest as at least as much of an art as being a successful hostess, and one she had worked hard to perfect. Her professional life since the demise of *Lady In Charge* had largely consisted in being what one might call a professional guest. There was little she didn't know about relaxed amiability, rapt listening, and moving from one group to another by a process of social osmosis, without giving offence to those she left or appearing to butt in on those she joined.

It was true, though, that a well-known face helped. She was more likely to find herself with an embarrassment of company than with no one to talk to at all. True to form, Norman Brake was already grinning wolfishly at her over a bowl of cashew nuts.

'Afternoon, neighbour!'

'Hallo Norman, how are you?'

'Up to my eyes in harvest, shouldn't be here at all, but that's the way it goes.'

'It's been a good year then,' opined Isla.

This was altogether too optimistic a slant for Norman, whose grin was now replaced by an expression of grim foreboding. 'We'll see. Got the family with you?'

'As a matter of fact no. The boys are at school for another week or so and Richard's ill.'

'Tell him from me he shouldn't go letting you out to parties on your own. Anything could happen.' The grin slunk back.

'I think I'm pretty safe here, don't you?' Isla looked benignly about her.

'Don't bet on it. By the by, you got a roofing problem, I saw it when I was up on the silos the other day, you want to get it fixed before autumn.'

Norman's conversation always followed this hot-and-cold pattern: a pleasantry was generally followed by an abrasive reminder not to get complacent. Isla thanked him for the tip, and listened politely to his sales pitch and informal estimate – Norman's areas of expertise were legion. She was not one of those who ever betrayed boredom by glancing around while being spoken to, but she sensed Scotch was at her side before he spoke.

'Isn't this terrifically jolly?'

'Hello Scotch – yes, isn't it nice. Do you two know each other?' She introduced them. 'Norman's our neighbour.'

'And a conscientious one, I bet,' said Scotch, 'but then who wouldn't be under the circumstances?'

Norman's eyes grew flinty. 'They know they can call on me. So how long have you known Barbara, then?'

'Not very long. In fact I feel rather déclassé among all these people whose friendship dates back to the dawn of time . . . My parents know them both quite well – my connection is that I share a flat with their daughter.'

Norman looked scandalised, but Isla thought she could detect a certain gloating satisfaction at having his prejudices confirmed. 'Petronella's a lovely young lady,' he asserted pugnaciously.

'Indeed.'

'Champion horsewoman, did you know that?'

'I did as a matter of fact. I hope to see her in action some time.'

'She can outride any man,' insisted Norman as though in an

argument, 'and sort out any horse.' He looked over his shoulder. 'She here?'

'She is – up the other end.'

'Well, if you'll excuse me, I'll go and have a word before I go.'

'Not staying for lunch, Norman?' asked Isla.

'Not me.' His expression changed to one of smug secrecy. 'I got my dinner being cooked for me later on back home . . .'

Isla was trying to unravel this as Scotch stepped in front of her with a thoroughly unrepentant air.

'Is he always like that or was it something I said?'

'You didn't have to say anything,' she told him. 'But the flat-sharing didn't help.'

'I was only filling in the background.'

'*I* know that. So how are you, Scotch?'

'Terribly well. By the way Ned Braden called me up after your dinner party to see if there was anything I could do for him.'

'And was there?' Isla's tone was cool but her heart skipped a beat.

'I don't know . . . Most of our stuff is corporate, but you never know . . . We agreed to keep in touch. Nice guy.'

'Yes he is,' she agreed. 'He and I go back a long way.'

'He said. He thinks the world of you.'

'Oh for heaven's sake . . .' Glad to be interrupted, she hung out her glass for more champagne.

'No, he does. Not surprisingly. But he worries about you.'

She laughed. 'Why would he do that?'

'He thinks you're not happy.'

'Ned likes a bit of drama, and if it's not his it might as well be someone else's.'

'So he's wrong?'

For some reason she said: 'No one's happy all the time.'

'Underlying happiness is the thing, though, don't you reckon?'

'Isla, my dear!' She was rescued, and engulfed, by Bill Fyler's smothering embrace. When she emerged, Scotch had gone. 'What's he been saying to you? He's only here on your recommendation, you realise that?'

'Yes,' said Isla. 'Thank you.'

'Now come along with me,' said Bill, gripping her round the shoulders. 'There are no end of people dying to meet you.'

Marjory was, as she sometimes humorously put it, 'out at the front' kneeling on a cushion on the pavement in order to weed the border beneath her windows, when a car pulled up behind her.

'Excuse me—'

'Yes . . .' Marjory clambered awkwardly to her feet. 'I'll be right with you.'

'I'm *sorry*. What a nuisance I am when you're getting down to it.'

'Not a bit of it,' said Marjory automatically. She wiped her hands on her skirt. 'Now then.'

The car was a white Renault Diane, with purple daisies stencilled on the side. The flowers reminded Marjory of the sixties, a period she did, alas, remember all too well – she'd been matron in a prep school. The driver was one of those wild-haired, oddly dressed women whose age it was impossible to guess. Too old to be pretty, too young to be distinguished – and anyway, not trying to be either. A very *nice* face however.

'I'm looking for something called The Bury . . .' The woman picked up a piece of paper from the passenger seat and squinted at it. 'Does that mean anything to you?'

'Plenty!' Marjory was pleased to be asked for something she was so readily able to provide. 'There's a party on there.'

'Right. I should have been there about an hour ago, but I shot past the turning off the motorway and wound up driving Lord knows how many miles out of my way.'

'I'm sure it will still be going strong,' said Marjory. 'Just follow this road to the bottom, turn right at the crossroads, and follow that one for about half a mile, winding about a bit, and you'll come to The Bury on the right. You can't miss it, it's a big old place, and there'll be cars.'

'Thanks, you're a star.'

'Have a nice time!' called Marjory as the car drove off. She watched it sputter away – the silencer was going. The woman's mop of yellow hair, dangling hoop earrings and broad mouth lingered in her mind's eye. She had no idea Bill and Barbara Fyler had such a colourful assortment of friends . . . Well done them, she thought, as she lowered herself once more to her cushion and began digging vigorously with her fork at the ground elder.

Isla, being near the drawing-room door at the time, heard the bell and used it to escape gracefully from Joyce Mather, who was giving her a plain woman's appreciation of the modern-dress Hamlet at the Donmar Warehouse. She walked across the hall – twilit and brown even on a fine summer's day – and opened the front door. The late arrival held out her arms in an embracing gesture and threw her head back.

'I'm here! I made it! I'm so sorry, my organised daughter would kill me for this, but I missed my turning on the motorway listening to *Desert Island Discs* –' she stepped over the threshold – 'is the car all right where it is, I didn't want to spend even more time parking it out in the lane when I was late already . . . ?'

A small white car decorated with purple flowers was parked facing the front door. Isla was reminded of a dog tied to a railing, patiently looking in the direction from which its owner would return.

'I'm sure that's fine.'

'If the owner of that great thing with the bull-bars wants to leave before me he'll just have to say pretty please, won't he?' The woman beamed at Isla as she closed the door. 'And anyway,' she held out her hand, 'Jen Delaney. It's so lovely to meet you at long last.'

Isla shook the proffered hand. 'Well, thank you.'

'And *happy birthday*.'

'Oh –' realisation dawned. 'It's not my birthday.'

'Not?'

'I'm not, as they say, the lady of the house. I'm Isla Munro. You want Barbara Fyler.'

Jen struck her forehead. 'I do, I do. I'm so sorry. Late *and* barmy. Sorry.'

'Jen!'

Nell rushed into the hall and Isla watched as the two of them exchanged an untidy embrace. 'I thought you'd never get here!'

'Join the club. I took a wrong turning. And I'm parked bang

in front of the four-wheel drive from hell, *and* I mistook this lady for your mother, so a great start all round!'

'You thought Isla was Mummy?' Nell boomed. 'You are about to find out what a totally hilarious mistake that is!'

'You do look a bit young for the job,' Jen allowed apologetically. 'But that doesn't mean a thing these days when absolutely everyone is fit, glamorous and getting their oats till they turn their toes up.'

'Come and take a sneak preview at your handiwork,' said Nell. 'The great unveiling can take place now you're here. Isla, you come too.'

Isla allowed herself to be led into the dining room. In the bay window stood an easel, draped with a sheet. Nell went over to it and removed the sheet with a flourish, revealing a painting of Portia, looking suitably baronial but recognisable.

'Ta-da!'

'Oh, yes . . .' Jen went over to the picture, peered at it, touched the gilt frame. Isla detected a sea change in her manner, from daffiness to focused professionalism. 'It's quite some frame.'

'I expect you think it's too much,' said Nell, 'but Mummy will go for it.' She turned to Isla. 'Jen did the painting.'

'Did you really?' Isla drew closer. 'You are clever. You've really captured something.'

'That is what I'm paid for.' Jen, arms folded, leaning forward, gazed through narrowed eyes at the painting. Isla felt that she had been gently rebuked.

'Of course.'

'The aged Ps will be completely bowled over,' declared Nell, 'don't you think?'

'I do,' agreed Isla.

'And I invited Jen so she could accept the glory that's due to her.'

'I don't know about glory.' Jen straightened up. 'That left eye is distinctly dodgy.'

'For goodness' sake,' said Nell, replacing the sheet, 'wait till you see Portia – the whole thing's dodgy.'

* * *

Everyone was summoned to the dining room, Nell clapped her hands for silence and made a little speech. Bill brought Portia in, towing her by the collar, and sat her by the easel. The painting was unveiled, to coos of admiration and a burst of applause. Barbara's delight was a joy to behold. Jen was dragged forward to be thanked in person. Portia and Jen were introduced. Isla was reminded of the 'Alice, pudding. Pudding, Alice' scene in *Through the Looking Glass*.

Throughout this little ceremony Isla stood at the back, with Angela Scott-Chatham next to her. Angela was a smart, high-lighted, Alexon-clad matron whom it was impossible to imagine giving birth, least of all to Scotch. When the speeches were finished she turned to Isla.

'Only in England!'

'How do you mean?'

'A portrait of a dog! Quite a nice portrait, but just the same.'

'I thought it was a very good idea of Nell's.'

Angela sipped and bridled. 'Well, animals are her *thing*, aren't they?'

'She's a very kind-hearted girl.'

'You know . . .' Angela took another sip. 'There are certain English women who contrive to go on being "girls" till they're old and grey, and Petronella is one of them.'

'Yes,' said Isla, who could feel dislike for Angela filtering like iced water through her veins, 'I know what you're implying. I believe the jargon term is "latency girls". But I can assure you that Nell is no such thing.'

Angela raised an amused eyebrow. 'I wasn't implying any-thing.'

'No,' said Isla, 'I'm sure you weren't.'

'We're devoted to the whole Fyler family,' continued Angela in a more conciliatory tone. 'And Scotch thinks the world of Petronella – he shares a flat with her, you know.'

'Yes I did know that. He's a lucky man.'

Angela looked as if she might be about to take issue with this, but was fortunately prevented from doing so by the arrival of Nell herself, sparkling with the success of her present.

'I'm so pleased I got that organised – hello Angela – it's gone down a storm with Mummy.'

'I can see I must go and take a closer look,' murmured Angela, drifting away.

'You did very well,' said Isla. 'And the artist is nice.'

'Isn't she? Because I didn't give her any time, you know, and she'd never met Portia, she did it all from snapshots.'

'So a real pro . . .'

'Exactly. That's why I asked her to be here. But I'm so sorry about Richard, what a shame!'

'He's much better off where he is,' said Isla. 'He'll live.'

Richard thought he would very probably die, and sooner rather than later. He'd woken from a deep, troubled sleep in the chair in the orangery, aching in every joint and with his neck so painfully stiff that he actually had to support his head with one hand as he straightened up. He sat for a full five minutes staring blankly at the papers which were now strewn around his feet in disarray. Then he rose heavily, and at once stooped to steady himself on the arm of the chair as a wave of giddiness overtook him. When his balance returned he walked slowly and carefully into the kitchen and ran himself three successive glasses of cold water from the tap, draining them greedily, some of the water trickling down his neck. As he put the glass on the draining board, his own hands looked huge to him – huge and separate, like great fish. He pressed them to his face, wishing he were anywhere but here, on his own.

As he lowered them, he blacked out. It was for no more than a couple of seconds, simply a long blink of unconsciousness, but he came to to find himself slumped sideways against the leg of the table. Shocked and shaking he hauled himself up and on to a chair. He was iller than he thought.

After about three minutes, he rose, carefully, keeping one hand on the table, and took the mobile phone from the wall. He sat down again heavily and began to dial the Fylers' number, but then thought better of it. The place would be packed with people, his excuses would be made, and anyway, what was he going to say – 'May I speak to Isla, I need to hear her voice'? It was too pathetic. She'd be back in a few hours.

He rang Jen again, just in case, and when Keith answered, he hung up. Almost at once, the phone rang, startling him so that he broke out in a sweat.

'Hello?'

'Oh, it's you – this is Keith – you called just now.'

Not for the first time, Richard cursed the call-tracing facility. 'Foolish of me, yes. I suddenly realised I'd dialled your number by mistake.'

'Yes, it happens, doesn't it,' agreed Keith, 'with numbers you dial a lot. Anyway, as you probably gathered, she's still out in the sticks.'

'That's all right.' Richard was tight-jawed. 'It wasn't her I wanted to speak to.'

'She'll be back some time this evening, is my guess.'

'It's not a problem. Excuse me, I've a call to make—'

'I'll tell her you rang.'

'There would be no point.'

'It's up to you.'

'I'm sorry to have disturbed you.' Richard rang off, breathing heavily. It occurred to him that Keith would be a nightmare to cross-examine in court, because of his lack of the merest shred of perceptiveness. It would be impossible to play on his weaknesses, because he didn't know he had them.

He fetched another glass of water and called Caroline. Giles answered the phone.

'How's it going?'

'Not too good – I've got some bloody bug or other. What are you doing there?'

'Setting up a crack kitchen.'

'I mean, you're there for the weekend?'

'Got here yesterday in time for the Grand Prix.'

'How's Marcus?'

'Seems all right. Eating. Do you want to speak to Mum?'

'If she's within hailing distance.'

'She's doing something strenuous to a button-back chair. Hang on.'

Richard listened to the distant voices, Caroline's brisk approach to the phone.

'Richard!'

'How's the chair going?'

'Terrifically hard work but I *hope* it's going to turn out beautiful.'

'I'm sure it will,' said Richard humbly. He had a deep respect for his former wife's competence in the field of home improvements. 'And the boys are with you . . .'

'Yes, I buzzed up and collected them yesterday and they're getting a lift back with friends tonight.'

'Giles sounded cheerful.'

'He's not long back from the pub. Marcus has staggered out of bed, shall I get him?'

'No, don't bother.'

There was a brief pause, then Caroline asked brightly: 'So what are you two doing today?'

'Isla's gone to an old friend's party up in Bradenham, I'm nursing germs here.'

'Oh dear, I am sorry. I wish we weren't so far away, then I could pop round with a possett or something.'

He laughed. 'Good heavens, I don't need attending to, and Isla will be back this evening. I'm simply feeling a bit sorry for myself.'

'Well of course, one does . . . How's work? Anything I should be watching out for in the papers?'

'One or two colourful ones in the pipeline, I've been attempting to acquaint myself with the papers today, but it's a bit like wading through treacle.'

'There's no earthly use in trying to concentrate when you're below par, you'll only get depressed. Make a hot toddy and look at an old film or something.'

'I may well do.'

There was another pause. 'Well,' said Caroline, 'I suppose I'd better get back to my chair.'

'Yes.'

'I really am sorry you're not well – why don't you go to the doctor tomorrow?'

'If I'm no better I shall.'

'Isla's well?'

'Absolutely.'

'Are you sure you're OK, Richard? You sound terribly depressed.'

'No, no no . . . I'm going to take your advice. Bye Caro.'

'Bye.'

Richard replaced the phone, turned on the answering machine and went back upstairs. Lying on his side in bed, staring at the drizzle-smeared window he shivered, not with fever but with pure terror.

9

'This is so pretty,' said Jen. 'I don't know how you can ever bear to leave it.'

'With the greatest difficulty, in my case. Not quite so much for my husband.'

They were sitting in the garden of Brook End drinking tea, having both left The Bury at the same time. Jen put her mug down on the grass.

'Do you mind if I smoke?'

'Please. I live with a smoker.'

'Crikey, I wish I did. I live with a man whose idea of a vice is to cycle without clips and a helmet.'

Isla laughed. 'Really?'

'But he's my lodger, so I suppose I should be grateful.'

'Yes,' agreed Isla. 'I imagine what one looks for in a lodger is a complete absence of all those things that would be a basic prerequisite in a lover.'

'Except in bathrooms.' Jen lit a cigarette, shook the match and dropped it in her empty mug. 'Where bathrooms are concerned I have a pretty high tolerance of curly hairs, toenails, grime rings and slimy flannels, provided they're all my own. Anyone else's – forget it.'

'So how does your lodger score on the bathroom scale?'

'A near-perfect nine point nine.'

'That,' said Isla, 'sounds like "ninety-nine per cent of all household germs" – it leaves a person wondering about the other one per cent.'

'Yes, but the perfect ten doesn't exist. In bathrooms.'

'In anything. Bo Derek notwithstanding.'

'Who?' Jen narrowed her eyes.

'Bo Derek? In that film?' It was apparent none of this registered. 'With Dudley Moore?'

'No, sorry . . . I'm hopeless at names. But what you say is dead right. Thank heavens. I mean – who wants perfection? How wearing it would be to share one's life with a paragon.'

'True.'

'Pardon my asking, but where's your other half?'

'He stayed at home. He wasn't well.'

'What, a real illness, or a cop out?'

'A real one.'

'What a shame. But you came anyway. I mean you didn't feel you ought to be at home administering cold compresses and lemon barley or anything? Forgive me, but I'm interested in marriages, never having had one myself.'

'Not at all.' Isla realised she could not only very easily forgive this person, but that it was a positive pleasure to talk to her. It was as though something she had been missing without knowing it had suddenly been granted to her, and it was delightful. 'It obviously wasn't anything dire, and the Fylers are very dear friends. Besides, we did compromise – we were going to come for the weekend.'

'Don't get me wrong,' said Jen, 'I'm not implying you're a heartless cow or anything, I just don't feel terribly *au fait* with the norm.'

'I don't think there is one. And if there is, it's not us. We make it up as we go along.'

'What a terribly good idea. So what does he do, your husband, when he's well enough to work?'

'He's a lawyer.'

'A solicitor?'

'No, a barrister.'

'Oh my God, not another word. I know one of those and the whole thing's a closed book to me. I feel ashamed of my ignorance but completely powerless to overcome it, do you have things like that?'

'Lots, far too many.'

'Such as?'

'Computers make me nervous. Fancy cooking. Changing tyres—'

'For heaven's sake, you try and change tyres?'

'Well, if you get a flat on some country road—'

'If you get a flat on some country road you wait till a well-built farm labourer happens by and burst into tears!' Jen watched Isla's face, joined in with her laugh, and added: 'No, I'm full of admiration, but I find the gap between knowing what to do and actually being able to do it is just too massive in my case so I've got pretty damn good at commandeering assistance.'

'A useful skill.'

'And do you and your husband have children?' Jen glanced about as if they might be hiding behind the furniture.

'He does, from a previous marriage, but they're more or less grown up.'

'Like the rest of us – more or less grown up. I've got a daughter. She's more grown up than me. A foot taller, a stone thinner, and able to read maps and run to time. I truthfully haven't a clue where she gets it from because her father's a disorganised sod as well.' Isla's almost too-serene composure must have prompted her to add: 'Yes you're quite right I did say I'd never been married. I wish I could say I regretted it, but I honestly don't. And Red is the most together young person one could wish to meet, she scares the living daylights out of me sometimes, so it hasn't done her any harm.'

'It must be lovely to have a daughter.'

'Do you know, it is?' said Jen, as though the strangeness of this had only just struck her. 'It's not how much alike you are, it's how different. Fascinating.'

'I can imagine.'

Their first small, but not awkward silence intervened, before Jen asked: 'And now I'm going to have to admit it, I recognise your face from somewhere but I don't know where. Are you stringing me along . . . have we met before?'

'No, not that I know of. Although, funnily enough . . .' Isla frowned. There was something familiar, some sense of *déjà vu* . . . 'No, I'm sure we haven't.'

'So where do I know you from? I have this ghastly feeling

you're going to tell me you're a cabinet minister or something and I shall be completely humiliated, not for the first time—'

'I'm an actress,' said Isla, who hated this sort of exchange, 'so it's just possible you may have seen me on the box, but ages ago.'

'That'll be it then!' Jen snapped her fingers in the air and, apparently perfectly satisfied with this explanation, changed tack. 'If you're a famous actress you should certainly be able to get people to change tyres for you.'

Jen could only think that she had never known the meaning of charm until she had met Isla Munro. Charm in its mystical sense, of a spell. She could not remember liking someone so instinctively and immediately, so much. She found that the other woman's beauty and style, instead of (as was usually the case) making her feel like an unmade bed, pleased and soothed her. They were restful. The expression 'easy on the eye' sprang to mind. It was easy to be with Isla – easy to talk, easy to listen, easy to look. She was nice in a way that one did not perhaps expect actresses to be nice. Her gentle good manners and natural reserve were like a gift. Jen wanted, hoped, to be liked by her in return.

'You've got a Scottish name,' she said. 'Are you Scottish?'

'My father was, although he spent most of his life in England. My mother was a Londoner.'

'But don't you feel those tartan genes swirling around? I'm sure I would, particularly now, when Celtic's all the rage.'

'Not really. If I feel anything I feel English.'

Jen nodded in the direction of The Bury. 'That was very English, wasn't it?'

'I suppose it was. Actually I thought it was a nice occasion. Warm. I like Nell a lot.'

'I do. She's a good egg. But tough – I bet she could shoot a stray dog.'

'She could. And wring rabbits' necks. And chase foxes on horseback.'

'Oh, no . . .' Jen closed her eyes. 'Don't. I hate that.'

'It's part of her life, the way she was brought up, you mustn't hold it against her.'

'Oh, I won't, I won't . . .' Jen lit another cigarette from the stub of the last. 'Life's too short, and anyway it's not her fault. But I hope she never bumps into my daughter, she wouldn't be half so charitable.'

Isla tried to picture this tall, stern girl. 'Does your daughter have a boyfriend?'

'Red? Not that I know of. No one would dare.'

'You make her sound frightfully intimidating.'

'Yes I do and she is slightly, but she's adorable. You'd love her, I bet you and she would get on like a house on fire.'

'And her father . . . ?' asked Isla cautiously. 'Are you in touch at all?'

'Sort of.' Jen frowned. 'He and she are. She's the one who makes the effort, invites herself for weekends, goes down there with a bunch of flowers. Usually winds up babysitting for them on Saturday night. The only reason I don't is sheer idleness, not animosity. He's a decent enough bloke, but history . . .'

'He's married since.'

'Isla, you never saw anyone so married. If you think you're married, you should see Mo and Julie. It makes me realise what a lucky escape I had. Sorry.'

'That's quite all right, I know what you're saying.' Isla thought of the Stainforths. 'We know a couple like that and they make us feel complete amateurs.'

Jen said: 'It may sound odd, but my lodger's a married type. He's not, but he might as well be. I sometimes wonder if he fantasises about being married to me.'

'I'm sure he does.'

'You think? But then he may well never fantasise at all. He keeps tropical fish.'

'Is that indicative of something?'

'They use them in dentists' waiting rooms, don't they . . . A sort of visual bromide. But he lives with the darn things.'

'There's probably a woman you know nothing about,' suggested Isla.

Jen waved a hand. 'No, you don't understand, this is Keith we're talking about.'

'I'm trying to imagine.'

'Impossible, it'll make your brain ache. Tell me about these children you've had to bring up.'

Isla, who never blushed, felt as if she might be doing so now. 'I haven't had to bring them up. They're based with their mother, and I just do my bit.'

'Wicked stepmother.' Jen struck another match and spoke as she held it. 'How old are they?'

'Seventeen and fifteen.'

'Ouch!' She dropped the match on the grass and sucked her fingers. 'Damn! But they must think they've died and gone to heaven with you for a stepmother. Do you like them?'

'I do, yes. And I find them interesting.'

'Like I find marriage.'

'I suppose so, yes.'

'Do you wish they were yours?'

The bluntness of this question took Isla aback, but not as much as it would have done coming from anyone else. She absorbed the small shock and looked aside, thinking.

'No, I don't wish they were mine. They're not mine, they're someone else's, and that's all there is to it. That, I suppose, is how I can afford to find them interesting. If they were mine they'd probably drive me to drink.'

'Are they like their father?'

'There are trace elements. But they've had a completely different kind of upbringing, much of it apart from him, and nurture's a powerful thing.'

'I never felt,' said Jen, 'that I was any good at nurturing. I never had a vision of how it ought to be. I never had a game plan. I just knew I loved Red and I hoped she loved me, and we muddled along, with me getting stressed-out from time to time and her putting up with it.'

Isla said, 'If when you asked me if I wished the boys were mine, you meant did I wish I'd had children of my own, the answer is yes. But I don't spend time feeling miserable about it.'

'What about the mother of his children?'

'She's amiable . . . and busy . . . and – this is going to sound unkind—'

'I doubt it.'

'Peculiarly sexless. I like her a lot, I believe we're friends, but there it is.'

'Maybe that's why. Why you're friends. Because she's sexless.

A sexless ex, what could be better?' She caught Isla's doubtful look. 'And anyway, they did it at least twice, didn't they, so you've got nothing to reproach yourself with.'

Isla still felt she had been tempted into an indiscretion, something she sought strenuously to avoid.

'Have you seen the time?' she said. 'If you don't start to head into London soon the traffic will be appalling.'

'You too,' said Jen. 'And you've got that sick husband to attend to.'

'As a matter of fact I'm going to give him a ring before I leave . . .' Isla rose. 'Can I get you anything before the long haul home? Another cup of tea? Coffee? Or something to eat?'

Jen threw her head back, hand to brow. 'Please, no more! I shall never eat again – your friends know a thing or two about carbo-loading.'

Isla, laughing, went into the house

Jen watched her go and sat for a moment. She was reluctant to leave, although she knew it was true about the traffic.

This time Richard answered the phone.

'Darling,' said Isla, 'you sound utterly miserable.'

'I am. I've had the creeps all day.'

'I've tried to ring, but first you were engaged and then the machine was on.'

'I'm sorry. I called Archie about something, but then I found I couldn't work anyway so I crawled back into bed. I should have come with you, all that's happened is I've got more and more morose.'

'Well, I'm on my way any minute now.'

'I can't wait.'

'She is on her way!' called Jen who had appeared in the living room behind Isla. 'And she's only this late because I've been wasting her time!'

'Did you hear that?' asked Isla.

'Vaguely, who have you got there?'

'A new friend. We've been gassing in the garden.'

'I'm glad you've had a nice day.'

'Everyone sent their love, you were very much missed.'

'Hurry back, won't you.'

'I'll do my best.' Isla put the phone down. Jen stood with her bag over her shoulder near the front door.

'How's the patient?'

'Depressed.'

'So you must fly. And I'm off. Thanks for the tea.'

'Not at all . . .' Isla opened the door and they moved outside. 'I enjoyed talking. We must do it again some time. It's not as if we live that far away from each other.'

'I already thought of that. Here –' Jen handed Isla a dog-eared business card. 'That's me. Give a ring and we can have a drink, or lunch or something. Maybe you've got a borzoi or an Irish wolfhound that you want recorded for posterity . . . ?'

'Not so much as a budgie I'm afraid.'

'Darn, all this time wasted . . . Be in touch, anyway.'

'I will,' said Isla, 'I definitely will.'

Jen raised an arm through the car's sun-roof as she turned into the lane. Isla studied the card, and slipped it into her jacket pocket. Feeling ridiculously cheerful she went round the cottage, locking up.

Richard felt slightly ashamed of himself. Now that Isla was on her way back, in what would certainly be frightful traffic, he felt better. It was like going to the doctor. He scarcely ever went, but when he did it was his experience that the mere act of turning up induced an improvement. He supposed it was something to do with help being at hand. He roused himself, sorted through his scattered papers and, acting on instinct, made a call to Archie.

'Archie, I'm so sorry to disturb the peace of your Sunday afternoon.'

'The what? Come on.'

'Well – whatever. I tried to get you earlier in the day but you were out.'

'In the park. Fergal's first go without stabilisers.'

'That would be it. I just wanted to check a couple of points before the conference tomorrow.'

'My pleasure,' said Archie. 'Excuse me one moment while I bar the door . . .'

Following a brief conversation, during which he asked several questions to which he already knew the answers, Richard took a bottle of New Zealand Burra Valley Sauvignon from the fridge and two green glasses from the cabinet, and placed them on a salver which he carried carefully into the orangery. With a good deal of effort, he also opened a jar of large black olives: he had always been a bit cack-handed and when the lid jerked open he slopped a good deal of the dark liquor over his hand and wrist. Upstairs in bathroom he washed his hands and slooshed cold water over his face and the back of his neck, then opened the bedroom window wide – it had stopped raining – folded the duvet back and straightened the bed. He put on a clean striped shirt and grey trousers and, sweating slightly, went back down to wait.

Jen got lost on the way home. The traffic, as Isla had predicted, was heavy, and she made the mistake of turning off the motorway and attempting a cross-country route. She had no road map with her – Keith had given her one for Christmas but it had never found its way into the car – and her bump of locality was poor. Signs for London were replaced by signs for villages and small towns of which she'd never heard. It was rather exhilarating. The fact of not knowing her own whereabouts had never bothered her except when there was the added pressure of an appointment at the other end. With nowhere to go but home, and the certainty that she would reach Selwyn Street eventually no matter what route she took, she pottered happily along the country roads, noting at one point that she had moved from Hertfordshire to Bedfordshire and, a little later, that she'd crossed back again. At eight o'clock she stopped at a pub in a village irresistibly named Long Wardle and had a lager shandy and a salad roll sitting in the garden. Jaunty band music was just audible in the middle distance. She thought how very pleased she was that she did not have a mobile phone, or she might have given in to the urge to call someone, or to allow someone else to call her. The great thing about having mislaid one's way was the sense of freedom. When she finished eating she left the pub and walked along the village's main street in the evening sun, drawn by the sound of music. She came to a field, bordered by a children's play area and what was obviously the village hall. A number of people were clearing up after a fête – an arena was still marked out by hay bales and ropes, there was an outer circle of tents of various sizes flanked by folded trestles and stacked chairs, and a barbecue made from oil drums still smoked villainously in the small car park, attracting a queue of late customers for cut-price burgers and hot dogs. A confetti of raffle tickets and sweet papers drifted with wisps of straw on the ground. 'Lily of Laguna' blared cheerfully from the PA system.

Two men passed, carrying a table between them. 'Looking for something to do?' asked one cheerily.

'Sure,' said Jen.

'Those chairs –' he jerked his head backwards in the direction of the tents – 'have all got to go back on the stage in the hall.'

'Fine.'

'Super, thanks.'

For the next half hour Jen carried stacks of three chairs at a time into the village hall and passed them to two boys in scout uniform up on the stage. She was assisted in this by a harassed young woman whose troublesome three-year-old orbited them as they walked, in imminent danger of causing an accident. The girl's cries of 'Paul! If you do that once more I'm coming to get you!' punctuated the task. The girl, the scouts, the two table-shifters and everyone else seemed each to assume that Jen was some village resident known to the next person if not to them. It wasn't until almost everything was put away and they clustered round the barbecue for leathery hamburgers and carbon-encrusted sausages courtesy of the management, that a man in a striped blazer turned to her and said: 'Good of you to come along, people tend to disappear at the end of the day and it can take all night to clear up without enough helpers.'

'My pleasure.'

'So whereabouts are you from?' His eyes widened questioningly as he bit down on a rampart of bun, oozing ketchup.

'North London – Crouch End.'

Her status as an outsider had not struck Jen as in the least noteworthy, but the man's eyes bulged even further as he swallowed, wiped his mouth and exclaimed: 'London?'

'That's right.'

'So what – you're staying with friends? Got a cottage?'

'No, just passing through on my way home . . .'

He placed a large, hot hand on her shoulder. 'Hey, get this! This lady's been sweating her guts out for the hall committee and she doesn't even live here!'

This announcement was met with a communal whoop of astonishment and a smattering of applause into which Jen protested: 'I enjoyed it. I needed the exercise.'

Willy-nilly she found herself being treated as a hero. A few chairs still stood outside the beer tent and the stripey blazer, the table-toters and the harassed mother (whose child had now been taken home by a large father in flip-flops) sat her down and opened some warm table wine.

'I'd better not,' she said, 'I'm driving.'

Virgin Cola was at once produced, expressions of appreciation reiterated, and instructions given to the southbound motorway. The fête, she was told, was in aid of village hall improvements necessitated by idiotic Euro-directives. It had not, however, in spite of good weather, been as successful as the year before. Stripey blazer expressed the opinion that this was due to the lack of a big draw.

'You need a name in there somewhere,' he said. 'Not every year, but every so often. Last year we had London's Strongest Man, he was absolute magic, do you remember?' Everyone agreed that he had been, absolute magic. 'This afternoon,' he added grimly, 'we had our dear district councillor. She's a very sound woman, great on potholes and footpaths but not big on charisma.'

Paul's mother said: 'Yes, but on the other hand it's no good having some celebrity who just comes along, makes the announcement, judges the fancy dress and pisses off. The best ones are the ones who stay all afternoon and are really good sports and join in. They get the right atmosphere going and no one wants to leave.'

This chat flowed round Jen who, being mellow and relaxed, was only half listening. She considered vaguely that she ought to get going, but that before she did she would need a re-run of the directions to the motorway.

'Don't suppose you know any celebs?' asked one of the table-men. 'Newscasters, sprinters, quizmasters?'

'No.'

'Gladiator?'

'Sorry.'

'Isla Munro,' said stripey blazer, to knowing groans. 'She's the one I want.'

'Actually,' said Jen, 'I do know her.'

This provoked an outburst of astonished laughter, above which stripey blazer was obliged to raise his voice. 'That's incredible! Incredible!'

Paul's mother leaned towards Jen. 'A fan, in case you hadn't noticed.'

'So, how well do you know her?' asked stripey blazer. 'Well enough to put in a good word for us?'

'Probably.' Jen considered this. 'I only met her today. But we got on. She's great.'

'Of course she is!'

'But that could be professional. And beautiful – even close to.'

'And could that be professional too?' asked Paul's mother. 'We live in hope.'

'No,' said Jen. 'The genuine article. Take it from me, we hate her.'

Stripey blazer was beside himself. 'Who sent you? Come on, this can't be a mere coincidence. You turn up out of nowhere, work like a Trojan, and then pull Isla Munro out of the bag. There are forces at work!' He put an arm round her shoulders and pulled her against him, her chair rocking dangerously on two legs. 'Forces, I tell you, that we wot not of!'

By the time Jen, with the aid of written instructions, was heading south on the motorway she had agreed to mention the Long Wardle fête to Isla should the opportunity arise. She reflected that she was going to have to do some homework – Isla was more famous than she'd realised. Had she perhaps seemed rude, or offhand, putting on a deliberate show of being unimpressed?

Keith was preparing next day's packed lunch in the kitchen when she got back. He took sunflower spread right to the edge of the bread and then scraped off the excess and placed it on the next slice.

'Good day?' he enquired, taking square ham from a packet.

'Yes thanks. Keith—'

'That's me.'

'Have you ever heard of an actress called Isla Munro?'

'Certainly have.'

'How? I mean, what's she famous for?'

Keith licked his fingers. 'For being famous, mostly. She did one of those comedy detective things ages ago, but now she's mostly photographed with endangered species and children in need, that sort of thing.'

'Would you say she was a big star?'

'She's very popular with all age groups.' Keith placed one round of sandwiches on top of the other, pressed down and cut the rounds into triangles. 'And she always seemed like a nice person, even dressed in those kinky costumes.'

Jen uncorked the half-full bottle of Spanish red on the side and sniffed it before pouring herself a glass. 'I met her today.'

'You never,' said Keith, dexterously wielding clingfilm. 'I don't know, you do see life.'

'You're right, she is nice.'

Keith put the sandwiches alongside a Golden Delicious and a banana yoghurt in his lunch box, snapped the lid shut and placed the box in the fridge. Washing his hands at the sink he asked over his shoulder: 'And did you meet the mysterious husband?'

'He wasn't there. What's mysterious about him?'

'No one knows who he is. She's managed to keep the whole thing in the background. It makes good business sense I imagine, if you're the woman that most men would leave their own wives for.'

'I suppose so.'

'By the by,' said Keith, 'Rumple of the Bailey rang, twice. The second time he claimed he'd dialled this number by mistake, but I wasn't born yesterday.'

'OK.' Jen moved towards the living room, but paused. 'I wish you wouldn't call him that.'

'Oh dear, is it rude?'

'Not particularly. But it's not very funny either.'

'Oh dear,' he said again, and slapped his own wrist. 'Sorry.'

Jen pushed the living-room door to, and put on an old but favourite tape. Cain, who liked Annie Lennox, and Abel, who was prepared to put up with her, joined their mistress on the sofa as she sipped the vinegary Spanish red and thought back to her conversation with Isla.

The cottage in Bradenham, with its textured whites and creams and Wedgwood blues, its deal table and rush-bottom chairs, its modern watercolours and sweet peas in a stoneware jug, was like a memory of water at the end of this hot day. It was strange to think that she had sat there for an hour or more talking all unwittingly to a woman who apparently occupied a particular place in the minds – and, it seemed the hearts – of other people.

When the phone rang she was slow to respond, and Keith was already halfway down the stairs.

'There you are,' he said. 'I thought you must have dropped off.'

'No.' He retreated as she picked it up. 'Hello?'

'It's me.'

'Hello.'

'Something tells me you're not alone.'

'No, but I shall be shortly.' She followed Keith with her eyes as he reached the top of the stairs.

'I tried earlier, did he tell you?'

'Yes.'

'He got on my nerves so much the second time I told him I'd dialled the number by mistake.'

'So I understand.' Keith's bedroom door closed. She continued to speak as she trailed the phone into the living room and heeled the door to behind her. 'Yes, he said.'

'I've got nothing to say,' he said. 'I just felt like hearing your voice.'

'That's nice.'

'Good day?'

'Yes – yes, lovely. Some intriguing coincidences . . . I'll tell you all about it.'

'You must.'

'You sound a bit down,' she said. 'Are you all right?'

'No, I've been here all day feeling crummy – look, I've got to go.'

'Bye.' She put the phone down at once, used to these sudden endings. And as she did so a small, cold thought, as forbidding as the first drop of rain on warm skin, made her shiver.

As Isla opened the front door, Richard was walking across the hall towards her, his arms outstretched.

'Darling . . .' she walked into his embrace. 'You look tired.'

'Better for seeing you though,' he said into her hair, moving her gently from side to side.

But Isla's experienced eye had seen the film of secrecy over his face before his smile dispelled it. Perhaps it was time, she told herself sadly, that she too had secrets.

10

The conference had gone well. Richard had been ruthlessly hostile to his author, and his palpable hits had revealed an unyielding bedrock of probity, in itself an unexpected bonus. What had emerged for the first time was that his client, though not a man to whom Richard instinctively warmed, had a strong sense of personal morality and believed fiercely not just that he was right, but that wrong had been done – a distinction which would serve him well in court. A whiff of victory was in the air.

He said as much afterwards to Archie, who was junior on the case, and Archie's smart pupil, Dilip.

'You certainly tested his resolve,' said Archie diffidently, whose own style tended towards forming a warm and yielding relationship with the client. 'He'll probably be asking himself, who needs enemies?'

Richard declined a butterscotch from Dilip and lit a cigar. 'I doubt it. He's an extremely imaginitive man, that's how he makes his living. But it was a pleasant surprise to find him so solid.'

'So are we going to see right triumph?' asked Dilip.

'It's altogether possible . . .' Richard exhaled luxuriously. 'And in court, I suspect. I don't think we're dealing with a settler, I think our man wants to make a high-profile stand.'

Archie accepted a sweet and spoke round it: 'And you relish that.'

'I do. Because I think we'll win. I don't believe this case is about nice legal points, it's about who appears to have the angels on their team. And our man, in my opinion, does.'

'Damn right,' said Archie. He spread his arms. 'I mean, just look at us.'

During the last fortnight in July, Isla and Richard began to free-wheel downhill towards their month off. They didn't generally go abroad in August – they usually managed Switzerland in the new year, and further afield – Antigua, Lamu or Goa – at Easter, or in early June, Richard's schedule permitting. In the autumn they took a long weekend at a country hotel in Wales or the Lakes. When the boys were younger – and even, to some extent, now – August was a month when, with the courts closed, they drew their horns in and made themselves available to Caroline so that she could go away without her sons or at least without worrying about them. Richard made facetious references to Shirley Valentine, though in fact the sort of holiday Caroline preferred was one centred around a shared activity. She had been landscape painting in Provence, mule-trekking in Spain, 'tombing and templing' up the Nile, and creative writing in Cornwall. Isla thought Caroline was brave for taking off on her own on these expeditions, and that they sounded fun, but Richard would always groan amiably.

'I can think of nothing worse than a project-driven holiday . . . !'

'That's because you lead a project-driven life.'

'So does Caro – all those cushions.'

'That isn't the same, as you very well know.'

'If there's a distinction it's an infinitesimally nice one,' he would say in what Isla thought of as his courtroom manner. There was no point in trying to use the 'Shirley Valentine' digs against him because, like an agony aunt, he would triumphantly point out that most romances were begun through a shared interest, and that Caroline was almost certainly hoping that her eyes, glancing up from, say, a potter's wheel in North Wales, would meet those of a fellow craftsman and that the rest, with luck, would be *karma*. Although meant affectionately, this was a streak of chauvinism in Richard which Isla elected to overlook.

In any event, August was a month for remaining quietly on hand, whether in Hampstead or Bradenham. This year Giles and Chris Beales had gone to discuss their business plans for an unspecified period in Ibiza where even all these years later, apparently, everything worth having in a holiday could still be got plentifully and at rock bottom prices. Marcus was working in an electrical goods warehouse on the North Circular. Caroline had opted for two weeks of archaeology, one of a number of courses available in an off-duty public school in Wiltshire, so Marcus's base would be at the Hampstead house. Isla told herself that these few weeks would be quiet, her own to do with as she wished. There would be few if any outside calls on her time, the village would be a ghost town and the West End unholy with tourists. Richard intended putting in some groundwork on what he called his literary scrap and otherwise taking it easy apart from a couple of golf breaks with cronies.

What she most wanted to do was invite Jen Delaney round, but when it came round to it she couldn't find her card. So in the interests of killing two birds with one stone she rang Nell's number in Swiss Cottage. In response to standard enquiries Nell sounded rather flat.

'Is everything quite all right?' asked Isla. 'How's Scotch?'

'Away.'

'And you miss him.'

'I'm afraid I do, it's like a mausoleum around here without him.'

Isla was pleased to hear this. 'So where's he gone off to?'

'Oh, some boring semi-work thing.'

'Semi-work?'

'I know, I know . . .' Nell sighed. 'He's gone on location with that Ned friend of yours, doing a car commercial up in Scotland – Scotch has agreed to do some PR for Ned, I believe, so this is what the politicians call a fact-finding tour.'

Isla's pleasure faded as quickly as it had come. 'But a brief one,' she suggested hopefully. 'I mean commercials take longer than they should, but not that long.'

'I think they're having a week's jolly at some country club in the borders, all boys together,' said Nell, with unconscious irony. 'And when he gets back I'm booked to go to Bordeaux with a girlfriend, so see if I care.'

Which would give Ned ample time to follow-through, thought Isla, and at once chastised herself for behaving like a middle-aged latterday Emma Woodhouse. She changed the subject to something less unwelcome.

'I wonder if you could let me have Jen's telephone number. The artist? Only we promised ourselves a lunch and I've lost the card she gave me.'

'Absolutely, toot sweet. Hang on a mo.' When Nell had passed on the number, she added: 'Could we do the same?'

'What a good idea – lunch?'

'Well, or anything – the pictures, a drink, even just a walk. There are things I want to talk about and you're such a brilliant listener.'

'It beats talking,' said Isla. 'Yes, I'd like to.'

'Perhaps – while Scotch is still away?'

'Fine.'

She's mad about the boy, thought Isla, as who could blame her? And he's up in the Highlands a-chasing the queer . . . They agreed that Nell would take a half day off from the gallery on Thursday, so they could meet at the Royal Academy Summer Exhibition.

Isla then called Jen Delaney. She'd assumed that Jen would elect to stay at home in August while the unfortunates still beneath the tyranny of school holidays joined battle for rest and recuperation elsewhere. There was no immediate reply . . . it would be frustrating if she'd taken off somewhere. She let it ring – Jen was probably working. Isla was going to suggest that her new friend come to the house in Hampstead for lunch in the garden one of these days while Richard was off golfing. She wanted to elicit the same delight and admiration that had greeted Brook End. Jen's singularity made her approval a rarer and therefore a more desirable commodity than that to which Isla was used.

She listened with a sense of happy anticipation as the phone continued to ring, just across the hills and valleys of north London, in Selwyn Street.

At two o'clock Jen was surveying the almost-finished portrait of Horace, Lady Saxby's basset, while eating a slice of pitta-bread filled with lettuce and peanut butter. She waited till the phone stopped ringing, before approaching it rather as if it were a venomous spider. As she lifted the receiver and dialled one-four-seven-one she told herself that she must do herself a favour and invest, as Richard had so often suggested, in an answering machine.

She listened to the bland female voice deliver its information, and advise that she 'press three to return the call', but hesitated for a full minute before doing so. When she did, it was with a sudden rush of misplaced confidence – it was Richard's number for heaven's sake, Richard, who rang her all the time, and she had nothing but the vaguest and most ill-founded suspicions that it could be anything else . . .

When Isla answered, Jen was stunned, as much by the awesome accuracy of her intuition as by the voice itself.

'Hello? Eight-o-three-o?'

Jen sat there with the phone in her hand, unable either to speak or make a decision. Even to put the phone down would be a waste of time, since her call could be traced as easily as she had traced this one.

'Hello?' Isla asked again. 'Who is this?'

'I think I may have the wrong number . . .' she said faintly.

'Perhaps – Jen? Is that you?'

'Yes.'

'No, this is my number – it's Isla, I just rang you.'

'Oh.'

'You must have pressed three.'

'Yes. But I didn't – I don't know—'

'You didn't recognise my voice.'

'No.'

'Are you all right?'

'Well –' Jen saw an escape route – 'actually, no. I'm feeling very rough.'

'Oh, I'm so sorry . . .' Isla's sympathy was more chastening than the sharpest reproach. 'It's probably this thing Richard's had, it's going round.'

Of course the remark meant nothing, but Jen rushed to deny it. 'It'll be Keith – he brings all the latest bugs home from school.'

'Were you in bed?'

'No, but I was thinking about going.'

'Go. Now, at once. I'll call you back another time.'

'It's all right,' said Jen. 'I'm here now.' A near-suicidal curiosity pulled her irresistibly along like an underwater current.

'I was going to ask if you'd like to come over here for lunch one day? Say a fortnight today? Richard will be on the links in north Devon, and I'll be rattling around here for most of August hoping not to get any calls from the police about my stepsons . . . But anyway . . . Don't worry about it now. Concentrate on getting better.'

Jen thought that until that moment she hadn't known the meaning of shame. Her face burned and her eyes smarted. She felt as if she were bulging to bursting point with the infected mass of her deceit. She was only glad that Isla couldn't see her.

'Jen . . . ?'

'Yes.'

'Oh, you're still there, I thought perhaps you'd keeled over on me.'

'No.'

'You don't sound right. Please go and climb into bed, we'll talk another time.'

'No,' said Jen. 'There's no need for that. It'd be nice to meet.'

'That's marvellous!' Isla's pleasure was painfully genuine. 'No standing on ceremony, we can kick our shoes off good and proper. And tell you what I'll do, so that you don't have to stand there a moment longer, I'll send you our address, and directions of how to find us.'

Us, thought Jen. Us, us, us . . .

'You can give me a ring if there's any problem.'

'Fine.'

'So I'll see you then. Acts of God apart.'

'I'll look forward to it.'

'*Au revoir*. Get well soon.'

Jen thought she heard a small intake of breath as though Isla were about to say something else. She herself held the receiver to her ear for a second, listening. But the short silence was ended only by a click, and the long, dismissive buzz of the dialling tone.

Jen had, naturally, from time to time speculated on what manner of woman Richard's wife was. Although he didn't talk about her – from loyalty, she suspected, as much as from sensitivity to her own feelings – she had occasionally caught a whiff of her over the telephone line, like an evocative scent that lingers in a lift or on a staircase. Snatches of music, a light step in the background, a half-heard voice in the hall . . . From these tiny clues and trace elements she had built up a picture, as romantic and unfocused as a photograph taken through gauze. Rebecca-like, this glamorous but spectral being hovered on the periphery of her consciousness. This was a woman serenely confident, of coolly assured taste and elegance – someone who listened to Debussy, who wore clothes by Jean Muir, who had her own bathroom, who knew what to do with pine nuts . . . A woman who was respected by her hairdresser, and kept her shoes on shoe trees. This was a woman admirable in every respect – competent, talented and exquisitely decorative but (Jen always told herself) perhaps just the tiniest bit bloodless. A woman who could only contemplate sex after half an hour in the bathroom, who affected chaste, high-necked nightdresses and who believed it was good manners always to leave some food on the plate . . .

But now there was Isla, of whom she was sure only the good things were true. Jen wondered why she had ever supposed that Richard, of whom she was so inordinately fond, and to whose warm, weighty body, redolent of good living, she so often and so willingly succumbed, would marry anyone who wasn't – well – lovely. It was a simple enough realisation, but devastating. And Isla was so exceptionally nice. Jen recalled their conversation at the cottage with the wistful pleasure reserved for never-to-be-repeated happiness. Because now that the arrangement had been made she knew, of course, that she could never go. And that this marked the end of one relationship before it had even begun, and another after more years than she cared to remember.

Richard asked the resourceful Dilip to take charge of the telephone and walked down to the Embankment for a breath of air. He could hardly wait for the pleasant, sultry tedium of August to begin. It would be awfully nice to see the back of chambers for a bit. Also, he had to admit he was by no means A1. He had said as much to Archie that morning in response to some more or less rhetorical query about his health.

'Ah well,' Archie had said, in a stab at irreverent humour, 'all those years of unclean living are bound to catch up with you sooner or later.' He slapped his own midriff apologetically. 'Not that I can talk.'

On the Embankment, Richard sat down heavily on a bench. It was stuffy and he felt tired. A pair of mad-eyed joggers thumped by and he surveyed their sinewy shanks and sun-reddened shoulders with distaste. He could never have contemplated such a thing, which seemed to him to be a perverse mixture of the self-regarding and the stupefyingly dull. He had once been a proper, if not a serious, sportsman. Even now he played a wickedly unorthodox round of golf. The thought of exercise for its own sake was abhorrent to him – solitary and slightly shameful, like masturbation. And as for doing it in public . . . his shoulders twitched in an involuntary shudder.

He wondered, though, if there wasn't reason in what Archie had said. Sitting with his arms folded, he could feel the solid swell of his stomach and the stretch of his jacket across his shoulders. Maybe he should lose weight. Perhaps his heart, his whole system, was beginning to labour under the strain of carrying such a load. He went hot and cold at the memory of his lonely, ignominious collapse at the weekend. But the world of diet and weight loss was a dreadful mystery to him. He had recently been appalled by pictures in the press of a cabinet minister who had lost three stone on a regime of grapefruit, bran, mineral water and suchlike pallid, virtuous substances. Photographs of the politician in his unreformed state showed a man portly, certainly, but also prosperous, thriving and full of gusto. Next to this robust personage the slimmer version gave credence to the phrase 'a shadow of his former self' – a gaunt, hollow-cheeked, curiously wistful creature whose skin hung on him like an unironed sheet and next to whom his wife, an Australian blonde in the peak of condition, looked dismayingly dominant.

No, Richard would have none of it. Gravy lunches and custard puddings with chums in Middle Temple Hall were one of the smallish but utterly reliable pleasures of his chosen profession, as were drinks with cronies at El Vino's and the Athenaeum, and entertaining at home. Though Isla, of course, was sweetly chary of his health and attempted with utter tact and discretion to regulate his intake of what was not good for him.

Sitting there in the dusty, polluted sunshine, Richard for the first time experienced his body as no more than a sort of packaging, and one which was deteriorating with time and usage. He had never been especially introspective, nor a great worrier about anything much, especially his health, which he had always taken for granted. He was one of those who tended to joke about the muesli police and fitness fascists, and who reckoned that the pleasure and wellbeing that came from good living was infinitely preferable to the grey complacency of virtue. And until now he had no cause to change his tune. But maybe Archie was right, and the claret and Havanas, not to mention the mixed grills and treacle tarts, were coming home to roost . . .

Abruptly he got up and began to walk with big, agitated strides along the Embankment in the direction of Waterloo Bridge. He half heard a name called twice before he realised it was his, by which time a cab had pulled in alongside him at the kerb, and Donatella was leaning out of the window.

'Ricardo! Don't do it, I beg you!'

'I'm sorry . . . ?'

'Do not cast yourself into the waters!'

'I'm sorry Donatella I haven't the faintest idea what you're talking about.'

She opened the door of the cab and got out. She was wearing Levis and a red shirt, cowboy boots, gold hoop earrings. He saw the laughing faces of two younger men behind her. She kissed him with her usual gusto.

'You looked so sad and grim, my darling, we were quite sure you were planning to end it all.'

'I'm fine, thank you. I was just taking a walk.'

She pulled a stern face in mockery of his own. 'Then we must let you get on with it I suppose.'

'Well, anyway –' Richard was a little ashamed of his curmudgeonliness – 'you're running up a huge fare on my account.'

'Pah –!' Donatella's soaring hand poured contempt on money. 'I have earned it with the sweat of my brow, and now I'm on holiday. Tomorrow I am flying to stay with my family in Fiesole. You go!' she cried to her companions in the cab, one of whom, Richard noticed, was carrying a bottle. 'I shall pick up another one.' She slammed the door and tapped smartly on the roof with her knuckles.

Richard felt trapped. He glanced at his watch. 'I have to be back in chambers in fifteen minutes.'

'I know, I know, I know, I am not suggesting we check into the Savoy and fuck like ferrets.' She linked her arm purposefully through his. 'You are walking, and I shall accompany you, where shall we walk to?'

'Along to the bridge and back.'

'*Andiamo!*'

They set off. Despite the disparity in their heights there was no need for Richard to adjust his stride because Donatella lengthened hers amply. She smelt strongly of her usual man's cologne. Her bra, he noticed, was black and lacy, and (the memory was vivid) underwired, so that her fine bosom was cantilevered to an even prouder angle . . .

'What is all this walking?' she asked.

'I feel I need the exercise.'

'Poor old thing!' She squeezed his arm against the side of her breast. 'Is your wife not looking after you?'

'I decline to dignify that with an answer.'

She shrugged. 'I don't know why you keep doing it. Extra-ordinary. Crazy.'

'Doing it?'

'Getting married – once was enough for me, and it nearly was the death of both of us.'

'I don't "keep doing it" as you put it,' said Richard in some exasperation. 'I have been married to Isla for nearly ten years now. Our marriage is an outstanding success by any stand-ards—'

'Hah!'

He stopped walking and extricated his arm. 'What's that supposed to mean?'

'You are sounding very pompous, Richard.'

'And you, if I may say so, are being rather rude.'

'Come, come.' She turned him back the other way and began

walking again. 'You are pretending you have no secrets. That will never wash.'

'I'm not pretending anything, I'm speaking the plain unvarnished truth. And anyway, you force me to say this Donatella, it really is none of your business.' He heard himself protesting and knew that indeed it would never wash. Not with this particular ex-wife who now let go his arm, spun round and halted him with a hand spread on his chest. She had always frightened him a little physically, it was a large part of her physical attraction that if it came to a scrap he suspected she would be more than a match for most people, male or female. Now she mugged him with her famous glare – brows beetling, jaw upthrust, shoulders squared above folded arms – and he still found it thrilling.

'I make it my business!' she declared. 'You are not well, you are depressed, you have secrets – yes! – you are slobbing along the riverbank like a dickhead –' Donatella's use of idiom had always been arrestingly inexact – 'I do not see the man I married.'

Useless to point out that since their marriage had been a disaster, and was anyway many years behind them, it was hardly likely he would be the same person. And yet he had to admit there was something flattering in her assumption of ownership after all this time.

'I've been a bit below par, that's all. Working hard—'

'That's good for you! Stress is healthy. An intelligent being like yourself needs stress if he is not to become a jellyfish.'

'You may be right. At any rate, it's nothing serious.' He glanced at his watch. 'And I must get back.'

'I'll walk with you.'

'By all means.'

They crossed the road at speed. Though they were side by side he felt he was being led, and was slightly embarrassed when they met Archie emerging from Goodies to Go with a bulging paper bag.

'Caught in the act,' he said sheepishly. 'And Donatella, good gracious, what a lovely surprise . . .'

'Archie, Archie, Archie –' Donatella placed an explosive kiss on both Archie's pink cheeks. 'Now you must tell me how many children you have since I last saw you.'

Archie snorted with pleasure. 'For goodness' sake, we still only have the four – or is it five . . . ?'

'But there will be many, many more you may be bound,' declared Donatella as though she personally held the key to the Stainforths' procreative process. 'You and your wife are at the height of your powers.'

'Well, I don't know about that . . .' snuffled Archie, 'we just sort of muddle—'

Donatella placed a commanding hand on his arm and leaned confidingly towards him. 'What in the wild world is the matter with Richard?'

Wondering why in the wild – or even wide – world he allowed it, Richard submitted to their combined inspections, Archie's baffled, Donatella's searching.

'I don't know,' said Archie at last. 'What is the matter with you?'

'Nothing.'

'Pah –' Donatella stepped forward and gave Richard's left cheek a tap. Then the right, a little harder. 'Pah!' and the left again, still harder. 'Pooh!'

'Um – I get the distinct impression she doesn't believe you,' said Archie, conscious of a discreet, fleeting audience of passers-by.

'I don't,' Donatella affirmed. 'I do not!'

Richard, also aware of the audience, decided enough was enough. It was always too easy to fall beneath Donatella's spell and relinquish all initiative.

'I'm under the weather and I am going to see the doctor,' he said firmly. 'And now I really must get back to chambers.'

'As you wish. Goodbye.' Donatella began walking smartly away, the searchlight, as it were, switched off as abruptly as it had been switched on.

'Have a good holiday!' Richard called after her, but she only raised a hand, Fuhrer-like, palm uppermost, and walked on.

'Phew!' exclaimed Archie as they walked on together in the direction of chambers. 'What a woman!'

'She can be quite insufferably meddlesome.'

'But you must be a bit flattered, surely. I mean she obviously still cares about you.'

'Hm.' Richard was disposed to admit nothing. 'I think she may be what my sons would call a control freak.'

'Well, I don't know . . .' Archie puffed slightly on the stairs behind Richard, who was trying to disguise his own heaving lungs. 'She seems a great girl to me . . . your trouble is you've got an embarrassment of riches . . . First Donatella, shit-hot legal brain and every junior's fantasy lay . . . And now the sainted Isla.'

'And Caroline. Don't forget the mother of my children,' Richard reminded him as they entered the reception area. 'How would you rate her on the desirability scale?'

'She was lovely too of course,' said Archie. 'But she was more the sort of woman we could all aspire to if you know what I mean.'

'Like Alison?' Richard took a bunch of papers from his pigeon-hole. There were only two junior clerks in the office, and their intense attention to their VDUs advertised the fact that they were listening equally intently to the conversation. Richard studied his letters, Archie his own empty pigeonhole. No one looked at anyone else

'Um, absolutely,' said Archie.

Richard was pleased to find that he had no messages. Dilip had left a note on his blotter, timed at five minutes ago, saying that he had slipped out to buy a birthday card for his mother.

Richard sat down and rang his doctor, Jim Furmston.

'Wondered if you could run the rule over me Jim,' he said. 'It's donkey's years since I paid you a visit, so I thought perhaps . . . the complete MOT and oil change.'

'And what's made you jumpy all of a sudden?' Jim Furmston made a living at least as good as Richard's with this uncompromising cold-showers and wire-wool style of patient-management.

'I'm not in the least jumpy,' said Richard in a tone which demonstrated exactly how jumpy he was. 'But as the end of one's fifth decade hoves in view it would seem judicious to get the all-clear.'

'And if it's not?'

'You mean not judicious?'

'Not all clear. Same difference, some might say,' rasped Jim. 'You have taken that into account?'

'Of course.'

'Fine. I'll look forward to seeing you on Monday, then.'

Richard, his hand still on the phone, gazed out at the dry green trees and stately rooftops outside the window. He did not look forward to Monday. He thought of Donatella packing for Fiesole, never giving him a thought, damn her eyes. Light the blue touch paper and bugger off.

Dilip put his head round the door. 'Sorry for deserting my post – mother's birthday, you know how it is.'

'That's quite all right.'

'There were no messages.'

'Thank you.'

Dilip withdrew, then reappeared, holding aloft a KitKat. 'Like a bit?'

There was nothing Richard would have liked more at that moment but, mindful of his appointment with Jim Furmston, he declined.

Jen was packaging the Saxby basset for delivery when Richard arrived. She was so attuned to his approach that she did not actually need to see his car reverse smoothly into a space on the other side of the road to know it was there. The almost silent engine and gliding progress of the Jag, in this neighbourhood of chugging VW Beetles, Metros and reconditioned Minis created a perceptible change in the ambience like the arrival of a shark in a bathing area.

Her heart galloping, she stuck down the last of the bubble-wrap and propped the picture against the wall beneath the window. As she did so she saw Richard get out of the car, lock it with a snap of his magic key (the lights glinted minutely, suavely, to show the alarm was activated), smooth the buttons of his waistcoat and slap his jacket pocket in a characteristic mannerism, and cross the road towards Number 65 with a preoccupied air.

For a split second she debated with herself whether to answer the door . . . but then he would only let himself in anyway, and Keith was upstairs poring over ROA sheets to the accompaniment of Garth Crooks, and would be sure to give the game away

. . . Too late – Richard had spotted her now: he made a *'there* you are' face. She had no alternative but to go to the front door and let him in.

Leaving the door open, she walked back into the living room and waited for him there. Her pleasure in seeing him was intensified by her feeling that the doomsday clock must surely now be ticking. When his arms enfolded her from behind, and his head rested on top of her own they carried for the first time the poignancy of an experience whose days were numbered . . . She closed her eyes, letting his warmth flow through her and considered, also for the first time, the frightening possibility of love. When she hadn't needed to worry, she hadn't bothered to analyse. Now it seemed important to evaluate what she was almost certainly about to lose.

'That's nice,' he said, on the back of a gusty sigh. 'That's nice.'

For a second she found herself unable to reply, but she put her arms around his encircling ones and held on tight. It was the sound of Keith's door opening which helped restore her composure.

'Wait . . .' She went to the living room door and pushed it to. 'I'm seriously thinking of getting rid of him,' she said, thinking seriously of it for the first time.

Richard sat down on the windowseat and held out his hand to her, drawing her to him. 'Why . . . ?' he asked, putting his arms round her waist and his head on her breasts.

She dared to touch his hair, to stroke, soothing this time not him, but herself. 'I don't know. Loss of privacy. Naff music. Cycle helmet.'

Still without lifting his head, he said: 'He's a pretty decent bloke at bottom.'

'He is.'

'That's the trouble.'

'Yes.'

He gave a grunt of laughter. 'I don't know how you stick it.'

'Neither do I.'

Now he looked up, and directly into her face for the first time. 'I do hope it's got nothing to do with money.'

She laughed and ruffled his hair. 'Of course it's got *something* to do with money . . . That's why he's here in the first place. But I'm no longer so desperate that I have to have him living in my house and subjecting me to death by terrible jokes . . .'

'Mmm.' He pulled her head down for a kiss, and when he released her added: 'As long as you're sure. Because if it is money—'

'No, I'm sure.' She stepped away. 'Look, I'm going to fetch us a drink.'

She felt him watch her as she left the room quickly, smiling as she closed the door. But in the hall she paused to catch her breath. Money had never before been an issue between them. They exchanged only the smallest and most modest presents. Richard had never, ever suggested that he help to finance the least part of her life. His sure instinct in this area, in response to what was a feminine and emotional, rather than a feminist and political, sensibility, was one of the planks of their relationship. But now – she dragged her hands down over her face – the unmentionable had been mentioned. Suggested, already. In such small, deadly ways did everything change.

Keith was at the stove poking at a saucepan with a wooden spoon.

'Hi there! I'll be out from under your feet in two ticks.'

'That's all right.'

'No, because I know you've got company.' Jen fetched the scotch, the supermarket sauvignon and the glasses noticing as she did so the contents of the saucepan – egg noodles rehydrating in still water, like the fry of some monstrous pallid eel lurking at the bottom of a pond.

'That's all right, I'm not cooking.'

'How's the world of poodle-painting, I haven't asked in ages . . . ?'

'Fine.' She contemplated a noodle-joke in response to his poodle one. Went a step further and pictured Keith with the noodle-pan upended on his head, the noodles dangling round his neck, Crouch End's answer to Ned Kelly.

'Not too fine, I hope, or you may not want a lodger cluttering up the place –! Only joking,' he added. 'Now where's my stir-fry sauce . . . ?'

*   *   *

They sat together on the sofa, with their drinks. Richard sat at one end, his legs stretched out, Jen was curled up next to him. His arm was round her shoulders, the hand down the front of her shirt.

'So did you do the deed?' he asked.

'No.'

'There's no time like the present, you know.'

'You can't hit a man when he's cooking his noodles.'

'Perhaps not.'

There was silence for a moment. One of the cats – Abel – whisked round the door and into the log basket. Richard fondled Jen's breast. She could feel him becoming amorous.

'How's your wife?' she asked.

He'd mentioned money, she would mention this. The amorousness ebbed, and as it did so sadness, tinged with a bitterness she had never before felt, claimed Jen.

'Why do you ask?' he said.

'No reason.'

'Don't be coy, it doesn't suit you.'

'Don't tell me how to behave.'

He withdrew his hand, then his arm, pulled himself up on the sofa. 'I'm sorry if that's how it seemed, it wasn't intentional. I just can't imagine why you want to know.'

'Can't you?' She took a sip of wine to steady her mouth as well as her nerves. 'But she and I are as close as two women can be.' She saw the swift, pale lightning of fear, and from some long-ingrained instinct of protectiveness added: 'Without actually meeting.'

'I don't know what to say.'

'Tell me about her.'

He set his glass down. Covered his eyes with his hand. There was a long, painful silence. The shouts of boys on roller-blades on the pavement outside made it worse. Jen controlled her urge to embrace him, and tell him to forget it.

Massaging his eyes with fingers and thumb, he shook his head. 'No . . .'

'Why?'

He looked at her, his expression bleak. 'I thought you understood why.'

She did. It was like the money, only worse. But she wasn't quite ready to let go of it yet. There was something she needed to hear him say, no matter how much it hurt.

Casualness would be her weapon. It felt strange, because she was not given to indifference, either real or assumed. When she shrugged, it was like throwing a stone.

The stone found its mark. Inflicted damage. He looked away briefly and when he looked back she could see he'd gathered his forces.

'I don't want to discuss her with you, because I love her.'

'All right,' she said. Her turn now to tough it out. 'All right, fair enough.'

'Jen —' He reached for her hand but she moved it lightly away. 'What did you expect me to say?'

'Exactly that.'

'Well then. What are you trying to do?'

She shrugged again, but this time it was a mere inarticulate twitch of the shoulders, because she did not trust her voice.

'Can we leave it alone?' he asked gently.

A sharp response, 'Yes, you'd like that, wouldn't you' formed in her mind, but she beat it aside.

'How much do you love her?' Her voice sounded small and colourless, crushed by the weight of what she was saying.

'Jen—'

'No, I do want to know. It's important to me.'

He sighed. She felt his clear, clever, well-stocked lawyer's brain getting into gear, and when he spoke it was in precisely the way she expected.

'Well. If I'm forced to define it . . . I'd have to say that I couldn't contemplate life without her.'

'You couldn't live without her.'

'That's about the size of it.' The hint of playfulness that gave the game away.

'And what about me?' She tried to sound not plaintive and petulant but coolly, seriously enquiring.

'Oh . . .' He turned, tried to scoop her into his arms, but she held out her hand to fend him off.

'Mm?' She put her glass to her lips again. 'Could you live without me?'

She only had to wait a moment for his answer. But in waiting at all she knew, whatever he eventually said, what the answer must be.

August slouched on.

At the warehouse on the North Circular, Marcus toted microwaves and tumble dryers with a furious, scowling energy which belied his wasted appearance and impressed even his (initially sceptical) workmates. When they enquired with grudging affability what the fuck he thought he was doing ruining it for the rest of them, he gave neither an inch nor a smile, thus increasing his respect, if not his popularity quotient. In the evenings he returned to Hampstead and ate supper with his father and stepmother, hoovering up whatever was placed in front of him in a silence – only occasionally punctuated by curt monosyllables – which they learned to grade on an ascending scale from murderous to stable.

After supper he would submit with a poor grace to a phone call from his mother, who rang for her own peace of mind, but whose regular interrogations left her none the wiser. Duty done, he went out, only he knew where. But since he was always back by midnight, except on Fridays and Saturdays when he carried the milk into the house, and drank half of it straight from the bottle before retiring for the day, they tried not to worry. The absolute consistency of his morose humour and unhealthy habits, and his ability to sustain in spite of them a physically demanding job and an equally punishing social life, persuaded them that all was as well as could be expected.

Occasionally Richard tried to open up a fatherly discussion on Broader Issues.

'Have you,' he would ask over supper on the terrace, 'given any thought to what you'd like to do?'

'Do?'

'In the future. When you leave school.'

'No.'

'Any ideas at all?'

'Uh-uh.'

At this point Isla, agonised, would absent herself to commune with the dishwasher, clashing plates so she couldn't hear them in their pointless, bloodless locking of conversational horns. The worst of it was she knew that Richard's instinct was *laissez faire*, that he only conducted these interrogations because he thought he ought. It seemed to her that Marcus, though uncommunicative, had an agenda at least as serious as anything his father envisaged and, what's more, sufficient resolve to see it through. But there was no telling either of them, nor would she have dreamed of trying.

If she were to confront her husband, now or ever, there were more profound matters on which to do so than his behaviour towards his son.

Even had Caroline known Giles's whereabouts on Ibiza she was not being allowed to worry. Her eldest son had a well-developed sense of how to pre-empt unwanted adult enquiries, and rang her most days during that period in the late afternoon when he was least stoned.

He and his putative colleague, Chris Beales, had finalised their business plan during the course of a bar-crawl on their first day on the island. Since then they had concentrated their efforts on maintaining a state of euphoric, sun-baked near-oblivion – not a difficult task given the readily available quantities of drugs and drink, the all-night live music from a stream of red-eyed continental bands and the ever-changing *smorgesbord* of amenable women of all ages.

Having arrived with the superior notion (in case a get-out were needed) that the place might be a washed-up repository for sixties and seventies saddoes, they soon agreed that it was just about the perfect holiday. One week in and they both had the authentic look – tanned, thin and grubby, with thong necklaces, and spaced out expressions above the moth-eaten beginnings of teenage beards.

When Giles spoke to his mother he was careful to strike the right note. What that note was was something that came to him by instinct. As with the avoidance of the police breathalyser it was important, if one was not to attract unwelcome attention, to go neither too fast nor too slowly. An insistence on a series of blameless days frolicking on the sand, and early nights spent sleeping dreamlessly between freshly laundered sheets would arouse almost as much dismay as the truth. You had to give the fractious dog a bone to chew on. So he said things like: 'Nursing a bit of a hangover, the night-life here's tops . . .' Or: 'There are some amazing women – the one I was with last night is the daughter of that disgraced cabinet minister . . .' He meted out these titbits in the approved downbeat manner, knowing that Caroline would infer he was having a good time but not looking after himself. This kept her amused – the amusement appropriately tinged with maternal concern and a smidgin of disapproval. Had she known the extent of his debauch, the squalor of the overpopulated concrete pillbox where he returned, insensible, at dawn, or the sheer numbers of females who had shared his foetid bedroll, Caroline would have been profoundly shocked. As it was she reported back to Richard in glowing terms.

'It is so gratifying when you finally see the training beginning to pay off. Getting anything out of Marcus is like pulling teeth – it's as though to express an interest is completely beyond the pale. Whereas Giles, bless him, actually calls me and tells me how he's getting on. I'm sure it's all perfectly frightful, but at least he's in touch, and thinking about his poor old mother from time to time . . .'

Richard sympathised with her difficulties in communicating with Marcus, but took his older son's considerate behaviour with a pinch of salt.

'I should think,' he said to Isla, 'that it's in the time honoured tradition of "tell-the-old-dear-just-enough-so-she-won't-ask questions".'

'Probably,' agreed Isla.

'Still, if it makes everyone happy . . .'

'Would you rather that was what Marcus did? Involved you in some kind of passive collusion?'

'Well if you put it like that—'

'Made you a willing sucker?'

'No, of course not,' said Richard, aggrieved. 'It's just a skill Giles has, that's all, and I'm acknowledging it.'

'I like Marcus.'

'*I* like Marcus. But he is to communication what the Borgias were to catering.'

They let it go there. They rarely argued.

Claudia, now installed in her vacation job at Pleasurelands, was interested to discover that she didn't love children. This wasn't to say that she couldn't like them as individuals – there were a couple of Mo's brood, her half-brothers and sisters, whom she found genuinely congenial – but she couldn't declare, along with the bright-eyed majority of her fellow-workers, especially the female ones, that she 'really loved kids'.

The curious thing was that the children seemed to like her, or at least to attach themselves to her. They reacted rather as the domestic cat does, sitting cosily on the lap of the person who is least susceptible to its charms. As she walked or biked about her area of the compound each day she was invariably accompanied, Pied-Piper-like, by a squad of children who seemed simply to want to be with her. Perhaps, in this fun-led environment on the edge of the Cotswolds, where most of the staff were hell bent on fulfilling their every need, the children found something calming in her tranquil indifference.

Claudia was first to admit that she did not wish to be part of the Tiny the Tiger Club, which ran at the Leisure Plaza between ten and twelve each morning with the aim of giving jaded parents a much-needed breather. She was completely unsuited to the leading of singing and dancing, the telling of jokes, the running of competitions, let alone the wearing of the hallowed Tiny Tiger suit with its cheesy grin and odour of stale sweat.

Instead she'd opted for Site Ranger, a roving brief which involved patrolling her given quadrant, and checking that all was as it should be in this artificial world. This could entail anything from removing the overflow from litter bins to restoring lost children to their cabins (the word chalet was forbidden), to providing the answers to any number of random queries and demands pertaining to laundry, ten-pin bowling, lost bicycles and the opening hours of the John Peel Wine Bar. On Tuesdays and Thursdays she had to cover, on foot, that area of Ramblers Wood designated for dog walking, armed with a pooper-scooper and a black binbag. Holidaymakers were encouraged to perform this task themselves when walking their pets, but it was not a rule, so most chose to ignore the polite suggestion in the info-pack, and leave their dirty work for someone who was paid to do it. On these occasions Claudia would concentrate her mind on the green dress, the card from David D and the glossy catalogue of drop-dead clothes.

As to clothes, she missed, ferociously, her own idiosyncratic tat – its weight, its texture, its patches and layers. At Pleasurelands there was a uniform. As a Site Ranger she had the choice of black brushed cotton joggers, snowy 'PL' trainers, and a white polo shirt for cooler days, or black cycling shorts, trainers ditto and a giant white 'PL' T-shirt for hot weather. A black brushed-cotton bomber jacket and a jaunty red and black baseball cap could be worn with either of these ensembles, there was even a black nylon bumbag – horribly like Jen's – for personal effects. Claudia loathed all of it. The clothes, with their much-vaunted 'stylish comfort' felt as alien and restrictive as a spacesuit. And her height caused a problem – the girls' tracksuit pants were too short and the men's too voluminous. Though she felt a complete idiot she was assured she looked a knockout in the cycling shorts, which she topped with an XXL regulation T-shirt, tied on the hip. Fortunately the weather was good throughout August, so she didn't bother with the jacket, and never touched the bumbag. She wore her own wire-framed sunglasses and kept her hair as short as the Site Supervisor would allow.

But children, animals and uniform notwithstanding Claudia enjoyed her work. She liked being out of doors, she enjoyed the sensation of others being – in the main – happy around her. She liked the mobility, and the problem-solving. She became aware, over the first few days, that she had been taken on as the exception-that-proves-the-rule. There were three others whom she took to have been hired on the same basis: a dreadlocked black youth who served behind the bar and at table in the Country Club; an overweight Geordie girl at the bicycle depot; and a Hooray Henry who gravitated between the tennis courts and the boating lake and was proficient on both. Other than these, and herself, the staff of Pleasurelands was sprightly, smiling, white, and classless, with the in-your-face jokey energy of children's TV presenters.

Once she realised she was a maverick appointment, Claudia set about capitalising on the fact. It did not escape her that her area of the site included the so-called Executive cabins. Consequently, she comported herself like a potential starred first, the sort of girl the executive spenders would wish to see picking up stray lolly-sticks from their bit of the forest floor. She polished up her accent, strapped F R Leavis to the back of her bike and when on foot never broke out of a walk. It worked. She and her comet's tail of adoring children were treated like mascots around Fernie Hill, as the executive area was named, and the word was passed on to newcomers that Red (she had let her nickname be known) was rather a scream.

The same ploy was less successful in the staff quarters, until she made it clear by her behaviour there that it *was* only a ploy. She made no close friends, but she was accepted.

Towards the end of her second week, she was involved in an incident which would, but for one thing, have got her the sack. She was patrolling Ramblers Wood with her pooper-scooper, when she heard cries of anguish coming from near the perimeter fence. The Pleasurelands site was bordered by a wide, sandy track for cycling, walking and 'horse-riding' (Claudia always wondered what other animals were likely to be ridden in rural middle England), beyond which was a high chain-link fence, the uprights of which curved slightly inward to discourage trespassers or, possibly, escapees. On the far side of this fence was the rolling open farmland typical of the county, with sheep grazing between dry stone walls, and occasional islands of woodland. It was made clear to both staff and holidaymakers that any unauthorised incursions on to this land by either dogs or people would be viewed with the gravest displeasure by the local farmers.

Claudia rushed to the scene. The source of the shrieks was an elderly woman whose beribboned Yorkshire terrier – showing considerable stamina and initiative – had tunnelled out, and was careering across the field, scattering before it a highly satisfactory number of alarmed sheep.

'Oh Lord!' exclaimed Claudia. 'Damn!'

'Don't let him do it!' the woman cried, clutching the chain-link fence like a POW watching a doomed breakout. 'Don't! Stop him!'

For a split second Claudia thought the woman's distress was for the sheep, but then she saw the Land-Rover pulled up about two hundred yards away to the right of the scampering dog. A man in a cap and a green pullover was standing by the bonnet of the Land-Rover, levelling a gun at the dog.

Appalled that she might be about to witness the shooting of an animal in cold blood, Claudia took a deep breath and bellowed at the top of her lungs:

'STOP!'

She heard the click of the gun being cocked. The dog, yap-yapping, wheeled and headed excitedly towards the instrument of death, driving a couple of fat-bottomed ewes before it.

'STOP!' she shouted again, her voice breaking crazily in her effort to be heard above the dog's barking and the woman's wails of distress. The gun remained fixed, but she was rewarded by a small movement of the man's head as he looked her way. She jumped up and down, waving her arms.

'Stop! Don't! I'm coming! Wait there –' she said to the woman. Thanking God for the emergency skeleton key she'd so often cursed, she raced to the nearest gate, fought with the padlock, and was through, closing the gate behind her.

She ran faster than she had done in years, and not being particularly fit was fighting for breath by the time she reached the man. He had collared the terrier and was holding it roughly, by a handful of scruff and collar, at arm's length, the broken gun in the crook of his right arm. Without their tormentor the baaing sheep were regrouping fussily in the middle of the field. The man's face was flinty with rage.

'Give me one good reason why I shouldn't wring this bloody animal's neck here and now!'

'I'm sorry . . . I'm so sorry . . . He dug out . . . Sorry . . .' She put her hands on her knees and bent over to catch her breath.

'You should be bloody sorry, sheep-worrying's a criminal

offence. It's a bitch. Bitches are worse, and any terrier, even a lapdog like this, is a menace unless it's properly trained and exercised.'

Claudia straightened up. Her legs were trembling. 'I've said I'm sorry.'

'Yes, well –' Still holding the squirming and yelping dog, the man laid his gun in the back of the Land-Rover and took out a piece of rope, which he looped through her collar. He handed the end of the rope to Claudia.

'I'll be giving the powers that be a ring when I get back, have no fear.' Their hands touched briefly. Their eyes met. 'Hang on. I've just realised you're – who you are.'

'Yes. And you're –' She frowned, not about to betray a better memory than him.

He gazed at her. 'Anthony Saxby. Well I'll be buggered . . .'

'Oh, I do hope not,' said Claudia, with a coolness she savoured for hours afterwards. 'Not on top of everything else.'

She returned the dog, Tiny, to its tearful owner and went straight to Admin to report the incident before Anthony could.

'The dog dug its way out,' she explained. 'And it was only a small dog. I'm amazed it hasn't happened before.'

'Never mind,' said Sean, the supervisor, who was chubby and camp and in love with his work. 'We've got the maintenance team on the job, and sent some show tickets to Mrs Wilbram.'

'It's not her I'm worried about,' said Claudia.

'Sir Anthony?' Sean bridled. 'You leave him to me.'

Whatever masterful action was taken by Sean, it resulted in a call from Admin to the girls' block at about ten p.m., when a group of the Site Rangers had kicked off their trainers and were sitting playing poker on the floor of the day room: would Claudia please go to the office at once.

'Uh-oh,' said fat Georgia from the Bike Mart. 'A legover situation with our Sean . . . ?'

'The boot more like,' replied Claudia.

'Ooooh . . . !' they chorused at her touchiness.

In fact Sean was all smiles when she arrived, and Anthony Saxby was standing there with his hands in his pockets wearing a striped shirt and quite bearable chinos.

'Hello,' he said.

'Hello.'

'Sir Anthony wanted a word,' explained Sean with a twinkle.

'Perhaps I might –' Anthony turned his head slightly in Sean's direction while keeping his eyes on Claudia – 'take the young lady out for a drink, or is that completely *verboten*?'

'No, no – but back by midnight,' said Sean, 'with both shoes, preferably . . . !'

'Speaking of shoes,' said Claudia, as they made their way across the car park to the Land-Rover. 'I'm not exactly dressed for a date.'

'Who said it was a date?' He opened the door for her. 'It's just by way of apology for behaving like a pig this morning.'

It was a date, though. Claudia felt it in her bones, which were pretty accurate sensors. They went to the sort of country pub which only the natives know about, where her cycling shorts, extreme height and funny hair attracted not a flicker of interest from the other customers and where the barman greeted their arrival with a simple 'Evenin' Ant'ny.'

She had a Malibu, he a pint of flat, cloudy draught cider. Conversation was not particularly easy. They circled and sparred. He did not repeat anything which could be interpreted however broadly as an apology, and she was certainly not about to offer one – the holidaymakers' dogs were not her problem. His unreturned phone calls lay at the edge of their discourse like unattended baggage. He asked after Jen.

'She's fine.'

'My mother's cock-a-hoop with the painting.'

'Good.' He pointed to her empty glass. 'Want another of those?'

'No thanks.'

'I'm not surprised, it looks perfectly filthy.'

'I like it.'

'Yes, well –' he took a long swig of the cider. 'Each to his own, I suppose.'

'Absolutely.'

There was a short, deep silence, broken only by the slither and click of two youths playing shove-halfpenny at the bar. Claudia watched the shove-halfpenny: Anthony Saxby watched Claudia. She practised remaining completely composed under his scrutiny – she'd have to get used to that in the modelling game – but inside she burned.

'So,' he said, setting down his tankard with an air of finality. 'I'd better get you back before the jeep reverts to a pumpkin.'

She didn't smile. As they barrelled along the lanes, he glanced at her and asked: 'Shall we do this again? What do you think?' He was musing on the future rather than extending an invitation.

'I've no idea,' she replied in the same detached tone, though she did not feel detached. She recognised self-destruct mode, but it was hard to pull out of it without loss of face. Fortunately, he rescued her.

'Speaking personally, I'd like it if we did.'

'It's up to you.'

There was a brief silence during which she didn't look at him, but thought that he was smiling. 'Is it? Is it now . . . All right, I say we do it again.'

'Fine.'

'Tomorrow?'

'I can't tomorrow.' She felt she was being hurried, and she wouldn't be hurried.

'I tell you what, you ring me.'

'OK.'

She was trapped. In the reception car park – he'd offered to drive her to the block, but she'd read him the rule book – he got out a cracked and dog-eared wallet and handed her his card.

'I think you may already have it, but just in case.'

'Thanks.'

'It was nice seeing you again I must say.' He swung back into the driver's seat. 'And I'll look forward to hearing from you.'

Claudia opened her mouth to say something, but the Land-Rover's engine starting up stifled her remark at birth. He reversed, turned, and drew alongside, leaning on the open window and speaking loudly in his resonant aristocratic voice.

'I don't regret my treatment of that damn terrier, and I shan't hesitate to complete the job on the next uncontrolled dog I see worrying my sheep. But I say again I'm sorry that I was rude to you.'

Claudia walked slowly to counteract the beating of her heart. On the way she was accosted by two twelve-year-old girls who had lost their bearings on the way back from the junior disco. She restored them to their cabins and made her way back to the staff quarters through the moonlit quiet of the woods.

'Amazing, isn't it,' said Ned to his companion, 'how we manage to get this place to ourselves every time?'

'It is.' Scotch poured *blanc de blanc* and handed a glass to Ned. 'Is it them, do you think, or is it us?'

'Not our problem,' replied Ned. 'Lang may yer lum reek.'

'If you say so, squire.'

It was eleven p.m. on their last night. The two of them were comfy-cosy in the palatial Jacuzzi of the Loch Haye country club. There had been two skittish middle-aged married couples and a group of twenty-something female executives in the Jacuzzi when they arrived, but all these had since left and now they had the place to themselves. The Jacuzzi was housed in a sort of purpose-built gazebo halfway down the hill in a cluster of pines, between the soaring turrets and castellations of the country club (once the beating heart of a mighty fiefdom) and the capricious beauty of the loch. To reach it, guests had to walk some hundred yards down a path flanked by giant rhododendrons and azaleas, specially planted by the management to provide shelter from the prevailing wind. Large oilskin capes and golfing umbrellas with the Loch Haye logo were also provided. The effect of this short, secluded walk was to lend the Jacuzzi the air of an intensely private place designed for the taking of equally private – perhaps even proscribed – pleasures.

Ned, who knew the Loch Haye of old, was well aware of this atmosphere, and whatever he might say was not in the least surprised they had the place to themselves. In the pecking order of naughty-but-nice, two single men carrying a bottle of white wine far outranked marrieds with swapping on their minds, and left hen parties for dead.

He drank in the view: Scotch's head outlined against the unbroken smoked glass of the Jacuzzi's west wall. They themselves were invisible to passers-by, but this far north at this time of the year it was still not quite dark, and they could see the tumbling hillside, discreetly illuminated by uplighters, the ruffled silk of Loch Haye a quarter of a mile away, the opaque black mass of Ben Ormond, and the softer depths of the night sky, pricked with stars.

The shoot was over, but they'd taken a few extra days. And a few days, reflected Ned complacently, was all it had taken. Beneath the churning surface of the scented water he nudged Scotch's bare flank with the sole of his foot.

'Having a good time?'

'It's certainly different.'

'Life is one long learning curve, boyo.'

He grabbed Scotch's foot and placed it against his swelling member, massaging lazily.

'Tell me something more about this woman you share with.'

On this August weekday morning Isla and Nell found the Royal Academy Summer Exhibition packed with a cheerful crowd composed mainly of women, pensioners and tourists, all three categories frequently overlapping. The two of them moved from room to room with the throng, their pauses – and even their comments – largely dictated by what those around them were doing.

Collapsing on to the first free seat they'd seen in an hour and a half they agreed it was all a bit much.

'I never thought,' said Isla, 'that I'd hear myself saying things like "I could live with that", but it's catching. It has to be the least appropriate remark in the canon of art appreciation.'

'Yes,' agreed Nell, 'but you'd be amazed the people who come into the gallery with several k to spend and who make a choice based on the colour of their loose covers.'

'I suppose so. But I'm rather dismayed to find I'm becoming one of them.'

'What's so special about us? And anyway, what other way is there to respond to an exhibition this big and this uneven?'

They sat for a moment amid the shuffling and burbling procession of – Isla wondered what you'd call them. Not connoisseurs, certainly. Art enthusiasts? Viewers, as of TV? Spectators as in sport? Or simply punters?

'Let's go and eat,' she said. 'And more importantly, drink!'

They tried the Academy's basement cafeteria but it had already sprouted a queue into the corridor.

'Forget it. Come on.'

The dining room of the Ritz had never seemed more delightful, nor Isla's fame more welcome. A corner table with a view of the room was theirs, unrequested and without question, and the management's recognition and approval was evident in every discreet gesture.

They had buck's fizz. Isla raised her glass. 'Escape!'

'Freedom!'

They clinked, smiled, drank – and there followed one of those small, expectant pauses which occurs between people each of whom thinks the other is about to speak.

'Well now,' said Isla. 'I got the impression over the phone that you wanted to get something off your chest.'

Nell reddened. 'It's about Scotch.'

'I thought it might be.'

The blush faded into a more accustomed sternness. 'Did you?' She was almost accusing.

'Go on.'

'He's an absolute gem, you know.'

Isla's heart gave a little leap. 'And a real charmer.'

'Sod charming,' said Nell, with emphasis. 'Who cares about that? He's a bloody good sort.'

'I can believe it.'

'So why can't the parents? I mean, I'm not asking you to betray confidences or anything, but they talk to you and value your opinion – so what exactly is their problem?'

Isla hesitated while collecting her thoughts. A pearly trout was placed in front of her, and ravioli with fresh basil before the intently scowling Nell.

When the waiter had gone, she said: 'They're old-fashioned in the best sort of way. The idea of mixed sharing shocks them rather. They think he may be taking advantage of you.'

'Oh, please!' Nell, who had lifted her knife and fork, put them down heavily, clipping the side of her plate with a loud clang. 'Really! Do I look the sort to be taken advantage of?'

'Anyone's that sort in the hands of an expert,' suggested Isla gently. 'And you said how much you cared for him.'

'Er – no, I didn't actually.'

'Forgive me, but you—'

'I called him a good sort.'

'OK.' Isla smiled. 'Whatever you say.'

'God!' Nell sat in freeze-frame, outrage in place, as their Pinot Noir was poured. 'I can see I did right in asking you here.'

For the first time Isla gave houseroom to the idea that she might have been wrong, that the wish might have been father to the thought.

'I don't "care for" Scotch in the way you mean,' went on Nell.

'But in some way, you do?'

'As a chum. A pal.'

'Well,' said Isla, trying not to feel a fool, and wondering how she could, ever, have thought something which in the past few seconds had begun to appear preposterous, 'your parents will be pleased.'

'You're going to tell them, are you?'

'Not if you don't want me to.'

'But they asked you to report back?'

Isla spoke carefully. 'They were interested to know what my reaction was when next I saw you and Scotch together.'

'Which was weeks ago!' Nell stabbed her ravioli. 'So what have you said?'

There seemed to be nothing for it but the truth, and even as she told it how it was Isla could hear how sadly compromised she sounded. 'I said that you were in top form and Scotch was, as you've said yourself, a gem.'

'Handsome?' Nell munched furiously. 'Attractive?'

'Very.'

'*You're* attracted?'

'Good heavens, hardly, or at least only in the most distant way –' she would have protested even more excessively by adding that he was young enough to be her son, but Nell was on to her.

'There is no way to be distantly attracted. You're either mad for someone or you're not!'

At what point, wondered Isla, had the *savoir faire* passed from her to Nell? She was completely at sea. When the waiter hove

alongside and asked, 'Is everything all right, madam?' she misunderstood him and answered, 'Yes – yes, I'm fine, really—'

Without a hint of a smile he replenished their glasses. Nell
was quite pink again, but this time with passion rather than
discomfiture. Isla told herself to relax. Why feel defensive? Nell
had called this meeting. The ball was in her court. She invoked
the Mancunian Buddhist, settled her back against the back of the
chair, placed her feet side by side beneath the table and breathed
deeply . . .

'He's *terribly* attractive,' insisted Nell almost angrily. 'What
used to be called a ladykiller.'

'I suppose so. But nice, too.'

'Nice –!' Nell tossed her head back in a 'hah!' attitude. 'I don't
know about that.'

'You're right,' agreed Isla. 'That was the word we were always
told not to use in compositions when we were at school.'

'I'm desperately fond of Scotch,' went on Nell, rampaging
now, almost as though Isla hadn't spoken. 'But I'm not in love
with him.'

'I'm beginning to understand that.'

'You should – because I'm in love with you.'

Isla didn't think she imagined it. There was a subtle alteration
in the environment – a flinching and flexing of solid matter as
though a small earth tremor had occurred. Damask and linen
rippled . . . ferns and flowers trembled . . . the floor undulated
beneath their table . . . the wine glass grew soft in her hand so
that it bent and fell, splashing and splintering on to the floor.

The debri was removed instantly. 'Please don't worry madam,
another one is on its way.'

'Isla?'

'Yes.'

'Did you hear me?'

Perhaps she hadn't. Or perhaps she had misheard.

'No, I'm not sure that I did.'

'I said,' repeated Nell, freeze-framing again as the waiter
brought another glass and filled it for Isla, then continuing in
a fierce whisper, 'I said that I'm in love with you.'

This time Isla gripped the glass before it could turn soft, and took a long pull at her wine. Of all the situations she had ever been confronted with, both professional and private, this was the only one to have utterly confounded her.

'I don't know what to say.' Her voice was a dry thread.

'Oh, Christ!' Nell bowed her head and clasped her large, strong hands against her forehead. Isla noticed that there were already some grey hairs among the red. 'I knew I'd make a pig's ear of this!'

Her companion's embarrassment had the effect of restoring a little of Isla's composure. 'You haven't made a pig's ear of anything,' she said. 'You've just told me something for which I was completely unprepared.'

Nell peered up from under her clasped hands. 'But you can't have been! Not completely. *Surely*.'

'Completely.'

'Christ!' groaned Nell again. 'This is all so unbelievably horrendous!'

Isla drew more strength from the role of comforter. 'No it isn't.'

'What on earth must you think?'

'Well,' said Isla, 'now I do think, I feel flattered and privileged.'

Nell shielded one side of her face with her hand, grimacing. 'I hope no one's listening!'

'At the Ritz?' Isla shook her head. 'They won't be. And if anything's overheard, it will be by the most sophisticated eavesdroppers in the world. Our secret is safe.'

'Sophisticated – precisely what I haven't been, and am not,' declared Nell. Isla searched with her experienced instinct for ways to soothe, as a hand feels inside a bag for familiar treasures. She found one almost instantly.

'So tell me more about Scotch.'

'You asked about Nell,' said Scotch, leaning his head back on Ned's arm as darts of summer rain pricked the smooth wall of glass.

'Did I?'

'She's a great girl, and I won't hear a word against her.'

'Who, me?'

'She may be no beauty, but she's got this terrific energy—'

'And nice eyes. What people say about women who are out-and-out dogs. A great personality and nice eyes.'

Scotch slipped from beneath Ned's arm. 'Forget it.'

'No – look, I'm sorry.'

'She's a dear friend, the best,' said Scotch. 'And we live in perfect harmony.'

'Well I'll be hornswaggled . . .' Ned reached a hand around the back of Scotch's head and pulled it towards him. 'What bloke could possibly compete with that?'

12

'So there you have it,' declared Jim Furmston, on Richard's second visit. He switched the light off behind Richard's x-rays, and began washing his already spotless and well-manicured hands. 'Either you check in somewhere and get that carotid hoovered out, smartish, or you're going to have the granddaddy of a stroke any day now.'

There was an oil painting of a battle at sea just above the desk, and Richard fixed a thoughtful gaze on it as though assessing its value. Jim sat down beneath the painting so that the tumultuous goings-on it depicted – smoking cannons, blazing rigging, sinking rowboats and bloodthirsty hand-to-hand fighting on the quarter-deck to name but a few – appeared to Richard like a threatening thought-bubble hovering over his medical adviser's head.

'I'll get things moving, shall I?' asked Jim, tapping his Mont Blanc pen in quick march time on his blotter.

'Um – yes, sorry.' Richard, more shaken than he cared to admit, strove to seem preoccupied with other matters. 'What exactly would that involve?'

'Get you referred a.s.a.p. to see Martin Wheatcroft at the Brodrick, and then in to get the job done. You could be out of harm's way by this time next week.'

'That sounds a bit cheerless. Out of harm's way. I'll be out of harm's way when I'm six feet under.'

'Damn right. Depends which you'd rather.'

'It's such a ruddy nuisance, Jim. I've got a big case coming up next month—'

'Time for your understudy to have his fifteen seconds of fame, then.'

Richard transferred his gaze to the painting again. A good many of the mariners were in the sea, waving before drowning, as slatey crags of water bore down on them. It was awfully hard to tell which lot was winning.

Jim upped the tempo with his pen and crescendoed to a full stop. 'Better do as I advise, Dick.'

Richard pushed his chair back and rose. It was the only way to stop gazing at the picture. 'I'd like to talk to Isla.'

'That's allowed. But don't hang about, there is a degree of urgency.'

'It's hard to cultivate a sense of urgency from a standing start when none existed –' Richard looked at his watch – 'ten minutes ago.'

Jim stood up. He was by far the shorter of the two men but even the best bespoke tailoring private medicine could buy could not disguise the barrel-chested physique of an army PE sergeant. He put Richard in mind of a male version of Donatella, and had much the same unsettling effect. Richard half expected that if he faffed about too much he might receive a punishing blow to the solar plexus. Although, of course, that would somewhat defeat the object of the exercise . . .

'You rang me, not the other way round,' Jim reminded him, and at once held up a hand to silence argument. 'And no, I wasn't taken in by all that service and oil-change horse feathers. Men of your age who suddenly decide to have the full medical are without exception scared shitless.'

With a sense of urgency, Richard left.

Isla pulled into one of the unmade car parks on the edge of the heath before going home. She thought, I am turning into a foolish, fantasising, menopausal woman, and I got exactly what I deserved.

After their brief reversal and resumption of roles, she and Nell had got through lunch like the two well-brought-up, middle-class girls they were at heart, acknowledging that something untoward had occurred, not for a moment condemning it or (perish the thought) sweeping it under the carpet, but nonetheless trying discreetly to put clear water between them and this bit of local difficulty. At least, that was what she had tried to do. She was shocked to find she could be so – well, what Ned would have called tight-arsed. Nell, after her first fine frenzy, became almost tongue-tied and this enabled Isla to spin a web of nothingness, fragile but surprisingly effective, to cover their tracks. She had made some of the right noises about a 'dear, dear friend' and 'affection and respect' and Nell having her 'whole life before her' (whatever that had got to do with it), but she knew in her heart of hearts that it was guff, and dishonest guff at that.

And Nell had known too, and only bottled her feelings out of a commendable awareness of good form. On the pavement in Piccadilly, as a cab thrummed beside them, she made that clear.

'I did mean it, you know. I meant it, and it's true, and it's not going simply to disappear now it's been mentioned.'

'I realise that,' said Isla, who had been hoping that was exactly what would happen. 'We shall have to talk some more.'

Nell released her arm with a glum expression and said something like 'I suppose so'. Isla had waved her off and then fled, exhausted, to the car.

When Richard got home he thought at first that the house was empty. He poured himself a beer and considered ringing Jen. There had been something slightly out of kilter in her manner last time . . . a kind of self-consciousness which was entirely new, and which he sincerely hoped wouldn't last.

He carried the beer into the orangery, loosening his tie, and shrugged off his jacket. Seeing the shadowed and dappled green of the garden he sat down and on an impulse unlaced his shoes and discarded them, then his socks. He looked down at his big feet, which for a moment held the shape of the shoes, and were red in places and pale in others, moist all over with the sweat of a long hot afternoon. Poor old feet, thought Richard, you deserve a break.

The pleasure of the different textures beneath his soles – the smooth floorboards of the orangery, the licheny stone of the patio, the mossy ridges of the steps and oh, yes! the delicious, unmown coolness of the grass – was exquisite. He sat down on the bottom step with his beer clasped in both hands, clenching and unclenching his toes, feeling the strands of grass thread between them . . .

'What are you doing?'

It was Marcus, standing behind his right shoulder.

'Cooling off,' said Richard.

'Yeah. It was hotter'n hell in that place today.'

'Do you want a beer?'

'No thanks, I got a coke on the way from the bus.'

To Richard's utter astonishment, Marcus sat down, if not exactly next to him then at least nearby, on the flat top of the pillar that flanked the foot of the steps.

'Good day?'

Marcus gave one of his minimalist grimaces. 'It's a crap job. What can I say?'

'Stupid question.'

'Yeah,' agreed Marcus benevolently. He took makings from the pocket of his black jeans and began to roll a cigarette. Richard glanced furtively at the contents from beneath lowered lids. Having established them to be merely unhealthy rather than illegal, he felt a pang of remorse for his mean spiritedness.

'You're home early, aren't you?'

'Probably.'

'Any particular reason?'

'I asked them.'

Just in time Richard stopped himself from putting the obvious supplementary question, and was rewarded.

'I'm totally knackered.'

Alive to the possibilities, most of them unwelcome, Richard looked his son full in the face for the first time, and noticed that even by his own exacting standards he did indeed look knackered. The yellowish pallor of his face emphasised the grey-blue scoops beneath his eye sockets, and a couple of angry pustules decorated his chin.

'You do look pretty rough. Any symptoms?'

Marcus took a drag, coughed, took another drag. 'Not really. Just knackered.'

'You'd better get to bed.'

'No . . . What's the point?'

'I don't know – to rest, to recuperate.'

'I'd rather chill out down here.'

'Fair enough.'

They sat in silence for a couple of minutes. When Marcus had finished his cigarette he ground it out on the sole of his boot and shied it, like a dart, into the bushes.

'So what's up?'

Richard recognised this query as being quite distinct from the opening, rhetorical 'What are you doing?'. It indicated a modicum of real interest – it required an answer. If this went on, he thought, who knows where it might end? A pleasing vista of lively exchanges and intimate heart-to-hearts opened up before him.

'I was knackered too.'

'You've been looking like shit for weeks,' agreed Marcus equably.

'Have I?'

'You ought to see a doctor. You know what they say about blokes your age.'

'No,' said Richard, a tad testily. 'What do they say?'

'You start paying.'

'As a matter of fact I've been to see my doctor this afternoon.'

'Oh yeah?' Marcus made no attempt to disguise his scepticism.

'Yeah – yes. He says I'm in pretty good shape for a man my age.'

'Yeah? So what made you go then?' This brutal logic, so similar to Jim Furmston's, pricked Richard's conscience. He was going to have to come clean some time . . . On the other hand he hadn't even spoken to Isla about it yet.

'I may have to have a small operation – a sort of preventative measure.'

'Heart?' asked Marcus matter of factly.

'Er – no.'

'You can tell me, you know. I can take it.'

'I realise that, that's not the point. It's nothing of any importance, and anyway there's other people I need to tell first.'

'Have you told Mum?'

This was yet another new departure – an awareness of connections and relationships and their relative weights. Richard was astonished.

'No, but I will of course.'

'And it's no big deal.' There wasn't a hint of sarcasm in Marcus's voice, but there didn't need to be.

There followed another silence, broken by the sound of the front door. Marcus got up. 'Maybe I will crash for a bit.'

'Yes, you do that, a good kip does wonders.'

As Isla came out on to the patio she passed Marcus going the other way, and said hello, to which he responded with his usual nasal grunt. She went down the steps and bent to kiss Richard on the top of his head. He leaned briefly into her skirt.

'Everyone's home,' she remarked, sitting down by him. 'And I thought I'd find an empty house.'

'Would you rather have done?'

'Of course not. What brought Marcus back from the coal-face?'

'He's tired.'

'And you? What did Jim say?'

He hesitated. 'Not much.' He realised he had expected her to notice the hesitation, and was disappointed when she appeared not to, saying instead:

'Look at your bare feet.'

They both looked at them. He wiggled his toes, all nicely separate and splayed now that they'd recovered. 'I think I'll do the same,' she said, and slipped out of her thick-soled white deck shoes. She seemed to be bubbling over with something of her own, and her next remark confirmed this.

'If I tell you something, will you promise not to mention it to anyone else? To behave, in fact, as if you never heard it?'

'Depends what it is.'

'All right. I've just been having lunch with Nell.'

'Oh yes – how was the RA?'

'The usual curate's egg. Terribly crowded, so I bore her off to the Ritz – which was probably my big mistake.'

'You're going to tell me she ate enough for an entire sumo team.'

'Actually she hardly ate a thing.'

'Became roaring drunk and propositioned the waiters?'

'No, but you're getting warmer.'

'I give up.'

'She said she's in love with me.'

'Really?'

'Truly. And madly, and deeply if I'm to believe her. Which I do.'

'Well I must say it doesn't surprise me.'

Isla, who had been pulling at the grass between her feet, head bowed, glanced up at him. 'It doesn't?'

'No.' Richard put his arm round her and drew her into an embrace, a little awkwardly since they were both sitting on such a shallow step. 'Just about everyone I know is in love with you.'

'But Richard, she didn't mean she admired me, or was fond of me, or thought the world of me. She's *in love* with me.'

'Yes, I've hoisted that on board.'

Isla laughed. 'Well, I must say, I don't know what I expected, but this do beat all . . . I don't mind telling you *I* was – am – gobsmacked.'

Richard kissed her. 'It's one of your noblest qualities – you have absolutely no idea of the effect you have on people.'

'Yes I do. I'm not an innocent, and I'm certainly not noble, I'm a professional. But this was a shock. It's so intimate – so personal. It makes me look back on other occasions and wonder what was going on in her mind. And now that she's told me, what am I supposed to do?'

'Do you have to do anything?'

'I think so, if it's only to find a way to say no.'

'No to what? Did she try and force herself on you?'

'Don't be silly. She was sweet. Brusque, but sweet. Touching.'

Richard nudged her. 'She got to you.'

'She'd have got to anyone! I owe it to her to come up with some sort of considered response.' She felt Richard laughing. 'What's so funny?'

'I was thinking about poor old Bill and Barbara. Have they ever been barking up the wrong tree.'

Isla smiled in spite of herself. 'I know. Delicious.'

'All that outrage and suspicion squandered on the innocent Scott-Chatham.'

'I'm not sure innocent is how I'd describe him. He's in Scotland with Ned as we speak.'

Richard sighed heavily. 'Let them all get on with it, that's what I say.'

'But it's not only them, is it,' said Isla. 'It's me too, now.' Richard didn't comment. She stood up. 'I think I'll get myself a beer, do you want another?' He shook his head.

Passing through the hall she heard Marcus on the telephone. 'OK,' he said. 'Bye.' He emerged.

'How are you doing?' she asked.

'I was talking to Caroline.' He always referred to his mother by her christian name when talking to Isla, as though the appellation 'Mum' embarrassed him. 'She's back.'

'Did she have a good time?'

'I reckon. I forgot to ask.' Isla was on her way when he added, 'I think I might go home.'

She paused, turned. 'Of course – what about the job?'

'I've had enough of it.'

'Will that be all right?'

'Sure. Plenty more fish in the sea.'

Isla wasn't sure whether this comment referred to jobs or employees, so let it go without comment.

'So – when are you off?'

'I'll get my stuff together and . . .'

'Do you want a lift?'

'No thanks.'

He went up the stairs, taking two at a time, not leaping but with long, stalking strides. Isla thought that unlike the rest of them he was a self-contained, self-sufficient person, who made his own decisions without reference to anyone else and did not either seek their approval or fear their condemnation. She found that she admired that more and more, and she envied Caroline the sudden upsurge of filial feeling which was sending him home.

She returned with a glass of wine to find Richard, shoes back on, sitting in a chair on the patio. She picked her way gingerly over the rough stone and sat down next to him tucking her feet up on the seat.

'I'm sorry if I seemed dismissive about Nell,' he said. 'I agree it's a facer. But I still think you should do nothing.'

'Will I seem to acquiesce, though?'

'Yes. Why not? She can be in love with you whenever she wants. Doesn't mean you have to be in love with her.'

'I thought you'd be shocked.'

'I read the papers.' Richard shrugged. 'Even I am creaking towards the millennium with an altered perspective.'

'Yes.' Isla decided to let it go. Jen would understand how she felt. 'You're right. It's nothing to get worked up about. By the way, Marcus is going home.'

'You mean to his mother?'

'Yes. He was talking to her on the phone just now. A sudden pang of homesickness I suppose.'

Richard held out his hand to Isla and she took it, grasping it firmly to establish contact.

'There are days,' he said, 'and this is one of them, when I feel that marrying you is the only thing I've got halfway right.'

She moved his hand up and down gently. 'Don't be silly. But I'm glad you think that. We'll have to stick together, won't we?'

He didn't answer.

Next day, on the phone to Jim Furmston, he took an assertive line. It was his problem, after all, and his embolism. He was the customer.

'I've decided to wait till my case is over.'

He could almost hear Jim's eyes rolling heavenward. 'Why?'

'I've got too much on. In the meantime I'll clean up my act. Isla will be delighted.'

'Have you discussed it with her?'

'Not yet, a suitable moment hasn't presented itself.'

'Sod a suitable moment, Dick, I told you it was urgent.'

'If it was urgent yesterday it was urgent weeks ago, only we didn't know. I'm going to be as good as gold, cut down on the booze, throw out the cigars, go for long walks and catch some early nights.'

'So when will this case be completed – in your opinion?' Jim's voice was thin with disapproval.

'Shouldn't be more than a few weeks – hearing's set for the second week in September. I'll get back to you when I can give a firm date.'

'No, I'll get the wheels moving. I take it you can make the consultation at least?'

'That depends.'

'I'll get you an appointment with Martin Wheatcroft four weeks from now. You'll be in an opt-out situation, Dick. And I want to make it quite clear once again that this delay is against my express advice.'

'Don't worry,' said Richard. 'If the balloon goes up I shan't sue.'

'Too right you won't, old boy. You'll be dead.'

Jen was in uproar. What, oh what, was she going to do?

She spent sleepless nights raging at herself for allowing things to reach this point. And yet it was because they had gone on for so long, undisturbed and uneventful, that she had come to accept the situation as part of her life. She had told herself she was hurting no one because Richard so obviously loved his wife. But the offstage wife had become a full-stage player now, an individual – Isla, whom she had liked on first meeting and felt to be a soul mate. A state of affairs which she had never before thought of as deceitful she now plainly saw for what it was: shoddy, underhand, despicable.

She was by nature sanguine. She took her life on a day-to-day basis, as it came, and enjoyed it. She did not count money, or days, or problems or blessings. She placed no burden of expectation on those she cared for, including Richard, and in return they placed none on her. Red disapproved of course, but not vociferously, and at the moment she was too preoccupied with her own life to spare a thought for Jen's travails.

Jen didn't know what to think about Claudia's new liaison. *Sir* Anthony Saxby already! She'd known better than to take things beyond the 'oh, really?' stage when speaking to Red herself, but privately her reactions were more confused. One of the qualities she most admired in her daughter – and there were many – was her emotional self-sufficiency, her ability to behave not according to the expectations or wishes of others, but according to her own intentions. If sometimes this resulted in aloofness, well, it was aloofness of which Jen herself could have done with a bit more. All the same, the part of her which she recognised as conventionally maternal had worried slightly over recent years about Red's lack of a boyfriend. It was old-fashioned of her, she knew, but she couldn't help feeling that a young woman of such beauty, brains and character *ought* to have a man in her life. Had Red honestly not met one man who fulfilled her exacting criteria? Or was there some other more complex or less welcome reason for her self-imposed isolation? Had her own behaviour and experiences, Jen wondered, persuaded Red that all encounters with the opposite sex were likely to end in a mess?

So she couldn't help being pleased that some sort of relationship appeared to be getting off the ground. But Sir Anthony Saxby? Not for the first time she wondered what was going on inside her daughter's head, not to mention her heart. Not that he wasn't attractive, or nice, or – thank God – unattached, but he was old enough to be her own lover, let alone her daughter's. What was a man of his age and social status doing pursuing a student? She couldn't get a handle on it. But then she'd sweep these concerns aside. Cupid was a notorious practical joker, and one thing Red had proved was that she could take care of herself. Also – and Jen allowed this notion to creep in only in the very wee small hours – if she was going to find herself facing a future without Richard, then it would be no small consolation to see Red happy with a man of her own. But even as she contemplated this dim, vicarious pleasure she would catch herself doing so and weep for her lost confidence.

Her turmoil seeped into other areas. Having once more psyched herself up to speak to Keith, she once more backed off. It was a Sunday morning, when they generally wound up having a coffee together. He was down first, sitting at the kitchen table in his joggers and flip-flops, reading the computer section.

'Kettle's boiled,' he greeted her. 'And I took the liberty of buying some sultana cookies, help yourself.'

'No thanks. Keith—'

'Go on, they're the ones you like.'

'No. Thanks. I'm not hungry.'

'Have a paper then.' He pushed it across the table towards her. 'Get the weight off your feet.'

'I only just got out of bed.'

'Yes but it's Sunday.'

'Keith—'

'Mm?' He smiled, and raised his eyebrows interrogatively, but did not take his eyes from the page. 'What can I do for you?'

'There's something I need to discuss with you.'

'Right!' He folded the paper with a rustle, and tapped the seat of a chair. 'Make yourself comfortable, I'm all yours.'

It was hopeless. Even as she lowered herself obediently on to the seat she could feel her resolve ebbing away. Keith's face, the very picture of amiable attention, jaws rotating on a sultana cookie, was enough to bring home the shittiness of what she was about to do. What had he ever done to her, except pay his rent on time, keep decent hours, maintain his room as the most orderly in the house, take her messages, feed her cats, and buy her biscuits—

'Oh sod it,' she said. 'I'll have one.'

'That's right,' said Keith, turning back to the computer section. 'Where's your spirit of adventure?'

Richard came round – something else which she felt powerless to prevent – and behaved as if everything were exactly the same. She had to remind herself that for him, perhaps, it was. She'd hoped and believed that something of her own perturbation had communicated itself on his last visit, but he was at his most maddening and (she admitted) attractive – brainy, dishevelled, preoccupied, a creature from another planet. This was the Richard she found hardest to resist, and she failed completely to do so. After making love she was dismayingly weepy, unable to distinguish between love and the fear of losing it.

'Hey,' he said. 'Come on, chin up. I believe the received response is, Do you want to talk about it?'

Dumbly, she'd shaken her head.

After he'd gone, heading west in the Jag as free as a bird for a few days' golf in the country, she picked up the phone to cancel her lunch with Isla. With his voice and his touch uppermost in her mind she was utterly determined. A few simple words, and pat, now might she do it.

But she'd underestimated the effect Isla's voice would have on her.

'Hello? Jen, how lovely! And I'm all on my own, too. Richard's left for Wiltshire, my stepson's gone home, I was just thinking how much I was looking forward to our lunch. I've got something extraordinary to tell you.'

A dreadful surmise momentarily deflected Jen from her purpose. 'Oh? What?'

'No, I couldn't possibly waste it over the telephone. It requires the perfect setting – wine, food, and a couple of hours with nothing to do but talk.'

'That was what I rang about,' said Jen.

'You're not going to cry off?'

'I'm afraid I must.'

'Oh, no . . .' Isla sounded genuinely downcast. 'You have no idea how much I've been looking forward to it.'

'I know. Me too.' Already Jen felt herself losing her footing, slipping back, and every moment the exchange lasted she could only lose more ground. A few brief words and pat – 'I have to be somewhere else – work, I'm afraid.'

'Never mind. Let's pick another day.'

'I'm likely to be pretty tied up for the forseeable future.'

There was a short silence. Jen, holding her breath, had the impression that Isla was weighing up this remark, which had undeniably been one of those open-ended excuses bordering on rudeness. She regretted it but could think of no other way, short of blurting out the truth.

When Isla did answer her voice was gently teasing. 'All work and no play. You have to eat.'

Jen knew she'd lost. 'Yes. You're right.'

'Here's a suggestion – my diary's empty, so you say where you're going to be, and I'll meet you there.'

So the meeting remained, but relocated to south of the park, where Jen was, indeed, due to arrange a photo session with a Dalmatian. As she put the phone down she felt both exasperation and relief. Exasperation at her weakness, her susceptibility, her fatal hesitation; relief that she would be seeing Isla after all, in what would be relative safety.

The Wakefields generally received a lot of post – most of it for Isla, since Richard's tended to be work-related and went to chambers

– but in August the flood slowed to a trickle. Invitations for the autumn had already been received and dealt with, and those for the following year were pending for the end of the silly season. However, the day after she'd spoken to Jen on the phone there was quite a sheaf of envelopes to be opened.

With Richard away, she was still in her nightdress at eight o'clock. She stood in the kitchen spooning Greek yoghurt and honey with one hand and leafing through the mail with the other.

There were two postcards, one from Giles, addressed to them both, and another to Richard from Donatella in Fiesole. She read this one first, without guilt – they agreed postcards were fair game.

I am having a simply heavenly time, she had written, *and there is a young man here who is after me like anybody's business. Every night when I go to bed the birds are singing. My family all send their love. I am fat and brown and sexy. I hope you are better than you were by the river. Love to you Ricardo, Donatella.*

Isla shook her head. Better than by the river? But Donatella – whom she liked – had an idiosyncratic way of expressing herself and that could mean anything. She picked up Giles's card.

Hi folks. This is a blast, and the mix of people is the best. There are some really wild German lads, and a black transsexual known as Hottentotty. Jealous? Went on a trip to the mainland, but it was closed. Cash running out so back end of the month and all systems go on the party circuit. Ciao, Giles.

In addition to these, there was an invitation to the David D rail sale at the Great Titchfield Street showroom, which she set aside to enter in the diary. There was also that rarest of communications, a letter from her agent, Lori, at Prize Performers.

Dear Isla

I do hope you're having a wonderful summer. It seems like forever since we were in touch, but I've seen your picture in the papers a couple of times in recent months, so I know you're keeping busy without us. However, we've had some exciting news – a request for you to appear as a regular panelist on OVER THE PARROT – *the crazy quiz programme with Adrian Coote and all those abrasive young alternative comedians? It has already attracted an extensive cult following, but both producers and presenters feel it needs someone to help them 'cross over' to a more mainstream audience, and since you are the nation's fancy (their phrase), it's you they want. Of course, the thought may fill you with absolute horror. But the money is exceptional, and they are not even considering anyone else until they have your answer, so if nothing else it is a very pleasing compliment to your huge popularity . . .*

Though Isla read to the end of the letter, she did not need to consider the offer. She had already made up her mind. Lori was astute, and her own interests coincided unerringly with her favourite client's. The quiz show was the right thing at the right time. It would be different, it might be fun (or horrifyingly scary), and it would call on her to show a different side of herself from the one her public was used. She was going to ring Lori and accept.

The next letter she picked up was from Nell. It was written on Bury-embossed notepaper, in biro, with the address crossed out and that of the flat in Swiss Cottage substituted alongside.

My dear Isla

I'm just about to leave for France. I'd say what must you think of me? Only I'm pretty sure of the answer. What a prize idiot I must have seemed, ruining a nice lunch like that. I do apologise for being so ham-fisted, and thanks for handling it all so elegantly. (Isla winced at the memory.) *But having grovelled, I can't pretend I didn't mean everything I said. I told you before you dashed off that none of this will go away, and it won't. I love you dearly, that's the way it is.* (Isla found tears in her eyes.) *Scotch is due back tonight, and I know what he will say – go for it. So I am. If when you've read this and had a jolly good laugh, you think there is the remotest chance you could care for me, please get in touch. Otherwise I faithfully promise not to bother you.*

All my love my dear, dear Isla – Nell.

A jolly good laugh . . . Isla sat down at her kitchen table and wept as though her heart would break.

13

Not long afterwards, Isla went out to Bradenham for the day. It was on impulse. She craved the uncaring, unchanging quality of village life, the tractors doggedly dragging the fields towards autumn, the parish newsletter issuing polite hints about the Best Kept Village competition, and begging produce (packaged food will be fine!) for Harvest Festival. It had been a desperately dry year, but good for the roses, and even the dourest and most desiccated gardens sprouted heavy swags of blooms. By gates and driveways stood boxes filled with bagged-up apples and plums, accompanied by large felt-tipped notices, 15P A BAG, CASH IN TIN PLEASE. The pub was advertising Live Music Night with 'the outrageous' Fritz the Cat. Norman Brake was mowing the recreation ground on a small tractor, describing ever-decreasing circles on the smooth green.

Marjory's bike was propped by the front door of Brook End, and Marjory herself was pulling up weeds in the garden. She sat back red-faced as Isla appeared in the kitchen doorway.

'Oh my dear, I had no idea you were coming – I'm so sorry you had to find yours truly grubbing about in your border.'

'Not at all Marjory, bless you.'

'I love it . . .' She got heavily to her feet. 'Golly gosh, anno Domini is playing havoc with my knees . . . Actually –' she waved a hand at the flowerbed – 'the unwelcome visitors are beginning to retreat. It's June when you can't turn your back for a moment.'

'Cold drink?'

'A squash or something would be lovely.' She followed Isla

into the kitchen and sat down at the table. 'Isla, I do hope you don't mind my coming and going like this.'

'Of course not.' Isla snapped ice cubes into tumblers and ran cold water on to lime juice. 'There. It's nice to know the cottage has a friend when we're not here.'

'Yes, a friend, that's certainly how I'd like to be thought of.'

'And you must always say if it's getting to be a bind. I mean the bike, in all weathers . . .' Isla tailed off, not wanting to characterise Marjory as decrepit.

'It's my trusty bike that keeps me going! I'd be a complete crock without it. Besides, I come down here most days to cook lunch next door.'

'Next door?' Isla entertained a picture of Barbara and Marjory criss-crossing and near-missing in the kitchen of The Bury like a couple of fighter planes.

'For Norman,' explained Marjory.

'Norman?' Isla couldn't disguise her astonishment.

'Well,' went on Marjory hurriedly, 'he prefers his main meal in the middle of the day and so do I, and I enjoy cooking and it's much more fun to cook for two, so I began by going down on a Wednesday and it went on from there. On Sundays he comes to me,' she added. 'And I do a proper roast.'

'Lucky Norman,' said Isla.

'He pays his whack, of course, that's only fair.'

'Of course.'

'And during harvest things went a bit to pot, I resorted to salads and casseroles, but with the summer we've had most of that's out of the way now.'

'I saw Norman,' said Isla musingly, 'up at the rec. Mowing.'

'He does such a lot around the village that people don't know about. I tell him he needs a PR person.'

'Yes, he's not the easiest man to get on with. He's a good neighbour, but pretty crusty.'

'He adores you,' said Marjory. 'Simply adores.'

'But you and he get on well?' asked Isla.

'Awfully well. We're both plain-speaking types, we've lived in Bradenham all our lives, always lived alone – we're quite a pair, really!'

Isla wanted to say they were no sort of pair – that Marjory

was a bright, adventurous, open-minded woman who went on cultural holidays and who had forgotten more about gardening than most people would ever know; and that Norman was an ill-kempt, bad-mannered, old fascist who believed nothing was for nothing, and read the *Sunday Sport*. Instead, she said:

'Good on the both of you! Just you make sure he helps with the washing up.'

'We don't bother with that,' replied Marjory spiritedly. 'That's what I got the dishwasher for.'

Round at The Bury the portrait of Portia was in pride of place over the drawing-room mantelpiece.

'We moved an ancestor to make way for that,' grumbled Bill. 'And a not-half-bad-looking one at that. One of mine.'

'She was a terrible, tight-lipped old witch that none of us liked,' declared Barbara. She was in transit, wearing a royal blue suit scattered with dog hairs, and several thousand pounds' worth of diamonds.

'Tush – Auntie Fanny was one of the beauties of the county in her youth. You shouldn't speak ill of the dead.'

'Portia's dead too.'

'Oh Bar,' said Isla, 'no. I am sorry.'

'Can't be helped. And I have that to remind me. Now I must away, committees call. Bill knows where the cold lamb is. Bye, ducky.'

'Sod cold lamb,' said Bill as the door closed behind his wife. 'Let's go to the pub.'

But there was no hot food there either, the landlord of The Diggings informed them, because of the Live Music Night.

'What's that got to do with anything?' asked Bill.

'We're doing a pig roast this evening, I've only got Janice in the kitchen and she's on the coleslaw and jackets for later. You can have the Essential Ploughman's,' he added, with a commendable use of marketing-speak.

'What do you think?' asked Bill.

'Sounds fine.'

'Will that be outside?' enquired the landlord hopefully.

'Not on your nellie, in here in the cool and away from the fumes.'

His choice of words reminded Isla of what she had come all this way to say. As they sat at a corner table with their drinks – a pint for Bill and a spritzer for her – she said: 'Let me give you an update on Nell.'

'Hell, yes. What goes on?'

'She's in France with a chum at the moment, as you probably know.'

'That's right, now you come to mention it she did say something on the phone. So what about Scott-Chatham?'

'He's delightful—'

'He was at Bar's do. Pretty boy, I thought.'

There was a fairly acute social antenna, Isla reflected, concealed beneath the huff and bluster. 'He's delightful,' she repeated, 'but you have absolutely no need to worry.'

'So he is a pretty boy.'

'I have no idea, but he's certainly not after Nell.'

'Thank the Lord for that.' He cast her a sharp, scowling look. 'She's not fallen for him or anything bloody silly like that?'

'No. They're just firm friends, devoted to one another.'

'I see.' Bill dunked a forefinger into his tankard and retrieved a minute fly. 'So long as she's free to form an alliance with some decent, dependable bloke.' Twin ploughmans were set down before them. 'What, no pickled onions?'

It had been Isla's intention to spend a lazy afternoon at Brook End, reading her book in the garden, but in the event she couldn't settle. The conversation with Bill had raised the awful possibility of Nell's telling her parents the truth. She wouldn't, would she . . . ? But the thought nibbled away at her, and at about three o'clock she locked up the cottage and headed north to The Hayes, Lettaford, to visit her father-in-law.

'A visitor for you,' said Karen, adding coyly: 'A lady visitor.'

Alec leaned forward heavily and peered round the side of his chair. 'I don't know any ladies—'

'Yes you do.' Smiling broadly Isla went over and bent to kiss his upturned face as Karen closed the door. 'Stop pretending to be hard done by.'

He grabbed her hands and held them tight in both his. 'Isla my darling, is it really you?'

'Yes, and you're quite right to be taken aback, it's been a shamefully long time since I was last here.'

'It has, it has, but never mind that, this more than compensates, in fact it's made my day. Not,' he added in case she should think him too cheerful, 'that that's saying much.'

'Give over Alec . . .' She left one of her hands in his and with the other pulled up a tapestry stool and sat on it. The professional actor in her recognised the amateur one in Alec, and knew how this arrangement – him in the big chair, she perched on a stool at his knee – would appeal to him. 'You're looking awfully well.'

'Do I? I don't know. They did something ghastly to my hair.' He ran his hand over his head. 'They don't listen to a word I say.'

'It looks nice. Smart.'

'Hm.' He shot a look at her beneath beetling brows. 'You and your leading lady's flannel . . . You're as beautiful as ever. He doesn't deserve you.'

'He doesn't have to deserve anything. I know you find this impossible to believe, but I love him.'

'Incomprehensible, my darling. Last time he came out here he didn't even bring you with him, what good is that?'

'He was taking Marcus back to school.'

'How are those two?'

Isla was careful. 'Growing up, and we all know what that means.'

Alec snorted. 'We all know what it means these days. I remember a time when growing up meant shutting up, putting up, and waiting till it was your turn.'

'Times change,' suggested Isla. 'They're nice boys, in their different ways.'

Alec leaned towards her, creaking slightly. She could smell his lunch, and the stuff they'd put on his hair. 'Their mother's a very silly woman.'

'I like Caroline.'

'You don't have to say anything for my benefit. She's a silly woman and I don't give a flying fart who knows it. There's no one listening.'

'Sorry, but I do like her.'

'The trouble with you, my darling –' began Alec, but was

interrupted by the arrival of a teenage auxiliary with a tea tray.
'Ah, good, what sort of bikkies have we got?'

'Garibaldis,' said the auxiliary.

'I like squashed flies. Just stick it over there and my lady friend
will see that I'm saucered and blown.'

The auxiliary withdrew with the air of one who was going to
tell her colleagues that Alec Wakefield was a rude old sod.

Alec, who had picked up the expression 'saucered and blown'
from a patient decades before, and whose own forebears had, to a
man, sipped Darjeeling with the utmost propriety, consumed his
tea and squashed flies with gusto – blowing, stirring, slurping and
dunking with noisy relish. Isla knew how this habit infuriated
Richard, and refused to betray distate by the merest flicker of
an eyelid.

'More tea?' she asked, when he put his cup down with a rattle
on top of the *Daily Telegraph*.

'I may very well, in a moment. Tell me, are you going to stay
for dinner?'

'I'd like to but I can't. I didn't even tell Richard I was coming.'

'So you need his say so for a day out?'

'No, but he's away at the moment and he likes to ring in the
evening. Still, it's only three-thirty,' she pointed out, 'I needn't
go for another hour.'

'In that case,' Alec's face bulged and reddened as he hauled
himself to his feet, 'I want to show you something.'

'Can I get it?'

'I can manage.'

Isla replaced their cups on the tray and abandoned the stool
in favour of the other armchair. She watched as with painful,
jerky steps Alec went to the chest of drawers, and opened one of
the top drawers. He breathed heavily, with a little 'hoo' sound
as he stirred the contents with a large, slow hand, looking for
what he wanted.

'Here we are . . .' He took out a letter, closed the drawer and
returned with his jerky robot's gait to the chair, collapsing with
an explosive exhalation. 'Must you sit over there?'

'The stool's a bit hard.'

'You're getting old, like me.'

'That's right.'

'Humouring the old bugger. Too polite to argue, aren't you?'

'Yes, unless there's something worth arguing about.' Isla was an expert on not allowing Alec to rile her.

He unfolded the letter. Isla recognised Richard's handwriting, but said nothing. Alec scanned the pages for a moment, blowing thoughtfully.

'He wrote me the funniest letter . . . I didn't know what to make of it. Here –' he tapped the paper – 'what do you make of this? "I've not been feeling too jolly and may have to go in for an op in the forseeable future." Did you know that? No you didn't but then why should you, you're only his wife. At any rate it's of no account, he goes on, let's see, "but not till after my present case is completed, and the prognosis is good – just a little tidying-up to ensure my future wellbeing . . ." blah blah . . . keep the old codger quiet. I was a bloody doctor, I know a classic coronary presentation when I see it!'

Isla was shocked, and it must have showed, for Alec wagged a hand at her. 'Sorry my darling, didn't mean to put the wind up you. You're quite right he shouldn't keep things from you. You want to give him a good bollocking at the first possible opportunity!'

'I don't want to – quite the opposite. I just wish he'd confided in me. Did he think I'd have an attack of the vapours?'

'No, no, it's got nothing to do with you my darling. It's him experiencing the cold draught of mortality. He doesn't want to mention it in case he starts to feel poorly—'

'He has been feeling poorly.'

'There you are then, in that case he probably thinks he'll drop down dead if he speaks the word "operation" out loud.'

Isla could think of nothing else to say in the face of this abrasive dismissal, and more than anything she did not want to weaken in front of Alec, who in spite of all the 'darlings' did not approve of weakening. It was allowed in private but not to be evidenced in any way.

'But that's all by the by,' he went on, turning the page. 'It's when he starts getting all metaphysical on me that I can't make head nor tail . . . For instance . . . yes . . . here we go . . . "I would be interested to know, if you are prepared to tell me, whether you and my mother enjoyed a happy marriage. The reason I write to ask, rather than doing so in person, is because I wish to make it clear what I mean, in a way that were I to ask you to your face you would rubbish as legalistic nit-picking. None of your we-lasted-the-course-didn't-we claptrap, Dad. I want to know if you made each other happy, in every way, and if there were areas in which the answer is no, then why not? What went wrong? And if you never really stopped to consider whether you were happy, what is to be inferred from that? And which of you loved the other more? Because there always is an imbalance, I believe. I dare say you'll regard all this as the apotheosis of impertinence, and you're perfectly entitled to bin the whole thing and never return to it again, but I'm anxious to know. And obviously, at the risk of sounding pompous"' here Alec pulled a grimace as an aside to Isla, '"there are no right or wrong answers to any of these questions. Just answers. I had a contented and secure boyhood and was never in any doubt that you wanted the best for me . . ." There's a bit more in the same vein, what the devil do you think he's on about?'

'He makes it crystal clear,' said Isla. 'But does he say why he wants to know?'

'In a stew about his op, I imagine,' said Alec callously. 'I'll have that other cuppa.'

In her attempt to seem perfectly unruffled, Isla moved with exaggerated care and slowness. She could feel the old man watching her.

'You should be wearing something long and swishy,' he commented. 'Not bloody trousers.'

'Poor Richard.' She handed him his tea, keeping a hold on the saucer for a second until his hand steadied on the other side. 'He's doing so much thinking.'

'I confess I was baffled. It's not like him to get personal. Not like any of us. We didn't go in for it. One takes all that kind of thing as read, surely.'

'Does one?' she asked, genuinely interested.

'Are you being pert with me?'

She couldn't help laughing at his choice of words. 'Alec . . . no.'

'Why at this advanced stage, with me on the home strait and

him in the thick of it, should he want to know how many times a week his mother and I had congress?'

'He doesn't go quite that far.'

'That's what it boils down to. Candidly, I don't know whether to dignify the whole barmy litany with an answer.'

'Of course you must. He's your son. Your only child. How you answer's another matter and none of my business.'

'True.' Alec waggled his fingers for another biscuit and embarked on a fresh bout of dunking and slurping. Over the rim of his cup he rolled his eyes at the letter, now on the arm of the chair. 'Care to look at it yourself?'

Isla was tempted, but also repelled, her fearful curiosity shrivelled by the taboo of reading a private letter intended for someone else.

'No thank you.'

'Liar.'

'It wouldn't be right, I'm not going to, and that's that.'

'You want to know if you're mentioned.' It wasn't a question, and Isla did not answer. Alec smacked his lips. 'You're not.'

Jen drove to Pleasurelands to visit Claudia only to discover that it was easier for a camel to pass through the eye of a needle than for an outsider with no reservation to get past the reception team.

'I'm her mother,' she explained. 'I just popped down to say hello – she said this was the best day.'

'It's changeover day, yes,' said the young woman in a shirt buttoned and tabbed like a white hunter's. 'But I'm afraid you can't come in without a pass.'

'I tell you what,' said Jen, who was feeling slightly queasy and in no mood to be trifled with. 'Why don't you issue me with one?'

'We can do that, possibly. I'll beep your daughter and get her to come over. Take a seat why don't you, she shouldn't be long.' Jen sat down. 'Coffee?'

'No thanks.'

She wouldn't have minded the jobsworth welcome quite so much had she not been late already. She had not got completely lost – visits to the Saxby place had ensured that the route rang certain bells – but she had missed a turning and got embroiled in a lengthy diversion.

After about twenty minutes, during which trolleys loaded with everything from sheets to cartons of milk trundled back and forth, and VDUs flickered and glared behind the desk, Claudia appeared. Jen had not seen her in her uniform before.

'Is this what they make you wear?'

'Mum –' Claudia took her elbow in a grip of steel. 'Don't. This is my mother,' she said to the girl in the important shirt.

'Hello there!' said the girl, flashing a big professional grin as though they'd never encountered one another before.

Jen didn't return the smile. 'We've met.'

'Mum – I've got an hour and a half, what do you want to do?'

'You could show me around. If I park inside somewhere—'

'Cars aren't allowed in the compound. We walk or cycle.'

'Whatever. Although I'd be a bit of a liability on a bike.'

Claudia's expression indicated that she'd be a liability in any case. She steered her to the reception desk.

'I'm going to show my mother round, may she have a visitor's pass?'

A paper disc with a smiling sunny face and the word 'Visitor' was stuck to Jen's T-shirt and they went through a turnstile into the manicured woodland glades beyond. When Jen glanced over her shoulder she saw that this side of the reception area was cunningly camouflaged as a log cabin, so that no hint of administrative reality might intrude upon the happy holidaymakers as they pedalled and strolled between the evenly-spaced trees.

'It's like *The Lion, the Witch and the Wardrobe*,' she remarked.

'I'm not sure I see the similarity.'

'Creepy.'

'Oh, it's creepy all right,' agreed Claudia. 'I'll take you down to the boating lake, there's a fairly bearable café there.'

It was a much longer walk than Jen had anticipated. She was quite light-headed, and the soles of her feet, in well-worn espadrilles, were beginning to blister by the time they got there. On the other hand the exercise, taken at a brisk pace, seemed to have restored Claudia's mood, and she thawed still further over a cheese and mushroom toastie overlooking the gliding boats and scudding ducks of the lake.

'Sorry I was a moody cow.'

'Were you? I didn't notice.'

'They're pigs on that reception, Sub-Disneyland gauleiters.'

'They're only doing their job.'

'Yes, and it says something about the calibre of person who does a job like that.'

Jen tapped her half-finished spanish omelette with her fork. 'This isn't half bad. Sorry I can't do justice to it.'

'No, the grub's quite reasonable. Though the burger bar's to be avoided. Mad cow heaven.'

Jen had to laugh. 'My darling Red, what are you doing here?'

Claudia cracked a dark, sheepish smile. 'Funnily enough I enjoy the bit I do, except for dog-shit fatigues. I'm out on my bike most of the day, not stuck inside, and the poor devils of punters are a good-natured lot on the whole. After all they're here to enjoy themselves, and they've no alternative since they're more or less locked in.'

'And how's the social life?' Jen left Claudia to interpret the question as she would.

'You mean Anthony. He's OK.'

'Seeing much of him?'

'No, because I don't get much time off. But he's asked me to go to Paris with him next month before uni starts.'

'And will you?'

'I doubt it. Too much to do.' Jen tried not to look crestfallen, but failed, because Claudia added: 'If he's that keen he'll ask me again.'

'And you really like him?'

'Yes. I'm slightly surprised to find I do. I really do.'

'How old is he?'

'Forty-two, shock horror.'

'Age isn't important.'

'Good old Mum . . .' Claudia gave Jen an affectionate look over her milk-shake. 'So how's things in your camp?'

'Oh, jogging along . . .' Having come all this way to tell her daughter her plan, she now felt compelled to make light of it, perhaps not mention it at all . . . 'I tried to give Keith his marching orders the other day—'

'Hee-hah!'

'– but I failed miserably.'

'Mum!'

'I gazed into his bright, trusting little eyes and couldn't bring myself to pull the trigger.'

'He's got you on toast.'

'But he brings me in a nice little supplementary income, and is no trouble whatsoever, and even puts himself out to be kind—'

'Mum – it's death by nerd, and you know it. That awful nickname he uses to Richard, to his *face*, for God's sake!'

'He doesn't mean to be insulting.' Now's the moment, she told herself, spit it out. 'Anyway, I'm going to finish with Richard.'

In the pause that followed she thought, how teenagery and arbitrary that sounds. Wonderful, sexy, distinguished Richard, who has been my lover for more than ten years, and I say I'm going to finish with him as though our relationship comprised half a dozen trips to the pictures.

'I'm sorry,' said Claudia.

'It's got to be done.'

'But it's still tough.'

'Yes.'

She was struggling to hold it together, and more relieved than she could say that Claudia did not touch her, or even keep looking at her: mutual embarrassment at its most invaluable.

'What brought this on?' enquired Claudia in a reassuringly commonsense tone.

'A combination of things, too complicated to go into . . . I knew you'd be pleased.'

'That's an awful thing to say, as if I wanted you to be unhappy.'

'But you never liked my arrangement with Richard. I'm not complaining, Red, just stating a fact.'

'I don't like to think of you being used.'

'I never was.'

Claudia frowned with what Jen recognised as an unaccustomed effort at diplomacy. 'Mum – you might not know if you were.'

'Richard isn't like that.' This was too much, Claudia's eyebrows shot up. 'It's true. You don't know him like I do, Red.'

'There is such a thing as knowing someone too well – not being able to see the wood for the trees.'

'No, it's not like that.'

'Mum! For Christ's sake get real! It couldn't be more like that, it's a classic – he has everything, exactly what he wants, with everything neatly compartmentalised, and you – and presumably his poor wretched wife as well – know your places and stay in them! In the nineteen-nineties – it beggars belief.'

Jen lowered her voice, pushing her anger back down her throat. 'I'm important to him.'

'You're not important at all! You're a complete non-bloody-person.'

'That's not true.'

'Not you, I don't mean the real you, I mean this put-upon, obliging bit of stuff that he visits a couple of times a week and who meekly puts up with it. It's not like you, Mum, it's not the you I know.'

'But it *is*!' Jen leaned forward to look into her daughter's face, but Claudia turned away stubbornly. 'It is, this *is* me. I haven't exactly made a resounding success of more conventional relationships, have I? Has it ever occurred to you that this suits me? That I'm not equipped to deal with anything more committed? You may not like it, love, but that's the truth. It's not fair of you to turn your back on the aspects of me that don't suit you. It doesn't do either of us justice, can't you see that?'

Claudia kept her face averted.

'Red?'

There was a small sniff. Claudia put up a hand and swiped away a tear.

'Anyway,' she said. 'You're going to finish with him.'

'Yes.'

'Well – I'm sorry, really sorry, Mum, if it makes you unhappy. But thank God, is all I can say.'

14 ∫

They met at the entrance to the V&A. Jen, concerned that they might be going somewhere smart for lunch, had accordingly worn a skirt for the Dalmatian's photo session, where normally she'd have worn jeans. The skirt was ankle-length Indian cotton in reds and ochres, with a drawstring waist to which were attached a carillon of tiny brass bells. She'd teamed the skirt with a plain cream scoop-necked T-shirt, flat plaited sandals, a chunky coral necklace and brass earrings and bangles. Unfortunately there was no escaping the baggage she had to carry for a morning's dog-watching – camera, folder, satchel. She could never aspire to elegance, but she knew what suited her. And it was one of those days when she knew she looked all right. As she strode rapidly – she was late – along the crowded pavement she sensed that she drew the odd appreciative glance – no traffic-stopper, but a person with her own style.

Isla, wearing lean jeans and a faded chambray shirt with the sleeves rolled up, was standing on the steps of the V&A, talking to a handsome old man whose face Jen recognised. There was a long-handled rush basket over her shoulder.

'Hello,' she said, 'don't you look nice? This is my old mate Percy. Percy, this is the artist Jen Delaney.'

'Madam,' said Percy. 'My pleasure.'

'Hello. Have we met before?'

'You may know him from the telly,' said Isla. 'If you have one.'

'Of course, you're an actor.'

'From time to time,' said Percy, 'the vagaries of public taste permitting, I still justify that title.'

Isla patted his cheek. 'Be off with you, we're going to Alma's.'

Percy gave a little bow. 'That, if I may say so, is no place to take an artist.' He turned to Jen. 'But leave your sensibilities at the door, my dear, and you will have fun.'

Alma's, Isla explained en route, was no more nor less than an old-fashioned drinking club of the sort portrayed in the play *Absolute Hell*. And Alma herself was an old-fashioned drinker.

'In other words a hard one. She started the club just after the war so that she could surround herself with all the theatricals she liked so much without setting foot outside her own front door.'

'She must be a great age.'

'She must, but we don't talk about it.'

Jen thought Alma's quite wonderful. It was really no more than two large basement sitting rooms, one of which contained the bar. The brownish decor was spectacularly, confidently under-maintained in a way that invited complete relaxation. There were sagging sofas, freckled mirrors, fierce plants, hundreds of paintings and photographs, and a piano. A French window gave onto a small paved yard where at this early stage in the day a broom stood against the wall by a small pile of cigarette ends and broken glass.

Alma, as Isla had indicated, one could not have made up – from diamanté hairslide to ebony cigarette holder she was quite perfect. A comely black girl was introduced as 'Rosie, my main squeeze'.

'Sorry,' said Isla, 'but we want to eat. What are you poisoning us with today?'

'Poison no longer,' rasped Alma. 'Rose does the cooking these days. Get to the kitchen, woman, and be about your duties.'

Isla bought a bottle of wine and they sat down in chairs near the French window. There was no one else there. The sweet smell of louche-living permeated the atmosphere.

'I love it here,' said Isla. 'At night you can't get food, it's strictly booze, loose talk and low company. But for lunch it's the most sequestered spot in town.' She glanced invitingly at Jen over her glass. 'The perfect place for a serious exchange of confidences.'

Jen managed to keep the confidences at bay for some time. She had come out today with the intention of behaving in a way that was neither cold nor even slightly frosty, but cool. She had been invited – pressed to come, even – had declined due to pressures of work, and finally caved in under renewed pressure. All of this meant that the onus was surely on Isla to make the running and the conversation. She did not have to say or do anything – she was a guest. That this had not been the original impulse behind the meeting was something she tried to put out of her mind. She would behave like someone in retreat, and there would never be another such invitation.

But the moment she had seen Isla in her frayed and faded denim, Jen was reminded again of exactly why she had given in. She liked Isla – deeply and instinctively – and delighted in her company. It was hard to be cool and withdrawn when so much was forthcoming that was exactly right. The place, the ambience, everything had been chosen to please and amuse her, with an ease of manner that demanded no litany of gratitude, but which said: your being here is enough.

They talked about her work, and moved on from there to pets generally – dogs, and owners, and dogs versus cats. From there, however, she was unable to prevent a progression to families – specifically Isla's stepsons, Richard's former wives, and his father . . . Jen had to keep reminding herself that this was Richard, her Richard, Isla was talking about. She'd heard this cast of characters mentioned before, she supposed, but this woman knew them intimately, and had a stake in their lives, whereas she – well – perhaps it was true, as Claudia had said, that she was a non-person . . . She had to be careful not to chip in with 'But I thought –' or 'Isn't he –'. A little knowledge was, in this situation, a dangerous thing. She wasn't suited to being a passive listener and after a while it got too stressful. Rose's arrival with the food – conch, and fresh fish, cooked with okra and served with dumplings of cornmeal, banana and plantains, sufficient for half a dozen people – created the opportunity for a change of subject.

'My daughter's going out with a man twice her age,' said Jen, digging in. Isla suspected that this particular confidence had been preying on her mind for some time and finally found its moment.

'What's he like?' she asked.

'Nice enough. And loaded. He's landed gentry. A Sir, at any rate.'

'But do you like him? You have met him . . . ?'

'A couple of times. I did his mother's basset. And yes, I did like him. But it's funny to meet a man who is the right sort of age to go out with oneself, and then to discover he's pursuing your student daughter. And this isn't some Tramps-and-Annabel's wolf about town, but a serious, well-bred sort of chap who wears glasses and runs an estate. I don't know . . .'

She sighed and began eating ravenously. Isla helped herself as she considered the scenario. 'Do you think she's in love with him?'

'I couldn't possibly say. She's never been in love as far as I know. Not for want of offers, I might add, and I don't say that as a doting parent. She's a serious knock-out, God knows how that happened . . . But she's never been in the least interested in having a boyfriend. And now this. I only pray he's not some sort of father figure, and that it won't end in tears and be all my fault.'

'Of course it won't be. If it ends, as you seem to think it might, there will be some tears, but there's nothing wrong in that. And why should it be your fault?'

'How long have you got?' said Jen.

'Who is this man, anyway?'

'He's Sir Anthony Saxby. The seat's near Oxford, and very pretty it is too. But I could sooner see Red running for prime minister than presiding over Kersney Court.'

'Actually,' said Isla, 'I've met him. We were on the same table at a dull do and he more or less saved my sanity.'

'But what does he see in her?' persisted Jen. 'I mean of course I *know* what he sees in her, she's twenty-one and six foot, outrageously beautiful and sharp as a tack. But all that aside, what's he after?'

'Maybe she's a lovely, lovable girl,' suggested Isla. 'And different from the sort he usually encounters.'

'Maybe. Probably. But still the whole thing confuses me.'

Isla leaned back, one arm behind her head, the other hand balancing her wine glass on the arm of her threadbare armchair. 'It shouldn't. Simplify, that's the thing. Your daughter sounds wonderful, and she and her aristocrat have got a real love affair going on. Lucky, lucky them . . .' She closed her eyes for a moment and thought of Richard, in conference. Tried to sit inside his head for a moment, and look out on his world with his eyes. To know what it was that would make her, and her alone, indispensable to his life and his heart . . . But couldn't.

'Anyway,' she said at last, 'let me tell you the extraordinary thing that's happened to me.'

To Jen, the most extraordinary thing about it was Richard's reaction.

'I can't believe he was so unconcerned,' she said. 'After all, you'd just told him you have a lover.'

'Someone who's in love with me. Not quite the same thing. But he was almost – not interested.'

Jen lit a cigarette, tried to imagine Richard hearing this news, and found it was quite beyond her. In that exchange he was another person, one she didn't know.

'I'd have thought,' she ventured, 'that any man would find that sort of thing a threat, or repellant, or titillating . . . or perhaps even funny. But not uninteresting.'

'Perhaps that's not the right word. He took it in his stride.'

'Maybe,' said Jen, 'he had other things on his mind.'

'Yes, possibly. He's incredibly busy, and he hasn't been all that well recently, and then there's the boys . . . yes. That's probably it.'

'You could do much worse than be loved by Petronella,' said Jen.

Isla sat up. 'I realise that. And of course I'm only telling you this in the strictest confidence.'

'Telling me what?'

'Thank you.' Isla heard, at the same time as the echo of her own reply to Nell, the cock crowing. So much for the confidence she had promised to respect. Twice already she had breached it.

'I don't like myself very much,' she remarked as matter of factly as she could, trying not to invite sympathy.

'Join the club,' replied Jen, just as evenly.

That, thought Jen, was my cue – and I missed it. But then, if she intended to see neither Isla nor Richard again, what point would there be in delivering herself of the appalling truth? The trouble was she knew, exactly, what the point was – so that in the far distant future Isla, who had been honest with her, would know that her honesty had been reciprocated. And then they might – but no, it wasn't going to happen.

At about three-thirty they left Alma having her temples massaged with essential oils by Rose, and walked back to South Kensington tube, taking their time.

Isla said, 'I have enjoyed this. It was exactly what I needed.'

Jen agreed that it had been lovely.

'So shall we do it again?' Isla didn't need to look at Jen to know that she was fumbling for an excuse, just as she had on the phone. What was the matter, when they got on so well, when they enjoyed each other's company, when they were able to be so frank with one another – when they had the makings of the perfect honest friendship?

The silence was uncomfortable. And when Jen broke it, it was to say:

'I'm absolutely snowed under with work at the moment.'

As soon as she'd said it she realised how affected it sounded – 'snowed under with work', what was she thinking of? It was a phrase which set her teeth on edge even had it been true.

'I know,' said Isla. 'I'm going to be busy when the silly season's over, but we all need time off for good behaviour.'

Now Jen felt even more foolish – this woman was a famous actress, for crying out loud, with more calls on her time than she could possibly lay claim to. A change of tack presented itself and with it, an escape route.

'Have you got something exciting coming up?' Shit, she thought, I sound like the trainee at Hair by Angie.

'Yes, as a matter of fact. Mostly I coast these days on public speaking and commercials, but I've got a telly offer for a very modish quiz show with a tribe of off-the-wall young comics.'

'I'd be scared shitless.'

'I will be. But after all, they're the ones with something to lose, all thrusting and ambitious as they are. I'm there as a sort of national monument. As long as I don't say the f-word or throw up on camera I shall be OK. I don't even have to be funny, just bearable. It will be fun, it will be different – it will be much harder than it looks which is very good for me at my age.'

'I suppose,' said Jen humbly, 'that money doesn't come into it?'

'Yes it does.' Isla was firm. 'We have separate accounts, make no mistake. I was an independent woman for much longer than Richard was a single man. He's three times married, but I had to be dragged kicking and screaming to the altar.' There was a pause, which Isla broke by adding suddenly: 'And what about you?'

'Me?'

Isla laughed. 'Yes, you. You have your beautiful daughter and your independence. But what about love?'

What about it, thought Jen. 'I'm not really looking,' she said. 'In my experience it has to creep up on you or nothing. Seek, and ye shall find absolutely zip.'

'You're so right.' They arrived at the station and stopped, having reached the parting of the ways – Isla was going by cab to Church Street. 'But if I had my wish, someone wonderful would be waiting in the wings for you as we speak. Maybe you should take a fresh look at your lodger . . . ?'

Jen shook her head, covered her eyes. 'I can see I shall have to introduce you.'

'I'd like that.'

Jen realised she had been led into the gentlest of traps. 'Look,' she said, 'for heaven's sake, I didn't mean it.'

Lori was waiting for Isla in the Greek coffee shop next to Lalage's Art Nouveau. She was what men call a pretty woman, and women recognise as a smart operator. This afternoon she wore a bright red suit with a long, tight jacket and flirty pleated skirt, and a red and white scarf tied chicly on the shoulder. On seeing

Isla she rose with a broad smile and leaned across the table to deliver a kiss.

'Great to see you, did you have a nice lunch?'

'We went to Alma's.'

'Say no more. Can I get you a nice glass of Andrews Liver Salts?'

'Turkish coffee please. It was good as a matter of fact. Alma's got a new girlfriend and she cooked Caribbean.'

'My God, I'd better get down there before Alma trades her in. Something sticky with your coffee?'

'No thanks.'

Lori ordered and pulled a rueful face. 'This really isn't right, I should be buying you lunch somewhere memorable.'

'It was my suggestion,' Isla reminded her. 'And besides, we're old friends, we know each other quite well enough to do business over a coffee.'

'That's true,' agreed Lori. 'And that being the case, will you think ill of me if I fall for some baklava?'

Over coffee Lori ran through the TV offer, and produced the draft contract. Isla didn't need persuading but Lori pitched anyway. When the waiter brought over a white rose for Isla, Lori touched the velvety petals admiringly.

'You see,' she said, 'this is it. The whole world loves you. That's why these comics need you on board, they're no different to anyone else, underneath the crap they just want to be loved too.' She leaned forward happily, tapping Isla's saucer with her spoon. 'Let me tell you, you're about to conquer new worlds.'

At the lights at the bottom of Church Street Isla narrowly beat someone to a taxi and discovered, when he importunately jumped in after her and closed the door, that it was Scotch.

'Mind if I join you? My treat.'

'No, no . . .' She couldn't help smiling. The treat, she felt, was all hers. She watched him as he perched on the folding seat opposite. 'Why are you sitting there?'

'More respectful,' he said.

'Are you not safe in taxis?'

'You'd have to ask other people. But there is something intimate about a London cab.'

'Come on.' She patted the seat next to her. 'Don't be silly.'

In the short period before he got out at Queensway (and as good as his word about paying) Isla discovered that the intimacy of a cab depended on with whom you were sharing it. Scotch kept his eyes on her in a way which made her feel she might be blushing.

'What do Nell's parents say about me?' he asked.

'They think you're on the make.'

'I am, generally speaking, but not with Nell. She's not interested anyway. We gave it a whirl, the merest *boffe de politesse*, but that was it and all about it.'

'And Ned?'

'What about him?'

'That's for you to say.'

Scotch reached across and tapped on the glass. 'My stop.' As the cab drew up he opened the door and looked over his shoulder at Isla. 'What you don't understand about me,' he said, 'is that I'm terribly wholehearted.' He got out, and paid. Then leaned back in, took her hand, kissed it.

'And,' he added. 'Terribly, terribly patient.'

Knowing she was being craven, Jen went into the tube station and hovered for a moment by the flower stall. After a decent interval she verified that Isla had gone before leaving through the far exit, and walking up Exhibition Road towards the park. She wanted quieter vistas, the grass and the water. She was tired, and beginning to regret the mountain of rich food and half bottle of wine she'd put away at Alma's.

Inside the park she found a bench and sat for fifteen minutes, almost dozing off in the afternoon sun. Only pre-programmed avoidance of the rush hour prodded her into action again and she got up and headed northward.

The Serpentine Gallery was currently showing the work of Forbes Batson, an angry old man of the new wave. Jen had seen him on television. He wore a shabby suit and an air of venomous, born-again iconoclasm that could have outgunned a man half his age. It had been in all the papers that one of the installations in the exhibition featured Batson himself. She went in.

A trickle of people were stopping, starting, staring, in silence. The works on view were massive iron and concrete structures uncompromisingly labelled in letters and numbers – like cars, thought Jen. Or prisoners.

She found them impressive but unsympathetic. In the corner was the one containing the artist. It faced away from the rest of the exhibition so that you were obliged to occupy the relatively narrow space between the installation and the outer wall.

It was a huge spherical stone shell, whorled like a snail or an ammonite, about eight feet in diameter. In the centre was a cavity less than half this size in which sat Forbes Batson, in what looked like the same tatty suit he always wore, his back against one curving wall, his bare feet pressed against the other. His arms were folded, his eyes closed, but Jen had rarely seen someone more alert. In fact, she had the unsettling impression that it was she who was being watched by this bizarre, elderly foetus, rather than the other way round.

She glanced at the label. 'U2', it said.

At Marble Arch she went into Boots. Her purchase carried a slight embarrassment factor and she picked up some deodorant and toothpaste to dull its impact on the till-assistant, who couldn't have cared less. One person's intimate secret was another person's product. Or so Jen told herself as, with face on fire, she ran down the steps to the tube.

Richard wondered what Isla had made of the postcard from Fiesole. Donatella was naughty to write the sort of thing that was calculated to irritate . . . He was a little surprised to find his wife out. Standing in the library he glanced up at the portrait of her grandfather . . . No matter how much two people had in common in their adulthood there was a vast twilit hinterland stretching away behind each of them, leading to God knows what howling wilderness. He scarcely knew two generations back of his own family, let alone hers. It was unnerving. In any individual there might be lurking a rogue gene which could create havoc in an instant . . .

He poured himself a mineral water, put on John Williams, and went upstairs to change, with the tumbling chords rippling all round like water over stones. He was making an effort, and Jim Furmston's grim prognostications notwithstanding, he believed he felt a little better for it. Maybe it was only the cool, clean taste of virtue, but whatever the cause his waistband felt easier, his step lighter, and his head clearer than they had in ages. Perhaps Jim had been trying to put the wind up him – but no, a medico of Jim's standing was hardly likely to recommend an operation simply to play games. Still, it was hard to maintain the necessary sense of urgency when he felt so much better. And with his physical improvement there was an accompanying lift in his spirits. He slightly regretted having written that letter to his father. At the time the need to find out, to communicate, was strong upon him, but he had always been the first to advise his clients to say, do, or write nothing in the heat of the moment, and he had gone against his own advice. The fact that Alec had not replied indicated the extent of the old boy's embarrassment. God knows what might be going through his mind.

The phone rang. It was Caroline, in exuberant form.

'I had a wonderful holiday – we didn't actually find anything, but the people were all absolutely super, and the weather was perfect, and of course staying at the school was pretty much like staying in a top hotel – heated pool, gym, tennis, magnificent grounds, but for a fraction of the price!'

'I'm so glad.'

'And the chap in charge was a genius, an absolute genius – Daniel Hetherington, have you heard of him?'

'No, but that doesn't mean anything.'

'He's one of the top men in the field, but like all top people completely approachable, no side whatsoever. He spent literally hours one evening in the bar just talking about his work, giving away all his trade secrets . . . I haven't enjoyed myself so much in ages.'

'That's terrific. How's Marcus, by the way?'

'Oh, fine. I wasn't too chuffed about him packing in the job, but now to be honest I'm rather glad. It's nice having him around . . .' She dropped her voice to an intense whisper. 'He seems to be changing, for the better . . . stringing whole sentences together, that kind of thing . . . I do hope it's not a false dawn.'

'I'm sure it's not,' said Richard. 'Isla's always maintained he had the right stuff.' At once he could have bitten his tongue off.

'And so have I, always, so have I.' Caroline was predictably quick to rise. 'It's just that you long for the day it finally shines through.'

'What about Giles? We had a postcard.'

'Giles is back, and gone again, looking ghastly beneath his tan. He and the Beales boy have got themselves into a horrible flat in Earls Court.'

'Paid for how? Even horrible flats cost.'

'Don't worry, they're working in a wine bar while they build up what they call their client base for the party thing.'

'I see. What's the name of the wine bar, do we know?'

'Yes, and to my eternal shame I've already checked up on it. It's The Trellis in Ancaster Grove. They're not waiters or barmen or anything like that. They're the lowest form of kitchen life.'

'The perfect milieu in which to build up a client base . . .'

Caroline gave a tooting giggle. 'I should so love to be a fly on the wall, wouldn't you?'

On replacing the phone, Richard looked up once more at the general.

'Well sir. I think I shall take your granddaughter somewhere disgracefully swanky for dinner tonight.'

Isla hadn't wanted to go out. Having him home was enough for her. Over dinner, she realised that for the first time in weeks she and Richard were both completely happy – happy in small ways, about what they'd been doing and who they'd seen, and even the weather, but truly happy nonetheless. She felt ridiculously elated. Was this all it took to make the future rosy – lunch with a new friend, the promise of work, relaxed conversation? She hadn't mentioned the letter that Alec had shown her, and she knew now that she would not, at least for the time being – why spoil a good thing?

'Let's go away for Christmas,' she said. 'Let's fly to the sun.'

'You always said you liked a log-fire-and-pine-needles Christmas.'

'I do, but change is good. We mustn't get stuck in a rut.'

'As we get older, you mean?'

'We just mustn't.'

'So what'll it be – St Lucia?'

'Something like that. Perhaps more remote. The Maldives – we'll go native.'

Richard pushed his chair back and rose, slowly. He dropped his napkin on the table. She thought he was going to make coffee until he walked to her chair and stood behind her, his hands on her shoulders. She put her right hand up to his, and waited.

He said: 'It must be all this talk of sun, sea and sand . . .'

She lifted his hand, held the palm close against her face. 'And going native.'

Afterwards, as he went downstairs to fetch their unfinished bottle of wine – their first in a week under the new regime – Isla dared to think: this is almost perfect. Evening sunshine made the treetops in the garden glow, but the bedroom was bathed in a soft, reflective light. It was the end of August now, the end of those sticky, becalmed days, and the beginning of a new season. Turn, turn, turn . . . A quiet assurance claimed her. It was impossible, at this moment, to recapture the exact nature of the troubled uncertainty of the past few weeks but, like reputation, it was something whose impact on her life she only fully recognised now that it seemed to be receding.

Richard came back and sat down on her side of the bed to pour wine. When he'd given her her glass he didn't immediately pick up his, but put out a hand and stroked the hair back off her face.

'I love you, my darling.'

She smiled. 'I know.'

'Do you?'

'Of course.'

He leaned forward to kiss her. He'd lost some weight recently but he was still bulky enough to disturb the mattress, and she held her wine out to one side to prevent it from spilling.

'I don't tell you often enough, do I?'

'Once is enough.'

'But I want you to know I mean it. And I want you to believe me.'

'Richard . . . !' She began to laugh, but his face was anxious:

she was reminded of the letter and stifled the laugh. 'Richard, I do believe you. And it's the most important thing in the world to me.'

He gave a sigh of relief, and raised his glass in a toast. 'That's that, then. Here's to happiness. And Christmas in the sun.'

For Jen, there was a certain pace, a rhythm, to the long, hot journey back, a rhythm dictated by what she would do when she got home. She would close the front door, remove her sandals, drink a pint of cold Evian water as the cats wove silkily around her bare ankles . . . and then lie down on the sofa, with the curtains half-drawn and the windows open on to the street and try, for a mere fifteen minutes, not to think. She would meditate on nothing. She would remain still. She would simplify.

And to begin with it looked as though she would succeed. The cats materialised by the front door to welcome her with their 'Me, me, me!' and the house was quiet. Keith – recently returned from ten days under canvas on the shores of Lake Coniston with a group of friends from the Accordian Club – was at a staff meeting, and she expected no visitors.

But when she went into the kitchen she saw them – Claudia, Anthony Saxby and Keith, sitting in the back garden. She took a quick step back, but not quick enough.

'There she is.'

'Mum –!'

Claudia appeared at the back door. 'Mum?'

'Red – how lovely.' They embraced.

'Sorry to surprise you, it's my evening off so Ant suggested we come up and say hi. We did actually ring on the mobile, but you were out.'

Ant? thought Jen. *Ant?* 'Yes, I had a job and a lunch down in Kensington.'

Claudia tilted her head quizzically. 'Are you OK?'

'Fine.'

'Come on and join us then, we made a jug of Pimms.'

She followed Claudia out into the garden. Anthony and Keith were deep in conversation, but Anthony got to his feet as she appeared.

'I do hope this is all right,' he said pleasantly. 'There are few things worse than being wrong-footed in your own home. Especially after a long, hot day in town.'

And what would he know about that, thought Jen, demurring, but a tad frostily. She accepted a Pimms and sat down.

'I thought you had a meeting,' she said to Keith.

'I do, but not until eight.'

'Keith's been talking about the Lakes,' said Claudia, 'and we've decided we've got to go there for a weekend.'

'I was dragged up various fells and escarpments in torrential rain as a child,' remarked Anthony, 'but I don't remember much and those memories I do have are rather negative. Sheep, blisters, hardboiled eggs, wet wool . . . It'd be nice to rediscover the area – see it in a new light. Have you ever been?'

'Years ago.'

'Not with me,' put in Claudia.

'No.' Jen was disinclined to elaborate on the long weekend she'd spent with Mo, wrangling pointlessly about a relationship they'd both known was on the rocks . . .

'Can you blame her?' joshed Keith. To Jen's amazement something like a smile flickered on Claudia's face. It was clear that agendas were changing faster than was in her power to assimilate.

Anthony laughed agreeably. If this strange little gathering was anything to go by he was certainly the Fitters-in Fitter-in. A quality, she reminded herself, supposed to be characteristic of the aristocracy. 'I wondered,' he said, 'since we've turned up out of the blue like this whether we could compensate by inviting you out for something to eat . . . ?'

'Oh, I don't think . . . It's kind of you but it's been a long day—'

'Mum,' said Claudia. 'Supper? Somewhere local? Come on.'

'You tell her,' agreed Keith. 'She should get out more.'

'Right,' said Claudia.

Suddenly, Jen thought she might be going to cry. She pressed her lips together and hoped that no one would demand a response. Help came from an unlikely quarter.

'No, no, I'm with your mother,' said Anthony. 'I'd feel just the same in her shoes.' He smiled briefly, understandingly at Jen. 'There's always another time.'

'Yes,' she said, hot with gratitude. 'There is, and I'd like that.'

With easy politeness Anthony turned to Keith. 'I don't suppose you've got time to keep us company over a curry . . . ?'

Jen stared at him. A lot, as far as she was concerned, was riding on his answer. He couldn't, surely? He *wouldn't*, would he . . . ? Her stare became a glare.

But Keith rose to his feet, dusting the seat of his trousers fussily. 'No, no, no, thanks a million but I mustn't. Someone's got to have something thought through to say on the new guidelines, and no prizes for guessing who that will be. But thanks for asking just the same.'

Jen exhaled with relief. Even stranger than the realisation that there was a God was that Keith did possess some rudimentary social sensibilities. And thinking this reminded Jen that she'd been rather less than civil herself, when even the Pimms she was drinking wasn't hers.

'I do apologise,' she said, 'if I was brusque when I arrived. It's been a long day, but it *is* lovely to see you.'

'Says she,' said Claudia, with a touchy smile.

'No really, Red.'

Anthony dropped his eyes for a moment in discreet acknowledgement of this small mother/daughter thing. When he lifted them again it was to remark, with an equally discreetly lowered voice:

'You're fortunate with your lodger. He seems a nice sort of bloke.' At this, Claudia fell back on to the grass with her arms over her face. 'Did I say something?' Claudia, shaking with laughter, shook her head.

'He is,' said Jen. 'And you're right, I'm extremely lucky.'

'Mama and I used to do country house weekends, not so much now unless it's for shooting, and the live-ins don't baulk. But you wouldn't believe the assortment of chancers, bores and shites, pardon my French, that one gets on those. And there's no escape because they're paying top dollar. Two and a half days is the absolute limit of one's tolerance. And the disgusting habits beggar belief.'

Claudia leaned up on her elbow. 'Tell Mum,' she said, 'what you told me.'

'I don't think she'd want to hear.'

'Take it from me, she would.'

Jen, the Pimms taking effect, spread her hands amenably. 'What can I say?'

'It's not all that startling really . . . but we have found some rather strange things left behind in the bedrooms. Sex aids and so on. I think people imagine anything goes in a stately home.'

'Tell her about the briefcase.'

'I honestly think—'

'No, do,' said Jen.

'Well, ah,' began Anthony, 'we had this couple from Belgium on one occasion, they seemed absolutely charming and the last word in respectability, he was a dentist and she was a solicitor. Delightful people too, never put a foot wrong, appreciative, civil, we kept telling ourselves that if all our guests were half as nice our job would be a doddle. But after they'd left we found that this chap had left a briefcase behind. We rang his Brussels address, but no joy, and in the end, in some trepidation, we opened it to see if there was some other address or number where we could contact him . . . The whole thing was stuffed full of lurid photographs – of him, of her, of both of them together, and all in our tapestry room which is the most beautiful in the house. It was something of a facer, as you may imagine.'

'I can believe it!' said Jen.

Claudia gripped Anthony's hand. It was the moment Jen knew they had slept together. 'Don't forget the punch line!'

'What the photographs made clear,' said Anthony in his cool, patrician way, 'apart from the fact that they enjoyed a robust private life, was that she was a he.'

Jen shrieked. 'And you had no idea? No idea at all?'

'Not an inkling.'

Claudia hugged herself. 'Wonderful, isn't it? Think of Ant and his Mama sitting there of an evening in all their highly-polished splendour, talking of cabbages and kings and all the time those two . . . I love it, I just love it!'

'She loves it,' said Anthony modestly.

'And did they ever claim the briefcase?' asked Jen.

'Oddly enough, yes, and in person. Or at least he did. And

without a scrap of embarrassment – but then I suppose he didn't know we'd opened it.'

'We, yes – what about your mother?'

'She took it in her stride,' said Anthony. 'She's extremely broad-minded, as the very ancient often are. There's not much puts her off her stroke provided it doesn't scare the domestics.' He got up. 'And now we must clear off and leave you to some well-earned peace and quiet.'

'Steady on,' said Claudia, 'I live here, remember? I'll say when it's time to go.'

'You're right, how rude of me.' He meant it. He's the genuine article, she thought. A proper gent. No wonder she loves him.

'Only joking.' Claudia scrambled to her feet. She was wearing long, crumpled khaki shorts and a black cheescloth shirt, now covered in bits of grass. 'Cheers Mum, don't get up.'

'Of course I'll get up. But give us a hand.'

Claudia yanked her to her feet and she went with them into the hall and opened the door. Now, of course, she saw the Land-Rover parked opposite – an outsider in this street of clapped-out saloons, as rugged and soiled as the Jag was sleek and spotless.

Anthony followed her gaze. Said: 'I do have a car more suited to driving young ladies into town, but this was an unplanned jaunt, so we're in our sliggins and sloggins.' He held out his hand. 'It was very nice to meet you again. And next time you must let us buy you dinner.'

'I'd like that. Have fun. Drive carefully.'

She stood in the doorway, watching them cross the road as though they were a couple of teenagers. Claudia cavorted around him with her long strides, galloping alongside and walking backwards in front of him, a picture of animal happiness. Jen caught the words:

'. . . she's going to need to be broad-minded when I'm the lady of the manor, because I'm going to run the place as a . . .'

Jen closed the door without catching what Claudia planned to do. Things were moving too fast.

It was too late now for the cool water, the drawn curtains and the meditation. The moment had passed. She could just hear Phil Collins helping Keith to formulate his notes on the new government guidelines. Unusually she found the muted warbling a comfort. She had wanted the house to be empty – now she was glad she was not alone.

She carried her bag into the sitting room, leaving the door open, and took out the Boots carrier containing the pregnancy-tester.

Once, these little bottles had been a regular part of her life. Now it was years since she'd held one in her hand. Since coming off the pill three years ago she'd kept condoms in the house, and Richard had been conscientious. But they weren't teenagers, it seemed so unlikely, there was always the odd occasion . . . You were never too old to be careless. As she stared at the label, then unfolded the sheet of instructions, minutely printed in several languages, the enormity of it all rolled down over her like an avalanche.

The door upstairs opened and Keith's footsteps went across to the bathroom. Breathing rapidly, she thrust bottle, box and instruction sheet back into her handbag.

'*Oh, think twice,*' sang Collins, '*It's another day for you and me in paradise . . .*'

Jen was sweating. Fool's paradise, she thought.

15 ∫

Was there any feeling, Richard asked himself, as he shook hands outside Court Number 12 with the author and the author's family, like that of having won? It wasn't better than sex, because it wasn't comparable. A smooth victory in court was not about the loss of control, but the exercising of it. Competence, experience, judgement, and professional confidence met in a fine point, so that with a steady hand and a delicate touch you could tease out the perfect result.

This might have been a messy case, dealing as it did with a sibling rivalry which had festered for decades. But thanks to the conduct of counsel on both sides feelings had not been allowed to cloud the issue. The case had been as elegantly dramatic as a bullfight, a passage of arms in which pain and rage had been subsumed in the precise intellectual ballet of the process itself. Even Charles Spall for the defence was on a high – when his eyes met Richard's the expression of worldlywise regret, assumed for his client's benefit, was lit for a split second by a glint of pure exhilaration.

And the best of it was, thought Richard as he basked in the gratitude, no lives would be ruined because of it. His client had been awarded costs, which his brother was well able to pay, but damages of only £1,000 – not enough to disgrace the loser, or to prevent normal family relations being resumed in due course. Richard did not delude himself – his arguments had swayed the jury because his client was the better man, but the other side could leave with their heads high, believing whatever it comforted them to believe.

Archie was red in the face with pleasure. When they finally

left the author and his supporters, and were on their way to the robing room, he asked: 'Drink, Richard? We must celebrate.'

'I'll pass, thanks.'

'Come on, you must. It's a famous victory.'

'I don't know about that. But an extremely pleasing one.'

'Damn right! You were in top form, played an absolute blinder.'

Richard smiled. It was true. 'We had right on our side. Which doesn't hurt.'

'Well,' said Archie, 'you talk about angels, but you were the very devil in there. It was a pleasure to watch you work, eh Dilip?'

'It was,' Dilip agreed. 'It will be in all the papers.'

'You betcher it will!' Archie was irrepressible. 'Dilip, you'll come for a celebratory snort, won't you?'

'I'd like to.'

'Good!' Archie turned to Richard. 'Come on, won't you reconsider?'

'The very last thing I want is to cast a blight,' said Richard, 'I'm as pleased as the next man about the way things have gone. But I'm going to go home.'

'Yes, yes . . .' Archie opened the door of the robing room and stood aside for Richard. 'Can't argue with that. Not only is this man head and shoulders above the rest of us,' he said to Dilip as they went in together, 'but he has the most enchanting wife in England.'

Isla's voice was on the answering machine.

'Congratulations, darling! I rang chambers and Terry gave me the news. Not that I didn't know you'd do it all along. And I'm glad you did, because I think you had the good guy. Look, I'm at Television Centre with Lori, surrounded by unbelievably clever people aged about fourteen. It's fun but a bit chaotic, and now the wine's come out and we're running late. *So* sorry not to be there, I've got a driver outside and the minute we're done we'll head home at speed. See you then. Bye . . . Bye.'

Richard reached Selwyn Street in the late afternoon. Cain and Abel were sitting in the living room window like Staffordshire pots, more perfectly, contentedly feline than any real cats deserved to be. He even managed a small surge of affection for them. Cats after all, and these two in particular, were the very model of faithless constancy. They knew neither love nor loyalty, but they were always there.

He left his jacket and tie in the car, locked it, and walked over to the house. The cats, biding their time, betrayed not a flicker of interest. He let himself in and stood for a moment with his hand on the door.

'Jen?'

There was no reply, and no sound from upstairs. Cautiously he went as far as the kitchen door and looked across the kitchen and into the garden: no one there. The place was a little tidier than usual, he suspected Keith's intervention. It was mid-September, the state schools had been back for some time. Keith would be full of the vim and vigour of a new academic year.

Well, to hell with it. He took the bottle of scotch from the cupboard and poured himself a generous shot, topping it up with tap water. When he turned round the cats had come into the kitchen and were posing, tails raised, on either side of the door. With a drink in his hand, Richard's brief change of heart did not extend to opening tins of cat food.

'Sorry chums,' he said. 'I'm not the man you want.'

Their indifference was ineffable. Their only movement as he passed between them was a fastidious flinch of their coats, as if to avoid contamination.

In the living room he sat down in the armchair facing the window, and breathed in the familiar scent. With the conclusion of the case he felt he had proved something to himself. He was as good as they said. He could still cut the mustard. Both physically and mentally he'd held up well – *more* than held up. He felt a great surge of positive health and energy. If he and Isla were going to have a palm-fringed, rum-and-coconut Christmas it would be amusing to go somewhere quintessentially English for their October weekend – Sheringham, perhaps, or the Dales. And before that he'd humour Jim Furmston, go and see the head honcho, get things moving there. He could tell Isla about it when they were away, and with a bit of luck get the job done between then and Christmas. There was nothing now in the pipeline at chambers that Archie couldn't handle, and he'd be able to cruise into the new year a new man.

He ran his wrist over his forehead, then undid his cuffs and rolled up his sleeves. The heat was terrific. The country was crawling through a punishing Indian summer. But that was all right. Loosening his collar, Richard returned to the kitchen to look for ice. He was happy to be alive.

Jen was photographing a parrot in Muswell Hill. At least, she would have called it a parrot, but the owners, a retired couple in their early seventies in an immaculate mansion-block flat, were keen to impress upon her that Chipper was a sulphur-crested cockatoo.

'You mustn't get him wrong,' said the wife, Mrs Hastings. 'He'll be insulted.'

'And we wouldn't want to be responsible for his actions then!' Mr Hastings added.

'Why?' asked Jen, genuinely interested. 'What would he do?'

'Nothing really my love.' Mrs Hastings patted her arm. 'He's teasing you. But they're very intelligent animals. And they see life. We've had him twenty years, but he was at least that age when we got him. Think what he's seen in his time.'

'And heard,' said her husband. 'Heard's the thing.'

'He's extremely handsome,' said Jen as she packed up her stuff. 'And he'll be my first bird.'

By the lifts, Mrs Hastings addressed Jen with careful, near-silent enunciation – the flat door was open.

'When do you think you might finish?'

'I don't know . . . two or three weeks.'

'Only –' she drew Jen closer – 'he hasn't got long.'

'Oh I'm sorry. So you want this as a memento.'

'No. Doug. My husband. A few months, he's been told.'

'No – oh dear.' Jen was overcome with remorse and a terrible compulsion to laugh hysterically. 'That's awful.'

'He worships Chipper. Taught him the Chinese Alphabet, do you know it?'

'No.'

'It's a bit of nonsense, but Doug's got him perfect. He worships him.'

'I'll be as quick as I can,' Jen promised.

Down in the road she put her things in the boot of the car and locked it. Something made her look up and there were Mr and Mrs Hastings standing framed in their living-room window, waving to her. She waved back energetically, and then felt ridiculously embarrassed about walking away from the car as she'd planned to do, so unlocked it again, climbed in and drove round the corner.

She was only intending to go to the small supermarket she'd seen on the way, and of course now she was in the car there was nowhere to park. She wound up leaving it twice as far from the shop as it had been originally. It was a fiercely hot afternoon, and she felt limp and exhausted. She remembered this: low blood sugar. She was going to buy a large chocolate bar – something with peanuts – and eat the lot in one sitting.

Back behind the wheel she unpeeled the chocolate and bit into it in the sort of ecstasy only available to a person on their own and not being watched. Munching gluttonously, she thought about Mr Hastings and his beloved Chipper. The expression sick as a parrot crossed her mind. She herself didn't care for birds, the something reptilian about the flat black eyes and the grey scaly legs. But she would do a good job on this one. And by the time she finished, she would have reached her decision and done what needed doing. She had life, she told herself grimly, an embarrassment of it at present. Life she could do. Whereas that old man was staring death in the face with pressed shirt, polished shoes and neatly-parted hair. Chipper's portrait would be done in time as a matter of honour.

Richard wondered how long to wait. After the adrenalin high of the last few days the pressure was beginning to catch up with him and the whisky, after a period of relative abstinence, had made him rather muzzy. He wasn't sure now that it had been such a good idea coming over to Selwyn Street. He'd been disappointed to find Isla not at home, and had wanted to share his victory with someone. Now he was stuck here, on his own, confronting a drive home in heavy traffic in the stifling heat. It was actually quite uncomfortable. He was fond of this house but in these temperatures it was claustrophobic. In Hampstead, the sheer size of the rooms, the lofty ceilings and the spacious tiled hall kept the place cool. Even the garden afforded great pools of deep green shade . . . He massaged his temples fretfully. Here, with the front of the house practically nudging its backbone there seemed to be no area into which the sun wasn't pouring mercilessly, and the garden was a parched rectangle, the bumpy, yellowish lawn so dried out that it was already showing cracks.

He wished, too, that he hadn't had the whisky. He'd been pumping quite enough adrenalin without adding alcohol to the mix, and it had given him a headache. It was time to go. In the kitchen, washing his glass – he didn't want to advertise his abortive visit to the returning Keith – he actually felt unwell. Perhaps it would be sensible to leave the Jag and get a taxi home. But then there was the problem of collecting it. For the first time he experienced the flutterings of anxiety about how things were to be managed.

He was in the hall when the floor rose up at him, with a sickening rush, as though to bite his face off. There was a boom in his head, no pain, but a shock that eddied through him. Nauseous and disorientated, his vision blurred, he realised he was lying on his side. One arm was flung out in front of him. He could see the familiar hand with its signet ring and the trace of some childhood scar the cause of which was lost to history . . . but it seemed detached from him. He thought he might be bleeding and tried to drag the hand towards his head, but couldn't. His other arm was trapped beneath him. He was icy cold. There was a bitter smell and he realised he'd brought up a small amount of vomit, its grainy wetness was beneath his cheek. His eyesight seemed to be going, there was a dark halo around his field of vision. The white telephone, on the floor about two metres in front of him, gleamed in this strange chiaroscuro like the object of some doomed, mythic quest.

He had never been more helpless, nor more terrified. When he tried to make a sound he could hear something inside his head, a vibration that rattled round like distant thunder, but no sound emerged. Tears trickled sideways across his face, over the bridge of his nose, his cheekbone, his temple to join the mess on the floor.

In the eternity that was the next five minutes his consciousness shrank to a wavering pinprick, his senses shut down softly, one by one.

By the time the front door was opened, and the phone picked up, he no longer knew where he was nor who was with him: and nor, *in extremis*, did he care.

When Isla got back she was not entirely surprised to find that the Jag wasn't in the drive. Richard would probably be celebrating with the team. She, too, was on a high – her afternoon had been the greatest fun and she positively hummed with pleasurable anticipation at the prospect of the recordings. The exact nature of her role in the mix was something to which she gave considerable thought. She had at all costs to avoid looking like a middle-aged woman bowled over, and exploited, by all this sharp new talent. At the same time to be too competitive would be to risk appearing shrill. Poised, calm, centred, and yet on the ball was what she must aspire to, and of course to look appropriate – which meant, in this case, unimpeachably elegant. Her finely-tuned antennae told her that even the smallest attempt at off-the-wall modernity would be death, and that her colleagues, fans though they professed themselves to be, wouldn't hesitate to mock her mercilessly on air if she made mistakes. Ned, talking about his agent's failure to get him film roles would refer glumly to his inability to 'play with the big boys' – Isla now saw that playing with the small boys was equally dangerous.

She went into the library, and made, as always a brief invisible salaam to her grandfather. Before picking up the phone she saw that two messages were registered, one of them, as she knew, her own.

'Alison?'

'Isla! Thank God you rang, you've prevented me from attacking my eldest with a wok.'

'Oh dear . . .' Isla laughed. 'What's she done now?'

'Don't ask, I don't want to give it another moment's thought. How are you?'

'Terribly cheerful. I rang to say great news about the case – Richard's not back yet, and I needed to go "whoopee!" with someone.'

Alison made a sound of irritable dismay. 'Do you know I didn't even know? You shame me.'

'No, no, I had my reasons. Richard's been a bit low so I especially wanted this one to go right for him. I rang chambers while I was still in town.'

'That would explain why Archie's so late,' said Alison, 'they must be carousing together. So much for – hang on, here he is—'

Alison half-covered the mouthpiece and Isla heard a door bang and a muffled exchange before Alison returned in full force.

'– would you like a word with the returning hero?'

'Yes please.'

'Isla, hello.'

'Archie – well done. I'm so pleased. Is himself absolutely cock-a-hoop?'

'Quietly satisfied was more the sort of thing, and with some justification. He was in dazzling form.'

'He has a great team behind him, Archie, we all know it. Anyway, I imagine if you're back he can't be far behind so I'd better look out a bottle of something jolly.'

'No,' said Archie, 'actually he wasn't with us.'

'Not?' Isla was baffled. 'Where did he go?'

'Home, he said. He specifically said he wanted to get back to you. I told Dilip it wasn't surprising –' Alison made some mock-aggrieved protestation or other in the background – 'anyway, he left and we went to do a bit of damage at the Waterford.'

'I see.'

There was a silence, which Isla was too preoccupied and Archie too awkward to fill. Alison spoke in the background, and Archie said: 'It looks as if everyone's just missed everyone else.'

'Yes, it does, although I don't know why he should . . .'

'Let me.' Alison came on. 'He reacted like you, didn't he, and went to find someone to clink glasses with.'

'Yes,' said Isla, 'I suppose he must have done.'

When she'd put the phone down she stood still for a moment, letting her mind quieten. Her mood had travelled on a queasy switchback from exhilaration to trepidation and, she told herself, neither was appropriate. Life was not heaven or hell – it was

life. She glanced upward. The general's granddaughter. Brave
and calm.

She pressed the button on the answering machine and listened
to her own voice. Then the next beep. Then the voice of a strange
man, beginning to speak while '*Frère Jaques*' was still playing.

'Hello – hello? My name's Keith Burgess. This is a message for
whoever is there, concerning Richard Wakefield. I got back to
find he'd had a fall and was unconscious. He seems very poorly.
I've called an ambulance and we should be at the Royal Free very
soon after this. The time's five fifty-five. So we'll be at the Royal
Free – ambulance is here. Bye.'

The recorded voice said: 'That was your last message'. The tape
whirred, bleeped, whirred, bleeped again and restored the status
quo. The red nought stared up at Isla.

She leaned slightly forward on the edge of the desk. A wave
of panic reared up, fanned her, made her face cold, but she
got a grip. A fall was a fall. It happened. She must get to the
hospital.

When she was in the car and driving down the hill the
questions started to hit her like dive-bombing birds. Who was
Keith Burgess? And what had he meant by 'I came back' –
back where? What was his connection with Richard? His voice
– classless, a little prissy – was not one at whose provenance,
as it might affect her husband, she could begin to guess. And
what in God's name did he mean by 'very poorly'? To Isla that
indicated a bad cold, or a childhood complaint like chickenpox,
but clearly it meant more than that here.

Her mind was in turmoil, and her heart thundering, but she
drove with particular care and precision. Time seemed to roll
back, and she recreated the separate, single person she had been
before she became a part of Richard. That person had been pliant
and adaptable, but in control. Things did not happen to the Isla
of old – she made them happen, or she allowed them to. That
was how she wanted it to be when she arrived at Richard's
bedside.

She would not let the bad thing happen.

The note, on a piece of Keith's distinctive squared, light blue
paper, was Sellotaped to the newel post at the foot of the stairs.

It was written in capitals in thick black marker pen, so Jen could read it the moment she opened the door.

RICHARD COLLAPSED. CALLED AMBULANCE AND GONE WITH HIM. WE'LL BE AT THE ROYAL FREE. KEITH.

She didn't stop to think, but turned and went straight back out, almost crushing the startled cats as she slammed the door behind her.

She'd got as far as Bishop's Avenue when full awareness struck, and she pulled up at the side of the road. Her heart was pounding and she was shaking. She cudgelled her brain to try and find a clear path through her confusion. Should she go? Was Isla likely to be there? She couldn't remember if the note had mentioned another call, and cursed herself for not bringing it with her. Knowing Keith he would be systematic, go through all the necessary procedures in the correct order, and do what needed doing. His concern, quite properly, would be for Richard, and information – she could almost hear him saying it – would be on a need-to-know basis. There was no doubt she had needed to know. But now that she did, what was the right thing to do?

Gripping the top of the steering wheel, she banged her forehead down on to her clasped hands. The horn blared, and the shock made her eyes prickle with tears. Get a grip, she thought. Simplify.

What's the worst that can happen?

Isla found a parking space on her second circuit of the one-way system. She'd allowed herself five minutes to park legally before resigning herself to the possibility of being clamped. Her coolness was a learned skill, one she had never been so grateful for. As she stepped out of the car, a young woman with a toddler in a buggy approached her.

'Excuse me, are you Isla Munro?'

'That's right.'

'You must get sick of this, but I'm such a fan –' she held out an open dog-eared diary and a biro – 'would you mind?'

'Of course not.'

'My name's Wendy.'

Isla wrote *Good luck Wendy, with love from Isla Munro*. 'Will that do?'

'Bless you,' said Wendy. 'Good luck yourself.'

In the hospital foyer there was a drunk at the reception desk. Isla stood, breathing evenly as the receptionist remonstrated with him, and a security man was summoned to escort him away.

She spoke quickly, to stifle the delighted recognition in the woman's eyes before it found expression in words. 'I believe my husband's here – Richard Wakefield? I had a message. He was brought in by ambulance about an hour ago.'

'Hang on.' The receptionist consulted first a screen, then a handwritten list. 'Yes, here he is, Richard Wakefield. Hang on please.' She dialled a number on an internal phone and as she waited for an answer, glanced up at Isla. 'Are you who I think you are?'

'I don't know,' said Isla.

'I think – hello? I believe you have a patient admitted about an hour ago, Richard Wakefield? Mrs Wakefield is here, could someone come down?' She replaced the receiver. There were two more people waiting behind Isla, so she contented herself with a let-it-be-our-secret look. 'Take a seat.'

Isla sat. Back against the back of the chair, shoulders down, legs together from knee to ankle, hands loosely on her lap. When she saw a tall, red-haired doctor approaching, accompanied by a man in a tracksuit whom she didn't recognise, she knew they were for her, but did not rise, leaving it to the receptionist to point her out. The doctor came over.

'Mrs Wakefield?'

'Yes.'

'I'm Doctor Vulliamy, I've been looking after your husband. This is Mr Burgess who found him and accompanied him in the ambulance.'

Isla looked at the second man. 'Hello.'

He gave a nod, mouthed something.

Dr Vulliamy extended a solicitous hand. 'Shall we find some-where more private to talk?'

Jen rationalised it like this. If Richard had been in the house then the chances were Isla was not at home. If Keith had accompanied him then it was also likely that Richard's whereabouts at the time of his fall would sooner or later be known. Apart from anything else the Jag was parked in Selwyn Street. If the balloon was going to go up, then better that she should go up with it, with all flags flying, rather than propounding her deceit by flight and concealment. Claudia was right – her life had not to date been an exemplar of order and clarity: her motto might have been 'I Muddle Through'. Now was the moment to end the muddle. The truth was she wanted to see Richard, to know that he was all right. That was all. When she had her answer, she'd go. She wasn't going to look for trouble, but she would not strive officiously to avoid it, either.

Having parked in a loading bay behind Europa Foods, the first person she saw as she entered the hospital was Keith. He was sitting on a chair in the reception area and his face was turned towards the door so that their eyes met the second she came in.

When he stood up, there was something deliberate and dignified in his manner, it was immensely reassuring. As she walked towards him she realised that she had never in her life been more glad to see anyone.

Isla sat down on a tweedy chair with wooden arms. She noticed a begonia in need of watering; a poster for the Scanner Appeal Sponsored Walk; bizarrely, a red metal ashtray; a water cooler and a stack of paper cups; some copies of *Hello!* magazine; a squat wooden table at shin-height; and a plastic crate full of children's toys.

Dr Vulliamy sat down in an identical chair on the other side of the table.

'I'm so very sorry to have to tell you,' he said, 'that your husband died shortly after arrival.'

'What happened?' asked Jen. 'Where is he?'

'There's no easy way to say this, Jen,' said Keith, and the use of her Christian name alerted her to the enormity of the news. 'He's gone.'

*   *   *

'I see,' said Isla.

'He'd had a massive stroke, and he had another as we were taking him up to resuscitation.'

'Yes, I see.'

'He will have suffered very little.'

'I understand.'

'I'm so sorry.' He rose. 'Please stay as long as you like. I'll send one of the nurses in.' He went to the door. She didn't envy him his job. 'You can make a phone call from here.'

'Thank you.'

'Can I get the nurse to bring you some tea?'

'Yes please.'

'I am so very, very sorry.'

As he was about to close the door, she said: 'I wonder – if Mr Burgess is still there – do you think I could speak to him?'

'Of course. I'll see. And I'll be back myself shortly.'

Dr Vulliamy went back into the reception area, and deputed a nurse to organise tea and go in to Mrs Wakefield, whom he now realised, of course, was the actress Isla Munro. There was an amiable drunk still ambling about being a nuisance. No sign of Burgess. He went over to the desk.

'The chap who came in with Mr Wakefield, stroke victim – Mr Burgess, in a tracksuit. Any idea where he is?'

Keith said nothing directly to Jen as he drove them both home in the Diane. Before getting in, he'd had to make their peace with the manager of Europa Foods while she sat dumbly waiting to be taken away. Thereafter his silence was broken only by the odd comment about the traffic and apologies for grinding the gears. She couldn't stop crying, but he didn't offer a hankie, nor say it was a good thing, for which untypical restraint she knew she would, in time, be truly grateful.

In Selwyn Street she tried not to look at the Jag. In the hall of Number 65 there was still a scrap of Sellotape on the banister post and – something she hadn't had time to notice before – a faint smell of disinfectant. She went into the living room and plumped down on the edge of the sofa, her head on her knees. Her body, if not her mind, feared that if it leaned back and relaxed it would leave itself open to a body blow of grief with which it was not yet ready to deal. The cats, repulsed by the atmosphere, were nowhere about.

Keith came back with a mug of tea in one hand and a glass and whisky bottle in the other. He crouched down in front of her.

'Which would you prefer? Or shall I add this – to this?'

She nodded blindly. He put down the glass, splashed some whisky into the tea and tapped her on the shoulder before handing it to her. 'OK?'

Was she OK? OK was like breathing, like putting one foot in front of another . . . OK was the bottom line. But even OK might be more than she could manage.

Messily, through her crying, she gulped some of the tea. Keith sat down on the other end of the sofa, holding the bottle in both hands.

When she could, she said: 'Keith – tell me what happened.'

Isla felt sorry for the little nurse, who looked about Marcus's age. She pictured her returning to her lodgings that night and saying to her roommate: 'I had to do something really awful this afternoon . . .'

'Where do you live?' the nurse asked.

Isla told her.

'Oh, so not far.'

'No.'

There followed a long, screaming silence. The nurse said: 'Is there someone you'd like to call? Your family?'

'I'll make some calls later. From home.'

'Yes, of course. Only I was wondering about you getting back to your house.'

'I have the car.'

'I'm not sure you should drive,' said the nurse, suddenly more confident with practicalities to address.

'Well – whatever. I can walk.'

'If you're sure.' The nurse did something unnecessary to the buttons on her uniform.

Is that it? Isla wondered. Do I just finish my tea and go? The cool composure she'd striven for earlier had set around her like plaster of Paris. She couldn't find her stride, locate her feelings, achieve spontaneity. She was numb.

Dr Vulliamy returned. 'Mrs Wakefield . . . Would you like to see your husband?'

'Yes, please.'

The nurse shot to her feet, took Isla's cup and opened the door. Some sort of look was exchanged between her and Vulliamy as Isla emerged into the corridor. She felt his large, firm hand momentarily cupping her elbow, steering her to where she had to go.

'This way.'

She followed him, the Woman Who Has Just Lost Her Husband. But of course this was a busy hospital, how would people know? And if they did, she was an everyday phenomenon.

They went up in a lift in which, mercifully, there was no one else. She was ambushed by what she knew to be a foolish and irrelevant fear.

'Excuse me – will I be on my own – when I see him?'

'If that's what you'd like.'

'Yes.'

'Then you will be, but someone will be within hailing distance.'

In case of what, thought Isla. In case I faint? Have hysterics? Throw up? Turn violent? The fact was that they had a far better idea of what might happen than she did. She couldn't tell what she might do, or how she would behave. She wanted to see Richard in order to acknowledge his departure: to play the final scene. Except that she didn't know how to play it. Her inadequacy was pitiful.

'Are you all right?' Vulliamy's finger hovered over the 'Doors Open' button. 'I mean, do you feel strong enough for this?'

'Yes, thank you.'

He led her through heavy swing doors with glass portholes into a room that seemed to Isla to be crowded with equipment, presently pushed to the sides in her honour. A very young man in a green overall hovered. Richard lay on a table with a thick, clean white sheet pulled up to his chin and folded neatly back.

'This is Mrs Wakefield.' Vulliamy gave the young man a nod and he withdrew.

He cupped her elbow again. 'Sure you'll be all right?'
'Yes.'
'Take your time. I'll be right outside.'
Isla approached the table.

Jen listened intently. It was the second time Keith had described, in painstaking detail, what had happened.

'Yes,' he said, in answer to her question, also for the second time. 'He'd been here for a little while. This –' he raised the bottle – 'was on the table. And this –' the glass – 'is his. He'd washed it up.'

'I can't believe it,' she said. 'Why can't I believe it?'

'You won't for a bit. Or that's what I read.'

'It's the thought of him being alone . . .' The tears oozed forth again

'Um – just so you know. In the ambulance I stayed right out of it. Let the professionals get on with their job. He seemed, you know, pretty peaceful.'

Isla looked down carefully, beginning with the sheet and moving up towards his face. That was all it was, she told herself – just his face. Nothing behind it, any more. When she finally allowed her gaze to rest on it she did not see the fabled peace of the dear departed. This wasn't peace, it was blankness, absence. A soulless, heartless, rebuff to the living.

When she stretched out her hand and touched him it was both a farewell, and an acceptance of her own utter loneliness.

'His wife was at the hospital,' said Keith.
'You told me.'
'I had to look in his wallet – call someone.'
'You did the right thing.'
'This is a horrible situation for you.'
'Keith –' she looked him straight in the eye for the first time – her face gross with grief, his pinched and earnest. 'Keith, it is horrible, yes. But it's my situation. I made it. And now it's never going to go away, so I'd better learn to live with it.'

* * *

Vulliamy accompanied Isla back to reception and reunited her with the little nurse on bereavement duty.

'Shall I walk with you to your car?'

'No thank you. I'll be fine.'

'I'll see you out anyway.'

Outside the main entrance Isla thought – I am never going to see this girl again, it doesn't matter what she thinks of me. It's better to be clear.

She held out her hand. 'Thank you for your help.'

'Oh . . . that's all right . . . it's what we're here for . . .'

'Goodbye.'

She walked the hundred yards or so to the car with a fierce concentration which shielded her from interest and intrusion. She drove back to the house with the same concentration.

In the drive, the mellow sun now barred with evening shadows, she took in the fact that Richard's car was not there. And realised that of course where the car was, there was another woman whose life, from this moment, was never going to be the same.

'I'm going to put a hottie in your bed,' said Keith. 'And then I'll make us some supper.'

'Thanks.' She looked up at him. 'Thanks, Keith.'

'No, please. You stay there.'

She caught his sleeve and reached for the whisky bottle. 'Give me that.'

'Do you think it's wise?'

'I don't want to drink it.'

Reluctantly he released the bottle. When he'd left the room she drew up her knees and hugged it close.

It was the only thing, in the whole of this house which he had visited for twelve years, which belonged to him. A half bottle of scotch was all she had to remember him by.

Isla crossed the hall and sat on the bottom step of the stairs. The house lay quietly around her. It seemed neither desolate nor expectant. Like Richard at the hospital, it was simply empty. No one there.

For half an hour she did not move. She couldn't face any

- Sarah Harrison

other room but this when they were all full of what he'd left behind.

When she did at last stand up she went to the room Marcus had slept in. The bed was neat, made up with clean sheets since Marcus's departure. She lay down on top of it and lay there wide-eyed as the phone rang, every hour or so, below.

• 268

16

In the days between Richard's death and his funeral, the weather held, and late summer trudged into autumn in punishing heat.

With Archie's stalwart help, Isla organised those things which had to be done. The funeral was to be private, in Bradenham. A memorial service had been gently suggested by various long-standing friends and colleagues, but she couldn't make that decision yet. She wanted as far as possible to maintain the tenor of their marriage, which had been something separate and secluded, a life set deliberately apart from that which they led in public. Her determination to achieve this helped her to stay calm. Her strength, friends agreed, was remarkable – but then she was a remarkable woman.

And her high standards caused everyone else to raise their game. No one wanted to be the one to put a foot wrong, to make a scene, to fall short. The letters that arrived overwhelmed her with their expressions of love, and admiration, and solidarity. Immensely distinguished judges and barristers spoke not just of Richard's dazzling gifts but of his warmth, his humour, his kindness to his juniors, and (a rare quality in the legal world) his humility. No one failed to mention the strength and joy he derived from his marriage to her. 'He was a private man where you were concerned,' wrote one QC whom she had never met, 'but also the one man whose most sacred bond was never doubted.'

That had made her cry – 'sacred bond'.

Caroline rang, but had to hang up after three minutes, unable to continue. Her letter, which arrived two days later, was dignified and generous.

'. . . we both loved him,' she wrote at the end. 'But you were better at it than me, and I could see how happy he was since marrying you. I was pleased, in a way, not to have the responsibility for his wellbeing – a responsibility I could no longer discharge. It was good to know that it now rested with you, and you were so well qualified to discharge it. But he is the father of my sons, and we feel his loss dreadfully. The boys have been wonderful, both of them. I can only imagine what it must be like for you. Sorry I was such a wet dishcloth on the telephone, it's the last thing you need.

All our love and good thoughts
Caroline.'

Isla herself wrote to Donatella, who could not be relied upon to read the *Telegraph*, and who would otherwise hear the news on the legal grapevine, to let her know that she would be welcome at the funeral. She received no reply.

'You don't have to do these things,' said Archie gently. 'People can look after themselves.'

'I know they can, but I'm happy to do it.'

Archie, of course, was unable to argue with that. All that stuff was right out of his league. He had married the first woman he'd slept with, and she had remained, contentedly for both of them, the only one. He had not the remotest idea what was appropriate under these circumstances, and bowed to Isla's superior judgement.

Nell, still slightly flushed from her two weeks in the *gîte* in Bordeaux, came round with flowers from the garden of The Bury.

'The parents have written to you, and want you to know they're maintaining a watching brief on the rector.'

'That is good of them.'

'How are you doing?'

Isla was becoming used to this question, or something like it. 'I'm not really sure how I should be doing. Getting along. Going from day to day.'

'Sorry, stupid question.'

'No, not stupid. But hard to answer.'

They were in the drawing room – Isla found the brilliant outdoor light overpowering in these dark days. It was lunchtime, but Nell claimed to have had a sandwich on the way and Isla wasn't hungry. She ate something – not much – morning and night, out of a sense of responsibility.

The spectre of unfinished business hovered between them. Isla knew that early training and innate good manners would never allow Nell to touch on it in these circumstances. But she herself wanted matters resolved and was aware that at this moment her vulnerability was her strength.

'Nell, about our conversation a few weeks ago—'

'Isla please don't, please, I can't bear even to remember it.'

'But we both do,' said Isla gently. 'So I want to say that I have great respect for your feelings, and affection for you, Nell. I hope we shall always be the best of friends. But Richard is the person I love.' Her use of the present tense was calculated. 'I should have said simply that, ages ago. That's just how it is. It's not to do with you, it's to do with Richard and me.'

'I know that.' Nell's eyes shone uncertainly. 'I do know that.'

'So please don't say you're sorry, or regret anything. Let's allow each other to be who we are.'

Nell agreed, and they bumped cheeks gently, wistfully.

Three days after Richard's death Isla locked up the house and went with Giles to Bradenham. She had two purposes – one, to discuss the funeral arrangements with the rector, the other, a task she did not relish: seeing Alec. She had had an almost monosyllabic conversation with him on the phone, a medium which could not begin to encompass his distress and outrage. She had felt like someone performing an amputation without anaesthetic. They were both, she sensed, excruciatingly aware of the pecking order of grief. Her distress, kept in check for the occasion, made her cool. His, new and raw, made him brusque. It had been awful.

Giles was her driver for the day. She would have been content to drive out on her own but Giles, on leave of absence from the wine bar, was dispatched by Caroline to 'make himself useful'.

'He wants to help,' Caroline assured her, though Isla thought that it was probably Caroline herself who needed to be of assistance, and Giles who was subject to a three-line whip. He

arrived in Hampstead at eight-thirty, baggy-eyed after enduring rush-hour tubes across London. They set off at nine, in
Isla's car.

She was keenly aware of the slumbering social Vesuvius she
represented to her stepsons who had, after all, just lost their
father. As in the very beginning of her relationship with them
she felt that all she could do was allow them to make the
running, and this she did now. She was anyway so exhausted
that she could barely speak. But she had reckoned without Giles's
characteristic modus operandi, which was to talk his way out of
any given corner. In this instance he was determined to bring
misery to heel with practicalities.

'Just say if you want to stop, won't you?'

'I will, thanks.'

'If you fancy a coffee, or anything?'

'Thank you.'

'What time did you say the sky-pilot was due?'

'Oh – elevenish.'

'Bags of time then.'

'Yes, no hurry.'

He put on a tape, one he'd brought with him. 'Pet Shop Boys
– is this OK?'

'Of course.'

He tapped the wheel with his fingers. 'Mind if I smoke?'

'No, if we can have the window open.'

'It's OK, I'm better off without it.'

'No, it's all right – really.'

'I tell you what, I'm going to stop and get some sweets.'

'Fine.'

'Anything you want?'

'No thanks.'

It went on and on. She wanted to scream, but he was in pain
too. He drove with exaggerated care as if she were very old or
very ill. Several times, at traffic lights and junctions, he gazed
out of the window and she knew he was struggling with tears.

When they reached Bradenham, and the cottage she said:
'Giles, this is so good of you. I want you to know how much
I appreciate it. I'd have hated to come all this way on my
own.'

Then, at last, he'd had a big cry, sitting with his head in his hands and sobbing noisily.

'Fuck it . . . ! I never even had a proper conversation with him . . . Fuck, fuck, fuck!'

She'd put her arm round his shoulders but said nothing because she was crying too. When he'd regained his composure with the aid of several squares of kitchen towel, she said:

'Giles. Do you think you could read something at the service?'

'I'll try.' He blew his nose to cover the small bloom of vanity of which he was ashamed, but which pleased Isla.

'I'd like that. And I think your mother would, too. And your father would be tickled pink.'

'I'll give it a go.'

'Good.' She kissed his cheek. 'Look, why don't you go and call on the Fylers. Bill might like to go to the pub. When I've seen the rector I'm going to call on your grandfather. You can come or not as you like.'

'I'll come.'

'Then good. I'll see you later.'

She tried hard, when discussing the funeral, to imagine what Richard would have liked. Though not a regular churchgoer he was a traditionalist who believed in continuity, and the importance of the observances. He would have described himself as not merely Anglican, but Christian – something she herself could not have done – and would, she was sure, want something staunchly celebratory. She chose 'For all the saints', and 'He who would valiant be'. She avoided, in spite of the rector's suggestion, Crimmond, the phrasing of which no congregation ever got right, opting instead for 'Lead us, heavenly father, lead us'. She herself would read from *Cymbeline*: 'Fear no more the heat o' the sun, Nor the furious winter's rages . . .'

For Giles, subject to his approval, she chose Robert Louis Stevenson, the passage that opened with: 'That man is a success who has lived well, laughed often and loved much . . .'

The rector was impressed. 'I don't often meet a widow quite so sure of what she wants.'

'It's not a case of what I want,' said Isla. 'But of what suits Richard.'

As she saw him out she thought perhaps she had been

pompous. When the rector was behind the wheel of his Micra she leaned down, arms folded and said: 'You see a lot of this sort of thing, so you'll forgive me if I wasn't as polite as I should have been . . . ?'

'My dear Mrs Wakefield,' his whole face softened with emotion. 'Even if it were required, forgiveness is not my province, it's God's, and I haven't the slightest doubt that he would wish you to take it as read.'

'And you?'

Almost unmanned he waved a dismissive hand. 'No more.'

She rang the Fylers. 'May I have my chauffeur back?'

Barbara was gruff. 'Isla dear, won't you come and have some lunch?'

'It's sweet of you, but no. We'll grab a sandwich. I'm a zombie at the moment and I need to see Alec while I'm still holding myself together, and then get back to town.'

'It's only four days till the funeral. Can't you come and just be at the cottage – or with us?'

'I shall come to the cottage, but not tonight. There are still some things I have to see to. Don't worry about me Bar, I've got masses of support.'

'Eating?'

'Eating.'

'Sleeping?'

'Well enough. And without assistance.'

'Very well. Giles is going out of the door now, he's been walking Pepe. Anyway, you know where we are.'

'Dear Bar – of course I do.'

They stopped at a pub on the edge of Lettaford and ordered a large portion of chips, with a salad for Isla and scampi provençale for Giles. Isla ate three chips and picked at the salad as Giles shovelled down everything else with the aid of several wedges of garlic bread.

'Sorry to be such a pig.'

'You're not, I like to see you tucking in.' She phrased her words carefully: 'Caro said you were too thin when you got back from Ibiza.'

'Yes, well . . .' He grimaced. 'You know how it is. We had

a great time, but you have to decide what to spend your money on.'

'I shan't ask.'

'I wish Mum wouldn't.'

'That's what she's there for. How is she?'

'She's still crying a helluva lot. It used to do my head in when she cried, but this time we've got used to it. Which is a good thing, I suppose.'

'And Marcus?'

'Not speaking, so what's new. But playing the white man. He's been good with Mum. He just sits there and lets her run on.'

'That is good.'

'Someone's got to.'

Giles scrunched and unscrunched his paper napkin, smoothing out the creases with his fingers on the table top. Isla noticed that he had acquired a tattoo of a scorpion on his right wrist.

Still smoothing, and not looking up, he said: 'You haven't got anyone to run on to, have you?'

'Yes, plenty of people.'

'Like who?' He was almost truculent.

'Friends, good friends. You.'

He blushed scarlet. 'You haven't even mentioned Dad to me.'

'But I know I could if I wanted to,' she said, adding: 'I think about him all the time, you know.'

He didn't answer.

Back in the car, she asked to drive as far as The Hayes. It helped, made her feel more in control. She said: 'I thought of something you might read – at your father's funeral.'

'Yeah?' He was wary.

'If I let you have it when we get back, you can cast your eye over it and let me know. If there's anything else you'd rather, that'll be fine.'

'No, no, I'll go along with you.'

'It's not the Bible.'

'Whatever,' he said, but she detected a note of relief.

They pulled up outside the door of The Hayes. Giles peered out.

'Christ, it's ages since I was here.'

'He'll be enormously chuffed to see you.'

'You think?'

'I know.'

Karen said how very, very sorry she was – Richard had been such a gentleman, such a kind and good son and, she added solemnly, with a lovely sense of humour.

'How is Alec?' asked Isla as they followed her up the stairs.

'Taken it hard, but not letting on,' replied Karen. She glanced sympathetically over her shoulder. 'I'm sure you know all about that.'

She was a nice girl. But then Isla supposed she got plenty of practice at this sort of thing. From the corner of her eye Isla saw her touch Giles's shoulder, lightly but reassuringly, as he followed Isla into Alec's room.

'Good God,' said Alec. 'Who's this you've brought with you?'

'It's Giles, as you well know.'

Isla watched as Giles, uncertain what his greeting should be, inclined slightly for an embrace, then thought better of it and stuck out a hand. Alec took the hand and slapped his grandson awkwardly on the shoulder.

'Hello feller-me-lad. Pity we have to meet under such wretched circumstances.'

'Yes.'

Alec plumped down wheezily. Isla took the other chair and Giles perched on the windowsill.

'Anything I can get you?'

'Nothing at all, we stopped at a pub.' Isla decided, for all their sakes, to be swift and direct. 'Alec, we shan't stay all that long, but I did want to come and see you. We've both lost Richard, and . . .' She wavered. Giles folded his arms and stared with tremendous interest out of the window. She drew a breath. 'I wanted to say that we're all thinking of you, a lot.'

'Thank you, my darling.'

'Karen says you've been wonderful.'

Alec grumphed. 'What's one supposed to be? Hysterical?'

'Well – quite. But all the same.'

'I've done a lot of thinking. I was a pretty terrible father.' He put up a hand to silence her protest. 'No, I was, I harbour no illusions about it. But I believe Richard and I understood each other. We established a modus vivendi. Which is as good as many and a great deal better than some. Eh, Giles?'

'Absolutely. He talked about you a lot.' Isla had no way of knowing if this assertion were true. Richard had not talked about his parents that much to her, but perhaps it was different with his sons. 'He admired you,' added Giles. 'He said you bestrode his life like a Colossus.'

This, whether solid gold or base metal, went down a storm. Alec's spluttering burst of laughter was its stamp of approval. 'A lawyer's comment *par excellence*! Good old Richard!'

'No, it's a compliment,' said Giles. 'I know that, because I feel the same way about him. Both of us do.'

'He was a clever chap,' agreed Alec. 'Got to the top and barely broke sweat.'

'A hard act to follow.'

'You'll be hard put, bloody hard put. But that's what a young man needs.'

Watching Alec's change in mood Isla wondered whether Giles should not, after all, consider a career in advocacy. She said: 'Alec, would you like to come to the funeral? It's in Bradenham, and lifts can easily be arranged.'

'No, no, no, you're better off without me, I'm a frightful old wreck these days.'

'I'll come and get you,' offered Giles.

'Are you safe?' Alec turned to Isla. 'Is he safe?'

'We got here from London without a moment's anxiety.'

'I'll think about it.'

Giles stood up. 'Anyone fancy a walk?'

They spent another twenty minutes walking in the garden, and sitting on a seat in the shade of a chestnut tree. Isla found she couldn't talk, but Giles made up for it, asking questions about The Hayes, commenting on Matron's figure and making Alec chuckle by describing his recent holiday (all too accurately, Isla suspected) as a dope-fiend's paradise.

By the time they returned to the house, Giles was on a roll. 'So when shall I collect you?' he asked. 'If the service is at two?'

'No, no, I haven't changed my mind about that.'

'Come on,' said Giles, taking one liberty too many. 'For Dad.'

Isla stepped in. 'Richard would understand, whatever you do,' she said. 'You'll be with us in spirit.'

'That's right, my darling,' said Alec. 'That's right.'

Grandfather and grandson, restored to their earlier guardedness, said goodbye and Giles went to the car as Isla saw Alec up to his room. He was perspiring and obviously tired, his steps heavy and uncertain, but back in his room he gestured to her to wait while he went to his chest of drawers.

He closed the drawer and returned with a letter, addressed to Richard, and ready stamped. 'I wrote this in reply to that rather strange one he wrote to me,' he explained. 'But I have this senile notion that you might like to read it, on his behalf.' He gazed down at the letter, puffing.

'I would. Thank you.'

'Sure? I mean it's of no earthly interest to you.'

'It's of consuming interest. But only if you're quite happy for me to read it.'

He took her hand, opened it and planted the letter in her palm, like an uncle slipping a ten bob note. 'There.'

'Thank you.'

She kissed him, and saw a tear trembling in the creases at the corner of his eye, although his mouth was firm. 'Forgive me for not coming to the bakemeats?'

'Nothing to forgive.'

'I couldn't stand it,' he said, and turned away. As he stumped back to his chair Isla closed the door.

They got back to London before six, and had a drink together in the orangery – white wine for Isla, coke for Giles.

'Do you want me to stay the night?' he asked.

'No thank you.' She recognised at once the wording of an offer which had been put into his mouth by Caroline. Don't just rush off and leave her, suggest you spend the night there and come back in the morning . . . But all she wanted was to be alone, to mourn, and adjust, and think of Richard. She'd scarcely wept so far but tonight, she felt, might be the night.

'It's so kind of you Giles,' she added, easing his carefully concealed relief. 'But I have things to do, and to think about.

You're not hurt are you?' He shook his head. 'I knew you'd understand. But before you go,' she went on more briskly, 'let me show you the reading I had in mind.'

She watched him as he took the book and scanned the marked passage with a frown of concentration.

'It's OK,' he said, with the surprised, upward inflection that denoted unconditional approval. 'I can handle that.'

When Giles had gone she first took the messages off the machine – all affectionate enquiries, offers of help and expressions of sympathy – then switched it back on, locked up and went upstairs to the bedroom: hers and Richard's. She undressed, had a bath, and got into bed. Richard's books – Bill Bryson, Paul Theroux, a biography of Philip Larkin, were still on the bedside table, making her heart thump with pain. But she was still not ready to move them.

She opened Alec's letter carefully, prising open the flap without tearing it, conscious of her privilege. The old man had a strong, educated hand corrupted by a doctor's lifelong professional need for speed. Paragraphs, written in thick blue ink, started well and became less legible as they went on. Isla read carefully and systematically, wanting to be sure of the sense first time round, deciphering one sentence to her satisfaction before moving on to the next.

My dear Richard, he had written.

How are you? I understand from Isla, who was good enough to drop by recently, that your health's giving cause for concern. Be sensible, won't you? Prevention is better than cure – something I am more at liberty to say now that I'm out to grass and no longer have a vested interest in the damage.

I was a bit put about by your letter I must admit. Whatever prompted it? Not that you don't have a perfect right to ask, but ours wasn't a generation, nor is mine a temperament, that goes in much for navel-gazing, as you well know. To begin with my inclination was not to bother but on reflection I see that's churlish, so here's my answer for what it's worth.

Yes, your mother and I were happy. We were an extremely successful and contented partnership for over forty years, which I think bears out this assessment at a time when everyone seems to switch horses at the drop of a hat ... But anyway. You ask were we really happy, as if you automatically suspect me of evasion. And again I say yes, I believe we really were.

If on the other hand this insistence is your way of asking about fidelity, then the answer is no, or not in the generally accepted sense. Both your mother and I had other encounters at various times throughout our married life. Some of them evolved into lasting friendships. None of them affected our loyalty to each other or placed our marriage in any sort of jeopardy. Everyone concerned knew this. We lived as husband and wife to the end, and since your mother's death I have felt the world to be an empty place and myself a poor thing in it.

That is all I have to say. Except perhaps this. There is marriage, and there is falling in love. The first cannot exist without the second, but the second can, and does, exist without the first. Marriage, if that is what you choose, is nothing if not for life. And falling in love is part of life.

All this has left me completely buggered! The little girl approaches with a light supper and not a moment too soon. I very much look forward to your next visit, dear old boy, so don't leave it too long,

Your ancient but ever-loving
Dad.

Isla put the letter back in its envelope, sealed it, and placed it between Richard's books. It was a long time before she slept.

The main reason she had returned to London was to discharge the responsibility which, of all the sad responsibilities there were at this time, she most dreaded: that of contacting Keith Burgess and organising the retrieval of Richard's car.

The hospital had handed her a piece of paper with Burgess's name and address on it as she left the hospital, but she had not yet even taken it out of her handbag. No one, however kind and caring, could understand why it was taking her so long to establish where Richard had been taken ill, and the exact circumstances, although everyone else, like her, assumed it had happened in the street. He'd been involved in a high-pressure, high-profile case; he'd made, for some reason, a detour; perhaps stopped for petrol – or champagne; and the time-bomb which had been ticking for months had finally exploded. The mysterious but admirable Mr Burgess had been first on the scene, and to the phone. But it was so unlike Isla they said – Archie, Alison, the Fylers, Marjory – not to have been in touch with this good Samaritan earlier.

It was unlike her. But then, she was not herself. It was not only the past that was another country, thought Isla, this terrible, unrecognisable present was just as foreign, and she felt lost in it. She tried to draw comfort from those aspects of it that hadn't changed, that she could see. But there were things which would have to be learned if life was to go on, and she dreaded learning them.

Dully, she sat down by the phone with her piece of paper, and then realised that of course there was no telephone number written down. She dialled directory enquiries, but was told that no one by that name was listed – might he be ex-directory?

Isla cursed the pretensions of people who didn't wish their phone number to be known. What, if not to be contactable, was the point of having a telephone? By now she felt so strung out that she decided simply to get in her own car and drive to the Crouch End address. Even if Burgess wasn't there she could put a note through his door. Then at the foot of the piece of paper she noticed a PTO. On the other side was written: *Working hours c/o Gunner Grove Primary School* and – yes – a phone number.

A teacher – that explained the voice, the competence, the clothes. She dialled the school's number. She looked at her watch. It was ten a.m. Mr Burgess would be at work. But that was the number he'd left

A harassed female voice answered her call. There was a shrill hubbub in the background.

'I wonder,' said Isla, 'if I could speak to a Mr Keith Burgess?'

'He's with his class at present.'

'I'm sorry, I won't keep him a moment.'

'We're absolutely rushed off our feet, it's harvest festival practice.'

'I'm so sorry.' Isla felt she had to speak to him now if she was going to. 'Just for a second?'

There was a tight-lipped pause. 'Are you a parent?'

'No – my name's Isla Wakefield. Mr Burgess was kind enough to accompany my husband to hospital recently when he – when he –' she was suddenly, hideously ambushed by emotion, but the woman's attitude had changed in an instant.

'Mrs Wakefield – yes, of course. I do apologise. Hang on and I'll get him at once.'

Footsteps receded, distant voices cutting the hubbub. Isla struggled to take control of herself.

'Keith Burgess.'

The sound of his voice brought her round – Dr Theatre, she thought. 'Mr Burgess, it's Isla Wakefield.'

'Hello. I'm so sorry about your husband.'

'Look, I apologise for calling you at school, but I wanted to thank you properly for what you did.'

'There's no need at all.'

'And to ask you – not now of course, but perhaps we could meet – you know, how – and when—'

'I understand.'

'And then there's Richard's car, I wondered . . .'

'Yes, it's in my road. Safe and sound. You just say when it would be convenient and I can see you there.'

'Perhaps this evening – say at about eight? I have to call a friend to come with me so that I can drive the Jag back.'

'Eight o'clock's fine. Turn into Selwyn Street at the Crouch Hill end and the car's a hundred yards on the right.'

How, she wondered as she put the phone down, did he know?

Archie drove Isla to Selwyn Street. They didn't talk. It was a perfect late summer evening: even the lowly terrace-covered hills and littered pavements of this part of north London were placid and romantic in the slanting sun. But for Isla it was a haunted journey. Where was this? Why had Richard come all this way? What part did these streets and shops play in his life, that she had known nothing about? She sat paralysed with fear and grief in the passenger seat as Archie drove, stopped, fumbled with the *A to Z*, executed embattled U turns, and finally located Selwyn Street.

She consulted her piece of paper for the house number, but Archie said: 'There it is – is that your man?'

'Yes, that's him.'

Keith stood by the bonnet of the Jag and waved them down. 'Let me out, can you?' said Isla. She got out and Archie went on to find a space.

She held out her hand. 'I do hope you haven't been hanging about for ages – I had your address.'

'No, no,' he said, nodding. 'It's a nice evening, anyway.'

'Look,' she said, 'I must ask you what happened. In your note you said you got back from somewhere—'

'I'd been at a meeting in school,' said Burgess. 'I live just along there –' he pointed in the direction Archie had driven. 'When I arrived your husband was collapsed near the door.'

'But why was he here?' She looked around. 'I mean – what brought him here?'

Burgess went on. 'He must have been taken badly and tried to get help for himself. But not made it. I went straight in and called the ambulance.'

'I'm so grateful for what you did.'

'Anyone would have done the same. I'm only sorry that – sorry I couldn't do more.'

She looked at the Jag, touched the roof. It was warm from the sun, but a single premonitory leaf lay, undisturbed, on its gleaming surface.

'So then,' said Keith, 'I got his wallet out of his jacket pocket and left a message with you. That was it, really. He was conscious at that stage,' he added, 'I think.'

Isla couldn't bear that. She could think of nothing else to say. She simply wanted to be away from this place, away from this man – this stranger – who had been with Richard as he died.

Archie appeared, driving back from the opposite side of the road. 'Can't find anywhere here.'

'Let's go,' said Isla. 'I think we should go anyway.'

'It fills up with residents this time of night. You might find somewhere in Hazeldene, that runs parallel to this, though.'

'No,' said Isla. 'We must go. Archie, if you go to the corner and wait, I'll follow you.'

She took the key of the Jag from her handbag and stared at it.

'It's a remote control lock,' said Burgess.

'Yes, of course.'

'When's the funeral?'

'On Friday.' She got in. 'You'd be very welcome, but it's out of town.' She sounded anything but welcoming but she couldn't help it.

'No, I'm afraid I shan't be able to. School, you know. And I don't have a car.'

'Goodbye then Mr Burgess.'

'Goodbye,' he said. 'God bless.'

She had almost reached the corner when she saw Jen Delaney walking down the pavement on the other side. In her attempt to wind the window down she pressed the wrong button and started the windscreen wipers. The small flurry, and the impatient toot of a car behind her caught Jen's attention. Isla waved, but Jen looked blank and walked on.

In the rearview mirror, as she turned the corner, she saw Jen and Burgess meet, speak, and go into a house together.

And she knew then what she had instinctively sensed a moment earlier – that Jen had seen her, but pretended not to.

Back at the house she put the Jag in the garage and offered Archie a drink, which he refused.

'But I don't like to think of you here on your own,' he said, 'can't you get some company? Would you like me to doss down in the spare room?'

What she wanted was to lay her head on Archie's chest, and feel his arms round her, and sink into the warm, respectful safety of his embrace. Only the knowledge of his frightened desire and his decency prevented her. She kept her distance, kissed his cheek, sent him on his way.

With his departure, she could no longer deny what she'd

seen. It loomed up before her like a prowler stepping out of the shadows.

But oh! she thought, oh Jen! Did it have to be you?

17

'You have to speak to her,' said Claudia.

'I think about it all the time. And then I think – and say what?'

'I don't know, but it's been too long already. It makes me feel sick to think of it. It's making you sick – you look awful.'

'I'm tired.'

'Sick and tired, Mum!'

'Yes,' admitted Jen.

They'd been to the cinema to see a film about cross-generational female bonding. It was billed as the feel-good film of the decade, but it had done nothing for them, and now they were sitting in the Jollyboys Arms, which was the glummest pub imaginable. Jen sensed that Claudia, although sympathetic, was angry with her – for her continuing unhappiness, and even more for her indecision. Jen understood all this. Compassion fatigue had set in. Red was happy – at twenty-one, with looks, love and the whole of life ahead, one wanted to see one's own happiness reflected back from the faces of other people, not be confronted by someone beset by sorrow and apparently intransigent dilemmas. It was tiresome; it was frustrating; and it made a person feel guilty, which she really did not need.

Jen sat up straighter, settled her shoulders; forced a smile. 'It'll pass. Time will do its stuff.'

'So are you going to tell her then?'

Jen's nerves jangled. 'Tell her what?'

'How about . . .' Claudia shrugged eloquently, 'everything?'

No, thought Jen, not everything, And if not everything, better nothing.

'I think she knows anyway. We saw each other. We both knew. It doesn't get much worse, Red.'

'You like her a lot.'

'I did, yes.'

'Well, if you're going to be enemies now you could at least try and be the best of enemies – honest ones who've levelled with each other.' She paused, but went on when Jen didn't respond: 'And Richard meant a lot to you. You should square the circle. Why throw the baby out with the bathwater?' The choice of metaphor made Jen wince – it would have been funny if it wasn't so terrible. Claudia sighed with exasperation. 'You could at least *try* to make it right. *And*,' she leaned forward to lend emphasis to her next remark, 'I bet you anything she's thinking the same thing.'

'Maybe.'

'I'm going to get us the other half. Stay there and don't go away.'

Jen smiled grimly to herself. Go away? She was rooted to the spot. It was all so painfully predictable. She'd been ready to do the sensible, independent, single woman's thing, and have a termination. She'd screwed up her courage (among other things, she thought wrily) and fixed the date. But then Richard had died, and that changed everything. Because the tiny tadpole of life in her womb was part of him, his legacy, and she guarded it jealously. She could not even picture a baby – Richard's son or daughter – let alone a fast-growing, separate human being, running around independent of her: she couldn't think that far ahead. What she wanted was to keep this life inside her, all hers. Or hers and Richard's. She knew it was sad, and unhealthy, and wrong: that it was not a sensible, mature way to reach a decision. That it was *not* a decision, but a kind of stubborn drifting. But she couldn't help herself. And the result was that she was now eighteen weeks pregnant, borderline for a termination, and with her resolve weakening with every day that passed. Even were she to approach the clinic again they would, with some justification, be dubious about her reasons, and she would be less likely to put across any kind of convincing case.

As for the alternative, she would not look more than a week or two ahead. Claudia returned with their drinks.

'What do I owe you?'

'Forget it.'

'No, no . . .' Jen ferreted in her bag. 'I must.'

Claudia removed the bag and put it on the floor. 'I said, forget it, Mum. I've been earning for the past six weeks. And I've got this modelling job coming up. You never know – this time next year I won't stir abroad for less than five thousand.'

Here was cause for legitimate maternal anxiety. 'Will it fit in with college?'

'I wouldn't be doing it otherwise.'

'What does Anthony think?'

Claudia bristled. 'Does it matter what he thinks?'

'I suppose not, except that you're obviously keen on him.'

'I don't actually know what he thinks. Except that he regards my life as my own. He's the least controlling person I know. Did you realise he's older than you?'

'Yes.' said Jen weakly.

'You'd never guess, would you?'

'Probably not.'

'Nothing to do with looks,' added Claudia kindly. 'You're terrific for your age. But he has such an incredibly open mind.'

Jen began to feel better. The film, the drink, and her daughter's happiness were finally having their effect.

'He's very attractive,' she allowed.

'Yes,' agreed Claudia, 'that doesn't hurt.'

'Are you serious about him?'

'That's such an old-fashioned expression.'

'But you know what it means.'

'I've never felt less serious in my life. But he's the business, Mum. We get on so well it's ridiculous.'

For the first time in days – weeks – Jen felt a smile begin inside her before it showed on her face. She leaned forward and planted a kiss on her daughter's cheek.

'Be happy, Red,' she said. 'That's all that matters.'

The next day her spirits inched up a little more. The morning was fine, but with a first nip of autumn. She awoke feeling refreshed and energetic and – she noted with surprise as she spread Marmite on toast – not in the least sick. She chose to ignore the implications of this development, and simply to savour feeling normal again.

The usual routines had been re-established. Keith had left for school, and the Dalmatian required its finishing touches. Yesterday she'd been dissatisfied with it but this morning the painting looked fresh and alive, she felt enthused by it, and by the prospect of finishing the parrot for Mr and Mrs Hastings. This, she decided, would constitute her deadline. When the parrot was complete she'd make her final decision. After all, if she wished to have a termination a little later than was generally acceptable, she could go privately. She had some money in the building society, and if these circumstances didn't constitute a reasonable use of funds, what did?

Having negotiated herself an extension she threw open the windows, changed the sheets on the bed and cleaned the house with such enthusiasm that the cats left at speed, and took up positions on the pavement, looking huffy.

People warned Isla that after the funeral would be the hardest time. It might well hit her then, they said solicitously, she was going to have to give in to her grief a little, having been so marvellous throughout. Up till now there'd been a million things to think about, but with the organisational escape route out of the way, the permanence of her loss would become real. She must let go, they suggested, turn to her friends, allow people to help, not worry about ringing at two a.m. if that was what she felt like.

Isla conceded that they were right, but they were basing their kind advice on imperfect knowledge. She had a great deal to occupy her beyond the funeral. Lori had contacted her to say that there was no pressure whatever for her to fulfil her contract with the quiz show provided she could let them know within reasonable time. She had assured Lori that she intended to honour her commitment, and was looking forward to it. Work was therapy; work was identity – another of the incontrovertible assertions of grief management. And thinking about work helped her to postpone what she least wanted to do . . .

It was almost a relief when Ned, who had been unable to

attend the funeral, turned up on the doorstep with a bottle of malt.

Having clasped her in his arms for over a minute, he said: 'I know you don't drink this stuff, but I do.'

'I might well join you today.'

He poured them both a generous slug and they drank it at the kitchen table with a packet of tortilla chips between them.

'I'm sorry I couldn't make the observances,' he said. 'Work, for once.'

She wasn't sure that she believed him, but they had always allowed each other a lot of leeway.

'And I'm bloody sorry about Richard,' he added. 'He was the best. Tops. I shan't ask how you are.'

'Thanks.'

'But word is, my lovely, you're going to be the toast of the airwaves with all those toothsome young men in baggy trousers.'

'I don't know about that.' She smiled. 'How's Scotch?'

Ned lit a cigarette, buying time. 'You heard, then.'

'Nothing concrete. But Nell implied that he and she were just good pals. And when she told me the two of you were in Scotland . . . Well, I've known you a long time, Ned.'

'And you drew the obvious conclusion.'

'Am I right?'

He shook his head, blowing a long stream of smoke. 'I did my best, can't deny it. He's a smart lad, and a genius with publicity – got me my first half-way decent job in ten years, the reason I couldn't come to the funeral.'

'Proper acting?' It was a joke between them.

'Better than that – improper. I play a middle-class wife-beater who gets to snog the leading lady before beating seven shades of shit out of her. The *nihil ultima* of street-cred.'

'When shall we see this?'

'Next February. So you see young Scotch is the architect of my professional renaissance.'

'You do look well, Ned. I'm glad.'

'But sorry to disappoint – there is no "thang" going on.'

'Not?' Isla was surprised.

'I gave it my best shot, thought I was on a promise, but no.

His heart wasn't in it.' Eyes narrowed, he studied her face for a moment. 'Meanwhile – is gossip appropriate, or inappropriate? My judgement's terrible at the best of times, and clouded by alcohol it's completely palsied.'

'Gossip's comforting.'

Ned leered. He had always had the jawline, teeth and eyes for a good leer, although in *Lady In Charge* days it was known by the more excitable lady columnists as his 'wicked grin'. 'You may already know this – he and the redoutable Petronella have an understanding. He goes his way, and she goes hers.'

Isla trod carefully. 'I see.'

'Her parents aren't aware of this of course, and they've been getting a bit exercised about his intentions. Wonderful, wonderful –!' He threw his head back in delight, and Isla could see that he had invested in all-white fillings. 'Anyway, Scotch likes Petronella, they confide in each other, and he tells me – are we alone? – that she is about to fling wide the closet door.'

Isla digested this information with a large mouthful of malt. 'Oh?'

'Isla petal, can you imagine? I know you've met these people and I haven't, but Scotch has described them to me, and the comic possibilities of this scene are rich and rare indeed! Ah – I've overstepped the mark.'

'Don't be silly. I was just thinking about it.' She tried to lighten her voice. 'It's brave of Nell anyway. Do we know if there's anyone special?'

'She went to France with a solicitor named Frances Acourt. We think the bold Frances may be the cause of this *glasnost*.'

Not long after this Isla got back from a children's charity fundraiser to find Donatella in the back garden. Or at least, as she stood in the drawing room window eating a Danish pastry, a figure had emerged from the greenery at the end of the lawn, frightening her half to death.

She put the Danish on the windowsill and opened the window. 'Who is that?'

Donatella stopped, spread her arms wide, turned slowly on the spot. 'I admire your garden!'

'It's you – I'm sorry, I was taken aback. Come on in.'

Their mutual greeting was cool and included no touching. For the fundraiser Isla had worn a shirtwaister, a silvery lichen-green, and matching suede shoes with a Louis Quinze heel. Donatella was in a severe black suit, tailored to conceal rather than enhance, with a plain, round-necked white blouse. Though she had almost certainly worn the suit for a court appearance, Isla felt that her own clothes struck an unfortunate note. The air seemed alive with that combative prickle peculiar to Richard's first wife.

Donatella accepted a glass of iced mineral water. Fetching it, Isla took the remains of the Danish into the kitchen and disposed of it in the pedal bin. When she returned Donatella was standing looking at the photographs over the fireplace, her hands tucked beneath the back of her jacket like a country squire.

'Handsome boys,' she commented, without turning round.

Isla put the glass on the mantelpiece. 'They were then. And will be again. The younger one's going through a bad-hair phase, but it'll pass.'

Donatella didn't smile. 'Did they attend their father's funeral?'

'Yes, they did. Giles – the older one – read a passage in the service. Surprisingly well,' she added.

At once she knew that she'd been wrong-footed. 'You should not be surprised. He has inherited Richard's gifts.'

Isla squashed the desire to ask on what authority Donatella made this assumption, since she did not know the boys, and was herself a very distant part of Richard's past.

'I myself was in court,' she went on, loftily, as though choosing to overlook Isla's lack of forethought in this regard.

'It was a very small, private affair,' said Isla. 'But I've been approached about organising a memorial service, so . . .'

'I should like to have attended.' Donatella was on an unusually high horse and determined to remain there.

'Naturally. And Richard would have wanted you there. But we all understand the demands of the system.'

Donatella took her glass of water and sat down. She did not look at Isla, but gave the brocade seat of the Edwardian chair a couple of brisk swipes with her hand before sitting. 'I think not.'

'Oh yes. I'm sure of it. You always had a special place in his affections.'

'Please,' said Donatella, 'there is no need to patronise.'

'I assure you I wasn't.' My God, Isla thought, why am I doing this? What possible reason is there for me to try and put this rude, importunate woman at her ease? And what is she doing here?

Donatella crossed her legs; rested her arms on the arms of the chair; there was something regal in her position. 'I have known Richard for a long time. Longer than you, if I may say so, longer than the other woman – longer even than his sons.'

'I suppose,' ventured Isla, 'that we all know a different Richard.'

Donatella gave something like a snort. 'He and I were young – I know what he is really like.'

'Perhaps it's presumptuous for any one of us to say we have the complete picture.'

'A typical public-school Englishman,' went on Donatella. 'Repressed. Evasive.'

'Is that how he seemed to you? I didn't find him either of those things.' It wasn't quite true but she could no longer restrain herself from fighting back. 'The Richard I knew was passionate and open.'

'Oh, he was adorable, of course, adorable, adorable . . .' Donatella waved a hand to show that all that could be taken as read. 'But if you had seen him, as I did, walking the riverbank in despair, unable to take care of himself—'

Isla remembered the postcard. 'I'm sorry,' she said, 'I have no idea what you're talking about.'

'No,' agreed Donatella, vindicated. 'You have not.'

'I assume you're going to explain?'

Donatella pursed her lips. 'Do you mind if I smoke?'

'No.' Isla watched her as she lit a cheroot, blew out the match, dropped it in the ashtray. Every tiny movement tried her patience almost beyond endurance.

'Richard was a very sick man,' declared Donatella.

'He hadn't been very well, we talked about it.'

'He confided in me,' said Donatella. 'He was afraid to see the doctor. I told him not to be such a child, that to be in ignorance is to remain in fear.'

'That's very sensible advice,' said Isla, hoping if not to damn, at least to dampen, with faint praise. 'No one could disagree with that.'

'Except the adorable Richard. I believe he did nothing. I went on holiday to Italy. Only one week since I am back, I hear that he has died. Because he is too chickenshit to see the doctor!'

This outburst was accompanied by a sudden and dramatic loss of poise. Donatella's hand trembled as she took a final drag on the cheroot and then flung it into the fireplace, her jaw set pugnaciously, and she averted her head, but not quite enough to prevent Isla seeing the tears in her eyes. Isla's impatience and resentment ebbed as fast as they had risen.

'You're absolutely right. He was a fool not to look after himself better. And I was remiss not to tell him so. It wasn't only Richard that was evasive – we both gave each other too much space. It's a very English tendency.'

The truth of this statement struck her a split second after it was uttered. She blundered on in its backwash, fighting to keep down the great wave of grief that threatened to engulf her. 'Thank you for trying. We should neither of us blame ourselves.'

'Blame has no part in what I am saying.' The edge had gone from Donatella's voice. When she looked at Isla, it was without the invisible but impenetrable barrier that had been there before. 'It is all so sad. Poor Ricardo,' she said softly. 'Poor Richard,' she added, to show that she spoke from the heart, and for them both.

Isla rose. 'I wonder,' she said, 'if you would like something of his?'

Isla walked with Donatella to her black BMW convertible, which was parked in the road beyond the gate. The hood was down, and a leather pilot's bag containing, Isla supposed, legal papers, lay between the back and front seats. Donatella threw her black handbag down next to it and opened the driver's door, which had not been locked. The box containing Richard's gold cufflinks she put in the glove compartment.

Isla nodded in the direction of the bags. 'You're very trusting.'

'Correction, I am very forgetful. In court, brilliant, in life – a walking crisis.'

Isla, watching her speed away on a wave of Verdi, thought she might have meant disaster. But crisis, with its connotations of excitement and possibility, was more apposite.

In bed that night Isla decided that the next day was the day she would do it. She would go and see her husband's mistress.

18

She took the Jag. She wanted to recreate this journey that Richard must have made so many times, in the way that he would have done it. It was strange to realise that this car – his car – was exactly as it had been on the evening he died. There was an *Evening Standard* from the day before on the back seat. A parking docket on the dash. The radio tuned to Radio Four. A CD on the player.

She had made a deal with herself. There would be no going back. After all this time she wanted to stare the truth in the face, and hear it speak its name. But if there was no one in, then it wasn't meant to be, and she would come away, and never go back. She knew very well that the first impulse was honourable and brave, the second cowardly and prosaic, but the deal at least gave her a predetermined structure which meant there were no more decisions.

As she glided past The Spaniards she pressed 'Play'. At once the car was filled with the glorious, robust voice of Lesley Garrett giving 'The Laughing Song' everything she'd got.

Jen reached that moment when she knew she was finished. For the best part of an hour she'd been refining and re-touching the parrot painting – then the switch was thrown that said: 'That'll do'. She put down her brush.

'Another day another dollar,' she said out loud, although that wasn't quite how she felt. Each painting (though God knows it was not how she'd envisaged spending her time when she had long hair and aspirations) was a small triumph. At worst it represented a victory over sloth, at best a decent piece of work, honestly completed. Looking at the canvas she wondered how on earth most people coped with what was so often referred to as the rat race, but which she was sure required levels of courage and endurance that were far beyond her. The mere thought of having to be anywhere at a set place and time for three quarters of one's adult life filled her with panic and affright. Even Red's job at Pleasurelands had impressed her. She was sure she couldn't have done it. As for the law, with its endless demands for exact knowledge, unshakable confidence, flawless performance . . . it made her shudder. And look, she thought bitterly, what it had done to Richard.

She had been up early and lost all sense of time, since Keith had brought her a cup of tea on his way out at eight-fifteen. It was for this reason that she had just consulted her watch, and knew that it was eleven forty-three precisely when she looked out of the window and saw, with a queasy lurch of disorientation, Richard's Jag drawing up outside.

Isla had assumed there would be nowhere to park. All she could remember was how crowded Selwyn Street had been on her last visit with Archie. But now of course it was mid-morning and most people were at work. There was space to spare. She still wouldn't have chosen to park immediately opposite, but she was tense and flustered, and misjudged the numbering.

She didn't dare change her mind, she had to keep moving forward or her resolve would falter. Without looking about her she got out, locked the car, and walked across the road and in through the gate of Number 65. A cat, two cats, scampered across her line of vision, running ahead of her, and disappeared. At the front door step, which was covered in sunken red and black tiles, she raised her eyes.

The door was wide open, and Jen Delaney sat on the stairs, waiting for her.

'It was you, wasn't it?' said Isla.

She might, of course, have been referring to their split-second exchange of glances through the car window, but Jen knew that she wasn't. Like an old married couple, they understood one another perfectly.

'Yes.'

Jen watched as she closed the front door. It became darker, the source of light shifted from the street to the living room. Jen had put on weight in the last few weeks, but Isla had lost it. She wore the same blue shirt and jeans she had worn that day in the park. But now she was pale, pin-thin, frighteningly stressed-out.

She walked into the living room. She had no handbag with her, just a bunch of keys in one hand. When Jen followed her she found her standing in the window next to the easel, her back to the light.

'Can I get you anything?' asked Jen.

'You can tell me how long it was going on for.'

For ever, thought Jen. 'Some years.'

'Which years? How many?'

'I think – ten. Ten or twelve.'

A minute delay as Isla absorbed the shock. Jen told herself, soon this will be over. It will be the worst thing that ever happened, but it will be in the past.

'How often . . . ?' Isla cleared her throat. 'How often was he here?'

'Once or twice a week.'

'What time of day?'

'Lunchtime or late afternoon, usually. Weekdays.' It sounded so tacky, and she knew it had not been tacky. And yet to deny or assert anything would be to inflict further damage.

There was another pause, during which Isla turned her back on Jen and stood, arms folded, looking out into the street, where the Jag gleamed in the early autumn sun. The keys swung slightly from her hand.

'Why?'

Jen was taken aback. 'I'm sorry . . .'

'Why did he come here, when he loved me? When we were so happy?'

'We were friends,' said Jen. 'We were close, relaxed together, we made no demands—'

Now Isla whipped round. 'And you suppose that I did?'

'No – I don't know—'

'Do you have any idea,' Isla's voice dropped as she came

towards Jen, 'what I'm trying to say? Can you begin to understand?' Her voice was thin and bitter, compressed by pain. 'Why
do you think I'm here?'

'We needed to see each other. If you hadn't come here I should
have come to you.'

'You knew, didn't you? You knew who I was.'

'Not to begin with.'

'But you found out. You knew and you still carried on.'

'Isla, I'd found a friend, it meant a lot to me, I was terribly shocked when I discovered who you were. Shocked and
ashamed, not of me and Richard, but that I was deceiving you.
You will never, ever, know how sorry I am.'

Isla gave a small, sharp cry of anguish and dropped on to a
chair. The keys fell to the ground with a chink as she pressed
her hands to her face.

'I am so sorry,' said Jen again. 'I know how you must hate
me.'

Isla shook her head. Sobbed, or laughed, Jen couldn't tell
which, then looked up. 'No, I don't hate you. I'm too tired to
hate you. But I despise you. Which is sad, Jen. It's so sad, but
that's how it is.'

She looked round the room. Jen felt her gaze move over
everything, her possessions, her home – her life – like a spider
walking over her skin.

'He must have known this place so well. As well as his own
home.'

Jen didn't answer. She endured the torture of Isla's scrutiny.
The long, scraping silence.

'How long did you say?'

'About twelve years.'

'Longer than we were married . . .' Isla looked at her. 'You
knew Richard longer than I did.'

'Perhaps . . .'

'You must have known when he married me – did you?'

'I was aware of a change . . .' Her eyes met Isla's. 'Yes, I did
know.'

'So, you could justify it. Because I was the intruder. I was the
interloper, is that what you told yourself?'

'No.'

'Well what did you bloody tell yourself?' Isla had never, until now, raised her voice. The shock of it made Jen flinch. 'What did you say to yourself in the late afternoon or early evening –' she gave the words a cudgelling emphasis – 'when my husband had gone back to his wife?'

'I didn't think about it.' This was the literal truth, but Jen could hear herself how it sounded – dismissive, callous, insulting. 'I mean that I accepted Richard as he was when he came here. It was as if he only existed when he was here. When he left to go back to his life, I went back to mine. We never made any claims on each other—'

'That was generous of you.'

'I never wanted any more than I had, than he gave me. And if he had suddenly stopped coming here I wouldn't have gone looking for him.'

'What am I supposed to do – be grateful?'

'Of course not.'

'When I said those things – all those things –' Isla shook her head to dislodge the memory – 'you just listened and answered. Knowing what you knew. How could you do that? Did it make you feel superior? Powerful? Is that the only reason you pretended to be friendly, so you could sit there smugly and watch me humiliate myself?'

'No.' Nothing could be further from the truth, or harder to explain. Jen was defeated. 'Look, I think you ought to go.'

'I bet you do. All I can say is, my dear, that this hurts me a hundred times – a thousand times – more than it hurts you!'

It was the 'my dear' that freed Jen. The part of her that had been shrinking like a whipped pup, beaten down by shame, stirred itself and bit back.

'Don't dare to tell me how much I hurt!'

'Your feelings don't interest me,' said Isla. It was the exact opposite of the truth.

'I've been through hell!' shouted Jen, red-faced, tears coursing down her cheeks. 'Hell, these past few weeks! Because of Richard *and* because of you! I agreed to see you the other day because I didn't know what else to do – I liked you, for God's sake! Because of you I'd decided to finish with Richard. But then it was all done for us, wasn't it? It was fucking well finished for us . . . !'

Her voice broke. There she stood in the centre of the floor, the woman whom Isla could not hate: her forearms over her face, fists clenched, sobbing. Isla, who had barely cried, envied her. The contrast between Jen – passionate and demonstrative, and herself as she must seem to be – jealous, resentful, sarcastic – was not one she found comforting.

'I'll go now,' she said, and picked up her keys.

'No you don't!' Jen crouched down in front of her, clutching her wrist. Her hands were strong, there was paint on the fingers. 'You came here to act this stuff out, so let me do my acting!'

'Acting?'

'Yes – something you know all about! Let me say my piece!' Jen grabbed her other wrist, gave them both a shake.

'Let go of me.'

She let go, but knelt there right in front of her, barring her way. 'One of the reasons I cared so much for Richard was because he loved you. I knew nothing about you, I never asked about you, but the only time I did he said he couldn't live without you. I was a part of his life which he'd become used to, and attached to, but you were completely indispensable to him. Without you, I wouldn't have kept him. He'd have left. You made him happy, you made him what he was. He was fond of me but he never loved me. If I did love him I never stopped to think about it, and now it's too late, I try not to. But please, please, please –' the fists again, this time held up between herself and Isla in a gesture something between a plea and a threat – 'please believe that I wasn't wicked. I was stupid and weak, but I didn't mean to cause all this damage. It horrifies me, and I'm more sorry than I can say. But it was you Richard loved. You, you, you! Lucky you,' she added exhaustedly, sitting back on her heels, head bowed.

Isla was moved. She wondered if Richard, who knew this room so well, was standing near them, hands in pockets, collar curling, looking on. She remembered Donatella's words, 'Repressed . . . evasive . . .' It was he, Richard, who had lived these two lives, made this journey repeatedly, gone from that room to this, from her to Jen. Richard who had lit the blue touch paper and retreated into the perfect, sanctified safety of death while their lives blew up in their faces.

'I believe you,' she whispered. 'I do believe you.'

'Thank God.' Jen went on all fours to the sofa and dragged herself up on to it, thrusting her hands into her hair, closing her eyes. 'You absolutely must believe me, Isla,' she said fiercely. 'Because I'm pregnant.'

19

The baby that Isla had never conceived had gone from being a pleasant possibility, not officiously strived for, to a deep and secret regret, without any conscious transition. She had suffered no pang of sudden realisation, never been told in so many words by a kind and highly-paid doctor, nor had she spoken of it to Richard. It had not happened, and she had allowed it not to. If Richard had been evasive about other things, then so had she, about this.

She knew that Richard did not care. She was all his happiness, and this his perfect marriage. That was what he had so often told her, and she had believed him. Although she was sure he would have agreed to it, she did not want a child enough to jeopardise that, and to force him – both of them – to submit to the long, costly and humiliating process of fertilisation treatment. That was something about which she was squeamish, prudish even, and she had projected her own revulsion at the idea on to Richard. When the thought crossed her mind, as it did very rarely, she dismissed it instantly because he would not have liked it.

And then there had been the question of her age. Although she saw all around her the evidence that women these days deferred motherhood for a multitude of reasons, sometimes until their early forties, she thought it not a good idea. Her experience with her stepsons had shown her at first hand what it was like to negotiate the emotional minefield of adolescence, and she could not imagine going through all that with her own child (which she knew instinctively would be harder) in her late fifties or early sixties.

She was wary of considering herself 'good with' the young

– that way there lay, if not madness, then at least the lively possibility of being taken for a ride – but she could say quite honestly that she liked them. She was not easily shocked – the entertainment industry had seen to that – and she understood instinctively the value of preserving a respectful distance between the generations. She did not feel that she was in competition with them: she wished them well. There again she had never been exposed to the day-to-day battle of raising children. In the face of Caroline's panicky conscientiousness, or Alison's genial, daily subjugation of chaos, she felt only humility. Could she do that? Could she ever have done it?

At these moments she would think herself lucky to be absolved from duty, and to be able to bask in the happy sinecure of unofficial favourite aunt. But in between there remained the dull certainty that she would never know those challenges, nor how she would shape up, and she mourned what couldn't be.

When Jen said that she was pregnant she had been able to do nothing but walk away. She left the front door open behind her, crossed the road without looking – not hearing the scream and blare of a terrifying near miss – and drove away. Somehow, she got home. She supposed she must have negotiated other vehicles, T-junctions, traffic lights and roundabouts, but she was not aware of doing so. Other drivers screeched to a halt, swerved madly to avoid her, cursed her roundly – a middle-aged woman at the wheel of a Jag, the driver from hell . . .

She was in shock. Back at the house, delayed reaction sent her swooping into shivering nausea. She took Richard's Black Watch plaid dressing gown – one she had bought him from Simpson's – out of the bedroom wardrobe and wrapped herself in it. Then she climbed into bed, her hands, feet and face still icy and lay with her teeth chattering for almost an hour before she started to relax.

Of all her confusion of feelings, the one that thrust its way forward, not to be denied, was her anger at Richard. All her love, her sorrow, her unswerving loyalty, seemed thrown into question by that small accumulation of cells in another woman's body, in another part of London . . . That he did not, nor could ever have known, about this legacy of his, seemed all the more

wounding. It was so casual, so easy, the most natural thing in the world – but something she herself had not been able to do. Even the dignity of her widow's grief had been corroded by this bitter, bitter jealousy.

She raged against Richard, weeping, moaning, tossing and turning, wishing, like a child that it could all be not true, or a dream, or that time could somehow roll itself back to the recent past with all its happy possibilities.

Eventually, she fell asleep. When she awoke it was late afternoon and for a split second everything seemed normal, before the enormity of what had happened hit her with the force of an express train.

A bell was ringing. The phone had rung several times while she'd been up here, and she'd ignored it, but this she recognised as the front door. Habit impelled her to answer it. She got unsteadily out of bed and discarded the dressing gown. The sudden exposure made her start shivering again. She caught sight of herself in the dressing-table mirror and was shocked to see how old she looked – old, and thin, and pinched. Too old for denim. She snatched up a brush and dragged it roughly through her hair.

It was Archie. He was already moving away from the door, or pretending to, and turned round with an anxious look when he heard her open it.

'Oh – Isla. Did I disturb you? Were you resting?'

'I was, but you weren't disturbing me.' Being kind to Archie was a habit as ingrained as answering the front door. 'Come in.'

'Are you sure? Well, OK . . . seeing as how I . . . I just thought I'd drop in and see how you were doing, bring you salaams from Ali and me.'

'That's nice of you, Archie. Come in.'

She caught sight of the two of them as they passed in the large mirror in the hall. There was a ripple in the glass that subjected those reflected in it to an eery, momentary distortion. She was like a ghost in her own house.

Archie selected tea in preference to a drink – he'd had a lunch, he explained, and also had to drive home, but she mustn't let that stop her, if . . . He seemed to believe that she must be desperate to drown her sorrows. She made a pot for them both and Archie carried the tray into the drawing room. Whether or not it was her imagination, their footsteps seemed to echo slightly as if the house were only partly furnished.

'The house seems so empty,' she said as they sat down.

'It would do . . . of course it would.' Archie took his tea. 'It's bound to.'

She raked her fingers through her hair. 'I'm sorry, I look like death.'

'Not at all, you don't. You look a little tired and stressed, but who wouldn't? Ali and I just wish there was more we could do.'

She made herself smile. 'You've both been absolute bricks, and I know I haven't been easy to help. You don't know how you'll react to – to this – until it happens to you.'

'A couple of people have asked me again about a memorial service. I said I had no idea . . .'

'I haven't either. I can't think about it Archie. Just at the moment the mere thought of another ritual, sitting in church, putting on the right face, all that – frankly it's too much for me.' Her voice trembled and she put up a hand to cover her mouth.

'Please, please, I didn't mean – the last thing I was trying to do was apply pressure. I only mentioned it to let you know how much Richard and you are in people's thoughts. He was so much liked and respected.'

'Good. That's good to know.'

Archie shifted in his seat, put his cup down with a jingle on the piecrust table. Isla thought, I'm losing it, I'm losing my ability to put people at their ease. There was a picture of Richard on the table, taken a few years ago. He'd been playing tennis with the boys in Bradenham, and stood there flushed and grinning, with a towel round his neck, his hair standing up in a damp peak, an arm round each of his sons. Archie picked it up.

'This is nice of him, and of the boys.'

'It's my favourite,' she agreed. 'He looks so happy and relaxed.'

'I should take more exercise . . .' Archie sighed. 'But it's finding the time.'

'You have to make time. But once you have, it pretty soon . . .' She ran out of steam. 'Archie—'

He started, as though he, too, had been sleepwalking through this conversation till now. 'Yes?'

'Archie, I want you to know I'm not going to pieces.'

'Of course you're not!' The promptness and emphasis with which he agreed betrayed him utterly.

'I don't want you going away from here thinking I'm a wreck. I shall miss Richard to the day I die, but I can face my own life. I can look into the future. I have plans.'

'I'm sure you do, it's what we've all come to expect of you,' said Archie, as if he were the elected spokesman for all who knew her. 'But – you have to recognise – I don't want to sound like one of these frightful self-help books, but you must allow yourself time, not rush things—'

'Archie, please!'

'Sorry.'

'Don't be sorry. I didn't mean to bite your head off. But I have time, scads of it, reaching away into infinity. Time is not a problem.'

'Sorr- yes.'

'I've had a bad day, that's all.' She took a deep breath, brought her voice back down. 'And since you're here, I want to ask you something.'

'Please, I wish you would.' Poor Archie. 'Anything.'

'Did you know Richard had a mistress?'

He was incapable of dissembling, the most transparently honest person she knew. His appalled disbelief was painfully genuine.

'No . . . ! No, absolutely not, I didn't. In fact Isla, I must say—'

'Well, he did, Archie. For years. This isn't some kind of deranged, grief-stricken fantasy. I've met her and talked to her. Are you quite sure you didn't know?'

'Isla, I swear to you. I'm certain that no one –' He shook his head. 'I don't believe it.'

'You have to. It's true. But it's not the end of the world,' she added, as Archie continued to shake his head like a wounded animal. 'And it's nothing new, or in the least unusual.' She was being cruel, because Archie's new, fresh pain was a comfort to her, it showed her she was past that.

'But Richard,' he mumbled, 'of all people!'

'He wasn't a saint.'

'No, but –' Archie raised anguished eyes to hers. 'He loved you so much!'

It was Archie now who broke down, and she went and knelt in front of him and pulled his head on to her shoulder. She was ashamed for having exacted the words which above all she needed to hear, at such a cost, from such a willing victim.

On the way out, Archie said: 'By the way, Amanda sends her love.'

'Do give her mine – how is she?'

'A pretty fair old nightmare. Keeping Ali and me on the hop. But she thinks the world of you and she was devastated when we told her about Richard. I think she's writing you a letter.'

'How sweet of her.'

'Don't hold your breath, it'll probably never get completed, let alone sent. You must let us know when this TV thing's going to be on, she absolutely hero worships that chap with the funny glasses.'

'Adrian. I'll get her a couple of tickets, then she can come along and meet him.'

'Can you do that? Good lord, she'd be beside herself!'

'Tell her it's done. I'll ring her up when I know about dates.'

Archie took her shoulders tentatively and kissed her cheek. 'You're a star. In every sense.'

She walked with him to the car. Before getting in, he paused.

'Isla, about this other thing—'

'Yes?'

'I don't really know how to say this, and it will probably sound even more stupid than usual, but – um—'

'Archie.'

'If it's true –' he held up a hand, apologising for doubting her – 'and if you say it is then I'll take your word for it. If it's true, I honestly believe that it made no difference. You were Richard's, um, one true love. His guiding light. He was never completely happy till he married you. And then he was. Actually he was one of the happiest men one could wish to meet. If there was someone else, he must have had his reasons or whatever, but it was you he loved. That's all I have to say. Jesus wept, what a speech—!'

'It was a nice speech, Archie. One of your best.' She kept her distance, but smiled at him. She had used him shamelessly and yet he saw it as his privilege. He was a good, dear man.

'Oh yes, I nearly forgot what with – Ali wondered if you could stand supper next week?'

'I could do more than stand it. I'd love it.'

'Splendid!' His face lit up. 'With a bit of luck that'll make Amanda stay in and you can tell her yourself about the tickets.'

'I'll look forward to it.'

'*A bientôt*, then.'

'Thank you for coming, Archie.'

She played back her messages. The first, from Lori, was congratulatory – 'You were brilliant, a real pro. I'm so proud of you. Please let me know any time if you simply can't face something, and I'll be a junkyard dog on your behalf.' Barbara, who didn't like machines, was brusque: 'Are we going to see you? Brook End's looking a bit sad since Marjory took up with Norman Brake. Ring me back.'

She played the last message three times. 'Isla . . . ? It's Scotch. I'm thinking about you every moment. You and Richard were the business . . . What can I say? I wish I knew you better so I could help you more. Fare thee well, not goodbye.'

Isla went out into the garden. The garden in Hampstead they had always kept as a low maintenance green space – as many different shades and textures of green as they could manage, with two or three statues, and a pool and waterfall among the trees at the end. In the summer Isla filled the stone urns on the patio with pelargoniums, lobelia, trailing fuchsias and petunias, but the secretive, changing green shade was what she and Richard had liked. The Brook End garden was where Isla indulged her untutored enthusiasm for scented, old-fashioned flowers.

She walked down to the end and sat on the seat amongst the trees, looking back towards the house. Soon it would start to be chilly in the evenings, too chilly to sit out here beneath the overhanging trees. She found herself thinking of Selwyn Street, of Jen's small, busy, untidy house, and of the life she led there. Sometimes with Richard. She tried to quieten her heart, to let her mind drift, and settle. It was difficult, the control of pain by surrender, and she only partially managed it. But when, about twenty minutes later, she rose and walked back up the lawn to the house, she was aware of a glimmer of grey where there had been only darkness: the faint, tremulous dawn of something that was not despair.

Jen could no longer fight her pregnancy. Quietly, relentlessly it was taking her over. How could she have forgotten how it felt, this sea change? Now that the daily battle with sickness had gone, she was reduced – or elevated – to the role of support system for what was inside her. Her waistbands, those with fastenings, would no longer do up. She was sure that with Claudia that hadn't happened so soon, but then she had been much younger. She sewed panels of elastic into the sides of her dungarees. In the Wednesday market she found a couple of loose Indian tops that came down well over her seat. She bought some leggings two sizes larger than usual. That would have to do. Her hair became an unmanageable fuzz: she went to Hair by Angie in Crouch Hill and had it cut very short. Angie said it took years off her, but she was self-conscious, thinking it exposed the beginnings of a sagging jaw. Her bust burgeoned, she was voluptuous. When she was nudged by the notion that Richard would have liked her like this, she slapped it away, and fastened her mind, penitentially, on Isla: reed-slim, fine-boned, long limbed . . . It was a bad joke. If Richard had wanted more children, he would have had them with Isla.

That this baby was going to be born was no longer in doubt. She told Claudia because she didn't feel she could leave it any longer. Passive deception had been part of her life for too long. The response was diametrically different from that which she'd expected.

'Mum – that's brilliant!'

They were in the supermarket, but Claudia embraced her mightily by the petfoods.

'You're pleased . . . ?'

'Of course I'm pleased, what did you expect?'

'I don't know.' Jen was dazed. 'Not this. You approve, do you?'

'No I don't *approve*, in fact I disapprove strongly – you ought to have known better at your age, but a little baby! I'll help out, you know that, and since you've obviously decided to go ahead – well – enjoy!'

Propelled by the build-up of irritability around them they moved towards the checkout. Claudia picked up a pack containing a Thomas the Tank Engine cup, bowl and spoon. 'Let's get this!'

'It's a bit early—'

'It's never too early – let me, I want to. I'm going to start buying something each week between now and the baby.'

They reached the checkout and Jen paid – for everything, because Claudia hadn't got any money with her. Out in the car park as they loaded the boot, she said: 'Red – I'm not trying to put a dampener on the proceedings, but I can't honestly say that I decided to go ahead, as you put it.'

Claudia looked at her over the top of the car. 'Of course you didn't, you've never made a decision in your life.'

'Oh.' Jen gulped this down and got in. She leaned across to unlock the passenger door and Claudia got in next to her.

'Sorry, that wasn't meant to sound so rude.'

'No offence taken.'

'You do well, Mum. You're like Ant, you keep an open mind. Go with the flow.'

'This is hardly what I saw myself doing in my fortieth year.'

'We'll do it together.'

'You've got your own life, Red.'

'But you are pleased about it, aren't you? You must be.'

Jen started the engine. 'I'm resigned to it.'

'Hang on.' Claudia leaned across her and switched the ignition off again. 'I do hope you're going to be a bit more positive than that. Resigned is no way to embark on a new chapter.'

'I dare say I'll be positive in due course. But the truth is, right now I'm shell-shocked.'

'Yes . . .' Claudia pursed her lips thoughtfully. 'How far gone are you?'

'Eighteen . . . twenty weeks.'

Claudia glanced briefly downwards. 'You don't show.'

'That's because I'm working on it. I may not show, but I feel.'

'It's so exciting!' burst out Claudia again. 'I'll shut up now.'

They let it lie there for a while as they drove back to the house. Anthony was due to collect Claudia there at about six. Jen had got used to these early evening exchanges, and she liked Anthony. His ignoring of the vast differences in age and background between himself and her daughter she now saw not as the practised denial of an ageing smoothy, but as evidence of a certain dignity, and a respect both for Claudia and their relationship. He allowed his demeanour to speak for him, always putting Claudia first, according equal deference to both her and Jen, and slotting himself modestly into the pecking order at Selwyn Street like a suitor half his age. His manners were part of him, never faltering but never conspicuous, either. In what could have been a vexed situation, Anthony's humility was the sincerest proof of his love for Claudia.

Which was why she dreaded him knowing about her pregnancy. She cared what he thought, and feared that no matter how he concealed it, he would secretly be appalled. This in turn might have some subtly destructive effect on the relationship between him and Claudia. Explanations would tell him far more than he wanted to know, and excuses would, of course, be out of the question on grounds of taste and politeness.

Claudia's enthusiastic reaction did nothing to set her mind at rest. This was a circumstance in which she was by no means sure which would weigh heaviest, romantic passion or the wisdom of experience. She hoped it wouldn't be the latter. This was her pregnancy, her responsibility: it would be awful if it were to reflect on Claudia in any way.

This evening, Anthony arrived in his silver Mercedes. They were going to the National Theatre to see a new play which had caused a certain amount of outrage among the self-appointed guardians of the nation's morals. Jen, watching him from an upstairs window (she had deliberately contrived to be out of the way at this moment), reflected that nothing displayed the generation gap more clearly than what he and Claudia had chosen to wear for the theatre. He was immaculately suited, Claudia was in loose, baggy, striped trousers which looked like – and may well have been – men's pyjama bottoms, whose frayed ends flapped just above her ankles. She'd teamed these with a navy-surplus jumper and baseball boots: she looked extraordinary. They made an arresting couple who might very easily have been taken for well-to-do uncle and wayward niece.

Standing in front of the mirror tweaking at her bits of hair, and putting on bigger earrings – anything to detract from her waistline – she listened to the sounds of his arrival. Claudia's verbal greeting was laconic, but punctuated by what Jen thought of as kissing intervals. She heard Anthony say 'Hello, my darling' and 'Mm – mm'. The front door closed and they went through to the kitchen. There was a chink of glasses, and Claudia's voice again, rattling on nineteen to the dozen now they were out of earshot. Jen's heart sank. Abel was lying indolently against the pillows on her bed, washing a front paw with his eyes closed. Time-wasting, she sat down by him and began to stroke his slack, plushy flank. But he wasn't in the mood, and dabbed her hand away with an imperious paw, claws out.

When she went into the kitchen, Anthony was leaning against the work top, with Cain in his arms. He let the cat slither to the ground when she came in, and kissed her lightly on the cheek – they had progressed to that.

'Jen, good evening. I say, you're different.'

She touched her head. 'I needed a change . . . Oh look, he's covered your suit in hair.'

'That's nothing. By the way, congratulations, what wonderful news.'

'Thank you.' She was guarded.

'Everything they say must be true, you look absolutely tremendous.'

'Do I?'

'See?' said Claudia. 'Have a drink.'

She poured a glass of white wine. Anthony said: 'I'd have brought a bottle of champagne if I'd known.'

Jen took a sip. 'Perhaps we should reserve that for wetting the baby's head.' It was the first time she'd mentioned 'the baby' as a separate entity, something apart from her current condition. It felt strange but not unpleasant.

'Good idea.'

Keith came in at the front door. 'Good evening!'

'Come on in and have a glass of something,' said Jen.

'Oh I don't know, should I?' He stood in the hall, removing his cycle helmet. It left his hair flattened and a red mark across his forehead.

Anthony poured a glass and held it out. 'This do?'

'Go on then, you twisted my arm.' Keith glanced round at the three of them. 'Everyone's terribly smart, are we celebrating something?'

There was split second pause, before Claudia said: 'I'm going to be a big sister.'

Keith's face was a study as he unravelled this, grappled with his disbelief, and sought an appropriate response. He looked at Jen, pointed. 'Ummm . . . you . . . ?'

'Yes. In March.'

'Well!' He was actually blushing. 'You could knock me down with the proverbial! Congratulations.'

'Thanks.'

'So, my goodness, there'll be a few changes made round here I'll be bound.'

'Not too many I hope,' said Jen. 'Anyway, it's a long way off . . .' She changed the subject without drawing breath. 'These two are off to see That Play at the National, Keith, do you think it's likely to deprave and corrupt them?'

'I can't say I care if it does,' replied Keith spiritedly. 'I'm against censorship myself.'

Anthony laughed, and put his arm round Claudia. 'Jolly well spoken. We few, we happy few, are well on the way to being the last outpost of civilised values.'

We are? thought Jen. *We are?*

Isla invited Barbara to go to the David D rail sale with her. She needed friends about her who were solid and unsentimental. She knew that beneath Barbara's thornproof tweed façade there were emotional antennae as sensitive as any butterfly's, but she could be relied upon to take such an outing at its face value.

The sale was on a Monday, and she spent the Saturday and Sunday nights at Brook End, so that they could drive in together.

She knew at once what Barbara had meant about the cottage seeming 'a bit sad'. It was clear Marjory had been in and done her stuff – it was tidy, there was milk in the fridge and the immersion heater was on – but the windows were filmy, and the affectionate little touches were missing. There was no posy of flowers on the dining-room table, no scrawled notes bristling with exclamation marks . . . There was a dead fly on the bedroom windowsill.

And yet Isla felt more at ease in Brook End. This had always been her place, more than Richard's. It was less haunted. She left the doors open front and back, and flung open the windows. Then she put on some music – Ella singing Gershwin – and went out into the garden. It was six o'clock, hovering, in late September, on the edge of dusk. She could hear the secretive chuckle of the shallow brook, and the idle, intermittent barking of a dog up in the village. She took comfort from the sense of the wide, warm fields all around, of the birds roosting snugly in the trees and beams of The Bury, of the churchyard where Richard lay, his headstone not yet weathered but already a part of that kindly, dignified gathering. She felt at home.

Norman Brake appeared at the five-bar gate on to the lane as she inspected what would be her last parade of flowers before winter.

'Evening.'

'Hello Norman.'

'Everything all right then? She's been in.'

'Everything's fine. Isn't it a lovely evening?'

'It'll do.'

'I'll have to get busy on these borders tomorrow.'

'Keep busy, that's the thing,' he agreed. And then, on a pugnacious note: 'It doesn't do to leave a place empty all the time.'

'We don't – I don't. We've always come as much as we can. I dare say I'll be coming more often, now.'

'Dare say you will.'

'Come in why don't you,' said Isla, safe in the knowledge that he'd never once accepted such an invitation.

'Could do.' To her astonishment he opened the gate and entered, testing the latch fiercely as he closed it again. 'Can't stop, though.'

Having conceded this much to neighbourly sociability, it was clearly as far as he was prepared to go. He wouldn't even sit down, still less come into the house or have anything to eat or drink. He and Isla stood, a little awkwardly, just inside the gate.

'Good service, up there the other day,' Norman commented, by which Isla knew he meant Richard's funeral.

'It was, wasn't it. I think Richard would have approved.'

'Old boy did well.' This might have referred to Richard, the rector or any one of half a dozen others, so she confined herself to agreeing.

'You doin' all right then?' asked Norman.

'Not bad – you know.'

'You look all right.'

'I feel better for being here.'

'Working?'

'I've got some television work coming up, it goes into production quite soon.'

'They need someone halfway decent on the telly, it's mostly bloody rubbish,' he opined. And he should know, thought Isla. She was sure that *Over the Parrot* would fill Norman with fear and loathing, and changed tack before he could press for details.

'How is Marjory?'

'Tearing about all over the place. This place don't deserve her.'

In Norman's admittedly limited lexicon of praise, this constituted honours of the very highest order. 'She is absolutely wonderful,' agreed Isla. 'Every village needs a Marjory.'

'She won't be able to do so much around the place once she's a married woman,' said Norman, testing the gate latch again. 'She'll want to stop at home a bit more. With 'er 'usband.'

'Of course . . .' Isla nodded thoughtfully. Put out a probe: 'Lucky man.'

'I am,' declared Norman. 'But I got work to do.'

'I feared as much!' cried Barbara on the way into London on Monday. 'I told Bill I reckoned it was on the cards but he laughed me to scorn.'

'So long as they're happy,' reflected Isla. 'And Marjory does seem to be.'

'But she hasn't a clue! The woman's a complete innocent.'

'We don't know that, Bar.'

'It's anybody's educated guess.'

'She may not have a lot of worldly experience as we'd recognise it,' said Isla, 'but she's not daft. A lot of people with strings of relationships behind them are as foolish as the day they started out – that's why they keep on making the same mistakes. Marjory's sensible, and pragmatic, she feels she'd like to be in partnership with someone in the last quarter of her life –' She faltered slightly. 'And this is her chance.'

'But Norman Brake? For goodness' sake.'

'Maybe she'll change him.' This provoked a snort of scorn. 'You never know.'

'Yes you do. Still, you're quite right,' conceded Barbara, 'there's nothing to do but wish them well.'

It was some time later, when they were coming into London, that Barbara said:

'Bill and I have got to tell people some time, so I may as well start with you.'

'Yes?'

'Hold on to your hat – this is a bit of a shaker.'

'Spit it out, Bar.'

'Nell's a lesbian.'

Isla, travelling at under thirty, cruised, tranced, through a red light. 'Is she?'

'Bill's completely poleaxed. Completely. We both are, but women are a million times tougher than men.'

Isla pulled into the inside lane, in the comforting shelter of a container lorry. 'Did she tell you herself?'

'She jolly well did.' Barbara ran big, square fingers round the string of pearls that lay on her bottle-green Pringle jumper. 'Took more guts to do that than to take a novice round Burleigh, I can imagine.'

'Yes,' said Isla, 'I can imagine it would. Is she happy?'

'Well, do you know, I think she is?' Barbara sounded mystified. 'After a fashion. I don't suppose anyone outside the norm like that can be really happy, but she certainly looked bright-eyed and bushy-tailed. And not wearing a collar and tie, or anything, thank God.'

Isla had to smile. 'She hasn't changed, remember. It's just your view of her that's changed.'

'Oh God, don't start on that, that's all far too clever for me, there's quite enough for the old boy and me to digest without getting psychological about it.'

'I only meant, she's still your daughter.'

'Don't I know it! Pig-headed as ever. God in heaven.' Barbara shook her head. 'What the village will say I can't imagine.'

'The village will chew on it for a while and then move on to something else. People like their toffs to be aberrant. You and Bill are obviously being brilliant, they'll take their tone from you.'

'There's a girlfriend, of course.'

Isla fixed her eyes on the back of the container lorry, counting slats. 'Is there?'

'Oh yes, yes, yes. We haven't met her, but apparently it's some young lawyer woman that Nell went to France with last month.'

'Really?'

'Not the first. There was some tragic unrequited thing going on before this – it makes you look at your friends, I can tell you. And don't we feel ninnies for getting so worked up about the Scott-Chatham boy!'

'I told you not to worry about that.'

'You did,' Barbara gave her an astute look, 'but not, I think, with this in mind.'

'No,' Isla admitted. 'Anyway, this new relationship – it's mutual, this time?'

'Big thing, we gather, though Lord knows what we're supposed to do about it. I mean, what's the protocol? Sunday lunch? Dinner? Tennis – she's probably a whizz at tennis, so maybe that's best. And what about beds? Hall-elujah, the mind boggles!'

'Separate beds, of course,' said Isla, pulling out and speeding up, her heart lifting as she left the container lorry behind. 'It's your house, Bar, you must do what you feel comfortable with.'

'I'm not sure,' said Barbara gruffly, but quite equably, 'that the old man and I are ever going to feel comfortable again.'

'Yes you will,' said Isla. 'You will, because Nell's happy.'

* * *

At the rail sale there was one model you couldn't help looking at. She was inches taller than the rest, with the swan neck and small, imperiously tilted close-cropped head of a Masai *moran*. The clothes she displayed might have been blown on to her astonishing frame by some freak wind, so oblivious did she seem to them. She had a long stride and a natural aloofness quite unlike the affected blank stares of the other girls. No make-up, no jewellery. A wonderful female animal. She was, thought Isla, a girl who in any context you cared to name, would draw the eye and the attention.

'Call me old-fashioned,' growled Barbara without irony, 'but none of these girls is what you'd call pretty.'

The MC referred to the tall model as 'Red'. Isla found a list of the models' full names in tiny print at the back of the catalogue. No Red, but a Claudia Delaney. She was quite sure it must be her, the daughter Jen had mentioned that day in the park.

'If this is the type of girl they pay good money to, I reckon our Nell would be in with a chance,' stage-whispered Barbara. 'And look at these prices, my dear, for the sort of stuff you can buy at the county show!'

'Not really, Bar. This is the designer version. Pretend-county show.'

'Even worse!'

After the show they toured the rails. Isla was an instant focus for the *vendeuse*, but for once she could summon no serious interest in the clothes. In the end she bought a long tunic in cream shantung with a mandarin collar. As her gold card was processed, she said: 'You have one very remarkable model here today.'

'You mean Red – isn't she exquisite?'

'I'm not sure about that,' said Isla. 'She's too individual to be exquisite, and too emphatic, somehow, to be a model.'

'It's her first time,' said the *vendeuse* apologetically. 'She's a little rough round the edges.'

'No, it's a compliment, you mustn't change her – Claudia, is it?'

'Claudia Delaney.'

'She's perfect as she is.'

The *vendeuse* smiled thinly and returned Isla's gold card.

Barbara hrumphed to Isla as they walked away. 'Pardon me if I don't buy, there's not a lot here for an elderly size sixteen with animals to attend to.'

'There are some beautiful tweed jackets, Bar, look . . .' Isla paused by the rail of jackets. 'One of these would be perfect for you. And as for the price you ought to splash out sometimes. As we get older we need more expensive clothes.'

'Mrs Wakefield is right,' said the *vendeuse*, who had remained in hover mode. 'This jacket is a classic, a must-have for any woman's wardrobe.'

What a fool she was, thought Isla, to make her eavesdropping public, let alone use the phrase 'must-have' which ensured that this particular potential customer would not buy the jacket if it were the last one on earth.

'Not interested,' Barbara declared. And muttered, as they headed for the door: 'Ghastly, ghastly female.'

As they walked down a side road towards their meter, Isla saw someone she knew coming towards them.

'Oh look – hello!'

'Isla, how nice to see you,' said Anthony, clasping her hand in both of his.

'This is Barbara Fyler – Bar, meet Anthony Saxby. He and I met at an insufferably boring charity lunch.'

'How do you do.'

'We consoled each other by playing hangman during the speeches,' explained Anthony, 'but very discreetly.'

'Good works can be heavy going,' agreed Bar, 'but someone's got to do them.'

'Is that what you're doing today?'

'No,' said Isla. 'Today we're purely frivolous, we've been at a fashion show.'

'David D?'

'How on earth did you know that?'

'Because I'm here myself to meet a friend from there,' said Anthony, glancing beyond them up the road. His face broke into a broad smile. 'And there she is.'

They turned to see the tall model striding towards them. Even off duty she had the kind of walk that made them both step slightly to one side for fear of being mown down.

As she drew level, Isla felt her glance whisk over them. Anthony stepped forward – he was fractionally shorter – and planted a light kiss on the girl's mouth.

'Claudia, I want you to meet Isla Munro – and Barbara Fyler. They've been at your show.'

'Yes, I saw you there. Hello.' It was clear Claudia wouldn't have shaken hands, but Barbara thrust out a paw, and it would then have seemed rude to exclude Isla. The girl's hand was very cool.

'How do you do my dear,' said Barbara. 'Jolly good show, but horribly overpriced.'

'I bought something nice,' said Isla. 'And it was a good show. Well done.'

'This is pocket money for her,' explained Anthony with a touch of pride. 'She takes her finals next summer.'

'I'm quite sure,' said Isla truthfully, 'that you could make thousands at this game if you wanted to.' With difficulty she looked into, and held, the girl's eyes. Be direct. Be open. Face value. She was perfectly certain that Claudia knew.

The next remark confirmed it. 'I'm really sorry about your husband.'

'How sweet of you . . . I miss him.'

Isla caught Anthony's aghast expression. 'I'm most frightfully sorry, I had no—'

'Of course you didn't.' She gave him a quick, reassuring smile.

Claudia's gaze hadn't shifted. 'We all miss him,' she said.

'I'm hopelessly muddled,' said Barbara as they headed for King's Cross and her train home. 'What's the connection?'

'She's the daughter of your painter lady – the one who did Portia.'

'Good grief, you don't say! I should never have guessed, there isn't a hint of a family resemblance.'

'I suppose not.'

'The fairies must have brought her,' said Barbara.

20

Jen delivered the parrot to Mr and Mrs Hastings. And not a moment too soon, it seemed to her. Doug Hastings had become so thin it was possible to imagine death sitting next to him in his armchair. His decline since Jen's last visit was shockingly marked.

But Chipper lived up to his name, and Mrs Hastings was the same as ever – tightly coiffed, neatly clad, a rose-red lipstick bleeding slightly into the lines around her narrow mouth. The flat was immaculate. Jen was touched and impressed by their absolute refusal to let appearances slip. Even Doug's shoes were polished to a gloss, his socks clung to his stick-like shanks with the aid of sock-suspenders and the sleeves of his beige cardigan were ironed to a crease down the outside.

Mindful of its importance, she unveiled the portrait with a certain amount of trepidation, but their reaction was one of unfeigned, unreserved delight.

'It's beautiful, it's absolutely perfect,' declared Mrs Hastings. 'Hasn't she done a wonderful job, Doug? Look at him dear,' she whispered to Jen, 'he's quite overcome.'

And indeed he was. His eyes were shining with tears, and one gaunt, freckled hand covered his mouth.

'Chipper's a very easy subject,' Jen lied. 'I've really enjoyed doing it.'

'You have a wonderful talent,' said Mrs Hastings, taking Jen's hand in both of hers and patting it gently. 'What a thing it must be to have a real talent, and be able to give so much pleasure to others. Isn't she clever, Doug?'

Doug had now got enough of a grip to answer, but only to murmur that he didn't know what to say.

'You've done for him,' said his wife cheerfully. 'Will you have a drink with us, to celebrate?'

There was no point in demurring, the sherry decanter and three glasses stood on a lacquered tray on the side. 'I'd love to.'

She sat down. Mrs Hastings – she implored Jen to call her Avis – brought over the sherry, and a little basket full of cheese footballs. It was over twenty years since Jen had drunk sherry, but she found that she did so now quite happily. There was something immeasurably soothing about the Hastings – their cleanliness, their courage, their kindness, their adherence to all sorts of relatively unimportant standards which, when taken together, amounted to an almost superhuman achievement. People poured scorn on this sort of tidying away of the emotions but it had its roots in politeness, Jen realised, and consideration for the feelings of others.

'Where will you hang the painting?' she asked. They had some pictures – three Redouté roses, a harlequin, a mountain landscape and Wise Old Elephant – but the walls of the living room weren't crowded.

'Over the sideboard,' said Doug, strong on the practicalities. 'We'll put the mirror opposite.'

'Good thinking,' said Jen. 'That way you get two for the price of one.'

'Three if you count Chipper,' Avis reminded them.

'Three, of course.'

'You're looking well, by the way,' Avis went on. 'Isn't she, Doug?' This was another thing about them, they talked about her in the third person as though she were a child, and instead of finding it irritating, it was curiously comforting.

'She is,' agreed Doug. 'I'm not sure about the haircut, mind.'

'It's modern, Doug,' said Avis reprovingly.

'A bit too modern for me. But you've put on a bit of weight, and it suits you.'

It may have been the sherry, or the childlike feeling, or simply the benign, anonymous safety of this place – but whatever the reason Jen found herself saying, without a moment's pause: 'I'm expecting a baby in the spring.'

'No!' Avis's face lit up. 'You hear that Doug? She's expecting!'

'No wonder she looks so pretty,' said Doug gallantly, making up for the unintentional slight a moment ago.

'Do you have a family already?'

'A grown-up daughter.'

'She must be over the moon.'

'She is pleased, yes. I wasn't sure what she'd make of her middle-aged mother being pregnant, but fortunately . . .'

Doug said: 'I bet your husband was surprised.'

'Doug . . . !' Quicker on the uptake, or the intuition, Avis frowned urgently at him.

'I'm sorry, did I say something . . . ?'

'No, of course not,' said Jen, thinking on her feet. 'We're separated. But very amicably.'

'That's the way,' said Avis. 'No one wants a lot of nastiness.'

Jen prayed that they wouldn't ask any more questions, but of course there was never the slightest chance they would do anything so indelicate. She had given them a perfectly plausible summary of her situation and the rest was her business.

When she rose to leave, Doug tried to struggle to his feet. She didn't like to stop him, but fortunately Avis stepped in, with a firm but gentle 'No you don't.'

Jen held out her hand. His was very cold and dry, the thin bones rubbing against one another in their sheath of papery skin.

'Thank you my dear.' He was teary again, but in command. 'It means a lot to me. I can't thank you enough.'

She said it was her pleasure, and meant it.

In the hall Avis took an envelope off a side table and pressed it into her hand.

'I wish it could be more.'

This time Jen pointed out gently: 'It's my usual rate.'

'But it's worth ever so much more to us.'

'I'm so pleased. I really am.'

Avis opened the door, put it on the latch and accompanied Jen to the lift. In a lowered voice, she said: 'He's not got long now.'

It was spurious to express dismay, so Jen confined herself to: 'I think he's marvellous. So brave.'

'He is. He's my Doug.' The lift arrived, and she patted Jen's shoulder. 'You get along. But come back and see us, dear. We never had any children, it does us good to see people.'

'I will, definitely.'

She got into the lift, pressed the button. Avis waved – a small wave, because it was only a short distance.

'Bye dear. Don't leave it too long.'

Jen felt tired on the way home – dead tired, emotionally and physically. The oasis of calm which had been the Hastings' flat seemed to have left her more vulnerable to the churning uncertainties of her own life. And although at the time she had found their fortitude uplifting, she was now ambushed by a terrible attack of weepiness. So much so, that she had to pull into a side road to effect repairs, only to find she was facing the wrong way down a one-way street and was being soundly blagged by a driver coming in the opposite direction.

'I'm sorry, I'm sorry . . . !' she sobbed helplessly. The poor man's look of quite justifiable exasperation flattened into one of dismay, and then of remorse as he inched by.

He rolled his window down. 'There's a space up there – I should nip in quick while the going's good.'

There wasn't much nipping about it, she was in too much of a state, and blinded by tears. But she got there, and then collapsed, sobbing, on the steering wheel

When she did get under way again, she promised herself some serious self-indulgence when she reached home – a stiff drink, a hot, scented bath (she might even light a candle or two as suggested in the magazines), and an early night with the radio and her book. The picture of herself tucked up in bed, glowing from the bath, with the cats purring on the quilt, was so vivid and seductive that it was a doubly rude shock to discover on arrival that the candles were not a luxury but a necessity – there was a power cut in Selwyn Street.

Keith met her in the hall with a rapidly-dwindling stub of *bougi* on a saucer.

'I found this, but remind me where the others are?'

Together, in the small, wavering light, they shuffled into the kitchen and located the carrier bag, among other carrier bags in the bottom drawer, where Jen's assortment of candles were kept.

'I don't believe this,' she moaned. 'How long have they been off for?'

'Three quarters of an hour. It was light to begin with.'

'But not now,' snapped Jen.

'I rang them, and it's this whole part of the grid apparently. They're on the case.'

'You don't happen to know if the immersion heater's on?'

'No – yes. I mean, I do know and it isn't. I turned it off when I came in.'

'Keith!'

'I'm sorry, but you generally like it off during the day, and since you seemed to have forgotten—'

'I had, but – oh to hell with it. Maybe the water's still hot.'

'You could try,' said Keith.

She did, and it wasn't. Because the bath was now definitely out of the question she began to crave it quite desperately. She felt heavy and drained – the small of her back ached and her stomach was tight. She went and lay down on the sofa in the living room, put on a Clannad tape, and tried to relax, but couldn't. There was a sensation of pressure that she couldn't relieve. Out in the hall Keith was calling the Electricity Board again.

'. . . so you've got no idea when . . . ? I see. Right. No, I appreciate that. OK, yes, we'll just have to be patient.'

He came in. 'I tell you what I've got my camping Gaz burner upstairs. What say I make us a cup of tea.'

'Thanks. That'd be nice.'

He peered at her in the flickering twilight. 'Are you all right?'

'I'm just so tired . . . I've no reason to be so knackered . . .'

'Who needs a reason in your condition? I'll make tea.' He went to the door, then returned. 'Better yet, why not go and get into bed? I could do you a hot water bottle.'

She knew that it was a good idea, but the thought of moving, of going up the stairs, was too much.

'I'll have the tea first, and then see . . .'

'Okey dokey.'

She almost dozed off lying there, but it was an uncomfortable state of semi-consciousness rather than the welcome surrender of sleep. In the background she could hear Keith pottering about, up and down the stairs, clanking around with the Gaz burner, assembling mugs, tum-te-tumming away to himself.

When it happened, it took a few seconds for her to realise that the tiredness and discomfort had become something more urgent.

Keith put a nightlight in a saucer on the tray and carried it through into the living room. As he came round the end of the sofa he saw Jen's hand stretched up towards him.

'The cup that cheers,' he said. He put the tray down and proffered the mug. 'There we go . . .' He peered at her in the dim light. 'Hey there, anyone at home?'

Dinner with the Stainforths was a mixed blessing. So many things reminded Isla of being here with Richard. In this robustly domestic context he had always been quieter than usual, and less confident, aware of his own shortcomings. She found this awkwardness touching, and loved him for it. And Archie, of course, was – both literally and metaphorically – at home, his body language relaxed, his manner freer, in a way that was nice to see.

They all missed the untypical Richard who had been such a vital element in the mix, who had enabled Ali to faff maternally, and Archie to show off a bit, and Isla to demonstrate (she admitted it) her rapport with the children. In the big untidy house in Clarendon Road, Richard had been their gracefully bewildered audience.

Almost unconsciously they tried to compensate for his absence. They spoke a little louder, and moved and ate a little quicker. Where they had never even thought of it before, they each feared a silence and were concerned about what to say next. It was something of a mercy when, as they sat round the kitchen table over coffee, Amanda appeared.

'Hi,' she said from the doorway, to all of them. And then again, specifically to Isla: 'Hi.'

'Hi yourself.'

Amanda came in and took a carton of yoghurt out of the fridge, and a teaspoon off the draining board. She peeled back the lid and began eating.

'Pull up a chair,' said Archie. 'Join us.'

'I'm OK thanks.'

'I know, but—'

'Dad – I'm OK.'

'You know what,' said Alison, whose sure instinct for setting her daughter at ease meant she'd barely looked at her. 'I'd like to go and see this disgusting and offensive play at the National. Find out what all the fuss is about.'

'Let's go,' said Isla. 'Are you on for being outraged, Archie?'

'Sounds like a woman thing to me.'

'My friend Eve's seen that,' said Amanda. 'She went with her parents.'

Ali looked at her now. 'If that's a hint, the answer is no.'

'She said it was boring as hell.'

Isla laughed. 'There go our pretensions shot down in flames!'

'I'd still quite like to see for myself.' Alison got up to make more coffee. A faint wail came from upstairs. 'Archie, get that would you . . . ?' Archie went obediently and Amanda sat down in his place. She scraped the last of the yoghurt from the carton and set it on the table, where the weight of the spoon caused it to tip over. She licked the fine rim of white from her upper lip, and glanced briefly at Isla.

'I was going to write to you.'

'That was a nice thought.'

'But I didn't get round to it.'

'It was still a nice thought.'

'I'm sorry about – you know . . .'

'Yes.'

Alison stood the cafétière, plunger protruding, on the table. 'Do you want coffee, Mandy?'

'Yes thanks.'

She put another mug with theirs, and sat down. Isla studied her own hands closely. Out of the blue a phrase from the New Testament slipped into her head – 'Take this cup from me'. She wished someone could take the pain away. It lay like a sleeping beast inside her, occasionally leaping up to slash her and make the tears spring to her eyes. She smoothed the fingers of one hand between the fingers of the other, as though pulling on gloves. The Mancunian Buddhist hadn't covered bereavement.

'Isla – your coffee.'

'Thank you.'

'Mandy . . .'

Amanda put three spoonfuls of sugar in her mug and stirred. She then began putting the coffee in her mouth with the spoon.

'Don't do that love.'

She put the spoon on the table, and began flipping it up and down by pressing the handle.

'Mandy—'

'Will you still be doing that television show?'

'Amanda!'

'Mum – I wasn't talking to you.'

'No, it's fine.' Isla felt relieved. The beast subsided. 'Yes, it's all going ahead. Did Archie tell you I'm going to try and get tickets for you?'

Amanda dropped the spoon with a clatter. 'Brilliant! That is just so cool.'

'And you'll definitely be able to meet Adrian Coote.'

'Wicked. Thanks a lot, really.'

'My pleasure.'

Amanda abandoned the coffee, stood up and leaned across to kiss Isla warmly on the cheek. She smelt of cigarettes and strawberry yoghurt, and a small silver heart on a leather thong swung out of the neck of her shirt and tapped against Isla's face.

'Thanks!'

As she disappeared, Alison grimaced. 'Gone to phone the coven. I'm sorry – she's not a bad kid, but sometimes they have absolutely no sense of what's appropriate . . .'

'She was perfectly appropriate,' said Isla. 'She rescued me from gloom.'

Archie entered, looking over his shoulder with an expression of startled pleasure. 'Did I miss something? What did I do to deserve that?'

'What?'

'I got a kiss from Tank Girl.'

'Oh that,' said Alison. 'I hate to disappoint you, but you didn't do anything, it was Isla.'

Archie sat down and claimed his coffee. 'It must have been good.'

'It was,' said Alison a touch grimly.

Isla smiled. 'I just reassured her that I was going ahead with the TV series, and hadn't forgotten about the tickets I promised her. And the invitation to meet Ade Coote.'

Alison caught the surmise in her husband's eyes. 'Yes, I'm afraid she asked.'

'Oh no, I don't believe it! I do apologise for her – I don't know what gets into her sometimes, she's so totally self-centred—'

'If you can't be self-centred at sixteen, when can you be?' Isla shrugged. 'She's a great girl and she cheered me up.'

Archie and Alison exchanged a look.

'If you say so,' said Archie.

On the way home Isla reflected that it was quite true. The prospect of taking Amanda and her friends backstage to meet their idol gave her real pleasure. It was undoubtedly more blessed – and more fun – to give than to receive, and Amanda was the perfect recipient, greedily delighted with what was in store.

Other people's offspring were a constant source of fascination. What was so intriguing was not their similarity to their parents, but their striking separateness. Amanda Stainforth's chameleon changes from brusque reserve to charming effusiveness were not mere teenage caprice, and certainly nothing to do with Archie and Alison: they were her own. And Giles and Marcus bore no discernible resemblance to either parent. One of the things she'd loved about Richard was his capacity (he'd counted it as a fault) to allow these differences, and to let them be themselves and go their own way. His sons' individuality was their greatest tribute to him.

When Barbara had spoken of Claudia Delaney's being brought 'by the fairies' it seemed not a whimsical, but a perfectly reasonable suggestion. How else, on earth, could one explain the startling magic of the unknown factor?

Isla went to sleep with these reflections running through her mind, and woke next morning refreshed, for the first time since Richard's death.

She knew, now, what she would do.

It took some time for the phone to be answered, and the voice on the other end sounded wary.

'Hello . . . ?'

'Is that Mr Burgess?'

'It is.'

'It's Isla Wakefield.' There was a short intake of breath, a hiatus. 'Isla Wakefield? You helped my husband.'

'Yes, I remember.'

'I wonder if I could speak to Jen?'

'I'm afraid she's not here.'

She sensed that the choice of words was a careful one. No indication of where Jen was, nor for how long: no offer to take a message.

Isla was equally careful. 'When do you think I might be able to talk to her?' Non-intrusive, open-ended, unthreatening.

'Ummm . . . that's a bit hard for me to say, really.' She could almost hear the sound of matters being weighed up. She hoped Jen appreciated all this diplomacy.

She decided to take a risk. 'Look, this is obviously difficult. I didn't mean to put you on the spot. I'll call back.'

She was actually lowering the receiver when she heard him say: 'No, don't. Look, Mrs Wakefield, she's in hospital.'

There was one of those dizzying shifts of equilibrium which accompany a new perspective. Isla had been full of her own resolve, her intentions, her positive thoughts. Now, in an instant, they were relegated to second place. Rebuffed, she clutched at professionalism, acted concern for all it was worth.

'I'm so sorry! What's the trouble – nothing serious?'

'Umm. I don't know if you were aware of this, but she's expecting a baby . . . ?'

'I did know, yes.' She no longer needed to act. Her voice was flat as she asked: 'Is everything all right?'

'She had a threatened miscarriage. I had to get an ambulance.'

'When?'

'Night before last.'

'And – the baby?'

'She was still bleeding when I called this morning.' Isla heard, now, his relief at being able to talk about it.

'Where is she?'

'The Royal Free.'

'Do you think I'd be able to see her?'

'Umm.' The caution crept back. 'Possibly. I couldn't say.'

She saw his difficulty. 'Let me put it another way. Is she allowed visitors?'

'One at a time. I've been. Her daughter. You know.'

'I'll give the hospital a ring.'

'Mrs Wakefield –'

'Yes?'

'It's none of my business, but do you think it's a good idea?'

He was a patently decent man. Now was the time, thought Isla grimly, to put that decency to the test.

'Actually, Mr Burgess,' she said. 'I think it's a very good idea.'

To be returning to the hospital after such a short interval, and for such a different reason, was unnerving. This time, although she found a place in the hospital car park, she sat in the car for a full ten minutes before she felt composed enough to go in.

Until this moment, with only a hiccup during her conversation with Keith Burgess, she had managed to hang on to the clarity of this morning's feelings. But now, as she followed the signs along endless corridors her confidence wavered. The feelings might be clear, but how was she going to put them into words? And, if she managed that, how would they be received?

Just before the lifts on the ground floor, she spotted a room designated Hospital Chapel. One half of the double door was open, and there was no one there. Half a dozen rows of polished wooden chairs stood empty before a round table bearing a crucifix and a neat triangular arrangement of bronze and white chrysanthemums. Everything was spotless.

With a slight twinge of embarrassment she went in, and closed the door behind her. She sat down on a chair in the back row, out of sight from anyone looking through the door.

Inertia panic, she thought, was like stage fright, surely. The trick was not so much to rise above it but to sink below it, and to allow something more elemental to take over. She knew what she wanted to do was right. If she could only let go of the anxiety and freewheel, instinct would see her through.

She remembered an incident as a child in the Far East. They were staying with people up country, and gone out for the day into the jungle. During a walk with their Malay guide they'd come to a narrow bridge – just plaited rope and slats – over a ravine. She'd been absolutely terrified of going across. Her father had kept on saying: 'Don't look down, don't think about walking on the slats – look ahead and think of where you're going.' That, she knew, was what she had to do now. The mechanics weren't important. What was important was the objective, the future. She must look straight through the difficulties to the other side.

She took a red prayer book from the holder on the back of the chair in front, and opened it. Had she not known better she might have suspected Divine intervention, as she read the lines:

> 'Take from our lives the strain and stress
> And let our ordered lives confess
> The beauty of thy peace.'

A man carrying a grizzling toddler pushed the door open and looked in. She had the impression that the chapel was not what he was expecting. He raked it, and her, with a harassed look before retreating into the corridor, still jiggling the fractious baby, and letting the door swing shut.

Isla replaced the prayer book. That was it, she thought. There was much to be said for ordered lives.

She asked the nurse at the desk which room Jen was in.

'End on the right, nearest the window.'

'Is there anyone else with her?'

'Not at the moment. If another visitor does turn up we'll pop along and tell you – she gets rather tired if there's more than one at a time.'

'Of course – I understand.' Isla was about to go, and then paused. 'How is she?'

'Very down.'

'But the baby . . . ?'

'Baby's still there, just. And the bleeding's under control. But it could be a long haul if she's going to hang on to it.'

'Thank you. I shan't stay long.'

It was a six-bedded room, and all were occupied. Six stories, thought Isla: six disordered lives. Of the two window beds, one was occupied by a stout teenager reading a magazine. The other had the curtain pulled two thirds of the way round.

Jen was asleep. Isla was shocked at how pale and drained she looked – but also younger, almost like a child herself. She lay on her side, facing the window, with her arms flung up on to the pillow before her face, in rather the same attitude she had used when kneeling in front of Isla at their last meeting, except that now the fingers weren't bunched into fists. It was too warm in the ward, and airless, and her bedclothes were round her waist. She wore a large T-shirt with a panda logo on the front, but the slight swell of her pregnancy was clearly visible.

Isla laid her freesias on top of the locker. It was strange to be an unseen watcher – Isla felt at once privileged and a little ashamed to be intruding on Jen's privacy. An auxiliary pushing a tea trolley came into the ward. Isla thought the taking of orders and clanking of cups would disturb Jen, but she simply lurched on to her back, one arm over her head, the other, with its plastic identity bracelet, lying on the striped counterpane.

The auxiliary put her head round the corner, and gave a mock-start, hand on front, when she saw Isla standing there.

'Oh my goodness –' she whispered hoarsely, 'tea, dear?'

'No thanks.'

'What about your friend?'

'I don't think so.'

The auxiliary peered benignly. 'Bless her . . . sleeping like a baby.'

When she'd gone Isla sat down on the upholstered leatherette chair between the bed and the window. It was three-thirty. Outside the great concrete and glass ramparts of the hospital the afternoon was one of sunshine and wind-driven clouds that chased across the windows. A cloud of small birds swirled between the buildings, switching direction in perfect unison, with a glint of light on feathers, like a shoal of fish. Far below Isla could see the covered play area outside the children's ward, where a few small figures moved between the bright colours of the wendy house, the sandbox and the climbing frame. Some poplars grew in the patch of green framed by the internal walkways, and their thin branches streamed and tossed in the wind, shedding fluttering handfuls of tarnished silver-green leaves.

She sat there, quietly and at peace, for nearly an hour. Once, like an anxious mother, she felt compelled to get up and bend over the bed to hear Jen's breathing. But a nurse, popping in to check, smiled approvingly.

'Let her sleep. Best thing for her.'

Shortly after that, the nurse from the desk appeared.

'Excuse me—'

'Yes?'

'Mrs Delaney's daughter's here . . . I don't know what you'd like to do.'

'It's quite all right, I'll leave now.'

The nurse withdrew. Isla took from her bag the card she'd brought with her, and laid it beside the freesias. Then, without hesitation, she took Jen's hand in both of hers and held it for a moment, before replacing it gently on the counterpane and walking quickly away.

Jen woke to find Claudia sitting on the windowsill, her long frame silhouetted against the westering sun.

'Red . . . ?'

'Hello Mum.'

'How long have you been there?'

'About – fifteen seconds. Sorry, did I wake you?'

'Don't be silly . . . it's lovely to see you.' She stretched out a hand and Claudia took and clasped it before bending to kiss her. The gesture reminded her of something. 'Have you done that once already?'

Claudia pulled the pillows up behind her. 'What?'

'I don't know . . . This is embarrassing. Squeezed my hand?'

'No.'

'I must have dreamed it. I had such a strong impression, some time when I was asleep, that someone was holding my hand . . . That I was actually being led, very firmly, by the hand . . .' She pulled a shamefaced smile. 'Talk about sick fancies.'

'I don't know.' Claudia sat down on the chair and leaned forward, elbows on knees. 'As a matter of fact, Isla Wakefield was here.'

'When?'

'Just now. She left when I arrived.'

Jen dragged a hand over her face. 'Oh, God. How long was she here for?'

'I've no idea. She did say that you'd been asleep the whole time.'

'Oh God – Red – how did she seem?'

Claudia looked down at her hands, spreading her long fingers which were so thin the light seemed to shine through them. When she looked up she was very serious.

'She seemed – really nice. Lovely, actually. I was glad she'd been.'

'Oh God,' said Jen again. The helpless tears began to course down her cheeks. She seemed full to the brim with tears at the moment, the least little jolt and they spilled over. 'How could she bear it?'

'Very easily, I had the impression.' Claudia leaned over and took the envelope from the top of the locker. 'She brought the flowers. And I imagine this is from her.'

'You open it.'

'No, Mum. You.'

Claudia laid the card on her lap. It was addressed formally, though not correctly: 'Mrs J Delaney.'

Claudia, in a burst of embarrassed tact, opened the locker, got out a carton of apple juice, and poured some into her mother's glass. Then helped herself to one.

Jen slid the card out of the envelope. It was a photograph. A big, rumpled man, disordered hair, a beaming smile, eyes that stared with infectious delight into the camera lens . . .

Richard.

Slowly, she turned the photograph over. On the back, in black ink in a smoothly rounded hand, Isla had written:

'Jen – You can do it, and you must, for all of us. I thought you might

like this to put with any of your own. Isn't it good of him? With my love – Isla W.'

Returning to the Hampstead house that evening, Isla found a bouquet propped against the front door – stocks, delphiniums and white roses, sweetly scented. The accompanying note, scribbled on a torn-out diary page, read: *'I brought these with my own fair hand. Haven't been able to stop thinking about you. I'll be back. Scotch.'*

For the first time in weeks, as she opened the door and went into the house, she found it free of ghosts. And made up her mind, at that moment, to leave it.

21

It was a fine Sunday in June, in Bradenham, and the sun shone impartially on the just and the unjust.

On the path leading from the lychgate to the church, a scattering of confetti brightened the mossy gravel, and mixed with the fallen rose petals on the newly-mown grass to either side. Inside, a dozen or so of the faithful raised their voices in the old familiar tune and declared their avowed intent to be pilgrims. Their fervour was intensified by the presence of the flowers from yesterday's wedding. Nothing, the regular churchgoers found, increased a person's sense of virtue more than a mass incursion of the ungodly. Marjory's attendance record was, of course, exemplary, but Norman Brake's supporters had been strangers to the Anglican liturgy.

Isla was in the garden of Brook End. She sat at the wooden picnic table washing new potatoes for lunch. In the middle of the lawn was a plaid rug with her book lying on it, open and face down. Upstairs in the bedroom her wedding outfit of cream and navy hung on the wardrobe door, with her broad-brimmed hat on the shelf above, and her matching spike heels standing trimly to attention beneath. The wedding had been a delight, but even more delightful was to sit out here in shorts, shirt and sneakers, without make-up, and feel the first really hot sun of the year on her bare skin. Marjory and Norman would be in Corfu now, but though she wished them every happiness, Isla didn't envy them. At this moment she did not wish to be anywhere but here.

She plopped the last of the potatoes into the saucepan of cold water at her elbow, and stretched her arms above her head. Then she left the picnic table and lay down full-length on the rug. Her head nudged the book and she felt for it with one hand, and closed it.

From next door came the intermittent plop and ping of tennis on the Fylers' court. Marcus and Giles – who had both attended the wedding – were playing with Nell, and her friend Frances. She was impressed by how easily they'd accepted this relationship, and even seemed to admire and respect it. Running counter to this was the fact that she'd had to cajole, then order, them to visit their grandfather that afternoon. But they had agreed, and were going – whether in deference, still, to her widow's weeds, or respect for their father's memory, or because they wanted to get it over with, she couldn't say. She preferred to think that a sea change was taking place.

They'd travelled mostly in silence, but it was a peaceful one. In his baby seat in the back eight-week-old Harry slept, his mouth slightly pursed as though turning weighty decisions in his dreams.

As they came into Bradenham, he began to stir. Jen looked over her shoulder.

'Perfect timing. He knows when refreshments are due.'

'He's my kind of people.' The driver slowed to turn right. 'By the way, where did you get the name Harry from? Not the prince?'

'It's the second name of the friend who helped deliver him.'

'First name no good?'

She shook her head. 'Keith.'

'No good.'

'But his other name was Harold, so I compromised.'

'Nice idea.'

'Nice man.'

Isla took the saucepan of potatoes into the kitchen and put them on the stove. She had put up a noticeboard on the wall, because this was her home now, and she had a life here, and things to do. Prominent on the board were three invitations. One, already accepted, was to open the village fête at Long Wardle in July. The second was to a fork supper with Caroline, to meet (as Caroline confided in biro at the bottom) *Daniel Hetherington – my chap!*

The third was a fax. *'Would you like to see a play? Or a film? Or have dinner? Or would you be content just to sit there and let me gaze at you? Let me know what suits you best. S.'*

The Diane turned in, and stopped, 'Journey's end, everyone,' said Jen.

Isla opened the cottage door and stepped out into the sunshine. There was a burst of laughter and a shriek of protest from the tennis court on the other side of the lane, waves and smiles as the car doors opened.

Scotch got out, and released Harry from his seat. He handed the baby to Jen and let her go first.

Isla opened her arms wide, and walked forward to greet the three people who embodied, for her, the possibility of happiness in an otherwise uncertain future.